Health and Growth

Commission on Growth and Development

Health and Growth

Edited by Michael Spence and Maureen Lewis

Contributions by
Michael Spence
Daron Acemoglu and Simon Johnson
Sir George Alleyne
Jere R. Behrman
Hoyt Bleakley
David E. Bloom and David Canning
William Jack and Maureen Lewis

COMMISSION ON GROWTH AND DEVELOPMENT

© 2009 The International Bank for Reconstruction and Development /
The World Bank
On behalf of the Commission on Growth and Development
1818 H Street NW
Washington, DC 20433
Telephone: 202-473-1000
Internet: www.worldbank.org
       www.growthcommission.org
E-mail: info@worldbank.org
       contactinfo@growthcommission.org

1 2 3 4 12 11 10 09

This volume is a product of the Commission on Growth and
Development, which is sponsored by the following organizations:

Australian Agency for International Development (AusAID)
Dutch Ministry of Foreign Affairs
Swedish International Development Cooperation Agency (SIDA)
U.K. Department for International Development (DFID)
The William and Flora Hewlett Foundation
The World Bank Group

The findings, interpretations, and conclusions expressed herein do not
necessarily reflect the views of the sponsoring organizations or the
governments they represent.

The sponsoring organizations do not guarantee the accuracy of
the data included in this work. The boundaries, colors, denomi-
nations, and other information shown on any map in this work
do not imply any judgment on the part of the sponsoring organizations concerning the legal status of any territory or the
endorsement or acceptance of such boundaries.

ISBN: 978-0-8213-7659-1
eISBN: 978-0-8213-7660-7
DOI: 10.1596/978-0-8213-7659-1

Library of Congress Cataloging-in-Publication Data
Health and growth / edited by Michael Spence and Maureen Lewis.
    p. cm.
  Includes index.
  ISBN 978-0-8213-7659-1 — ISBN 978-0-8213-7660-7 (electronic)
  1. Medical economics. 2. Medical care—Finance. 3. Public health
administration. I. Spence, Michael, 1943- II. Lewis, Maureen A., 1952-
RA410.H37 2009
  338.4'33621—dc22
                                                    2009005640

Contents

Figures

Tables

Preface

The Commission on Growth and Development was established in April 2006, partly in response to two observations. We felt that the benefits of growth were not fully appreciated, but we also recognized that the causes of growth were not fully understood. Growth is often overlooked and underrated as an instrument for tackling the world's most pressing problems, such as poverty, illiteracy, income inequality, unemployment, and pollution. At the same time, our grasp of the sources of growth in developing countries is less definitive than commonly thought—even though advice is sometimes given to policy makers in these countries with great confidence, perhaps greater than the state of our knowledge would justify. Consequently, the Commission's mandate is to "take stock of the state of theoretical and empirical knowledge on economic growth with a view to drawing implications for policy for the current and next generation of policy makers."

The 21 commissioners included 19 experienced leaders from government and business, mostly from the developing world, and two Nobel Prize–winning economists. To help assess the state of knowledge, the Commission invited leading academics and policy makers from around the world to a series of 12 workshops, held in 2006, 2007, and 2008 in Washington, D.C., New York, and New Haven. A series of thematic papers, as well as 25 country case studies exploring the dynamics of growth in specific countries, was commissioned. The Commission also met several times in Washington, Singapore, New York, and Suzhou. The workshop papers reviewed issues such as monetary and fiscal policy, climate change, inequality, growth, urbanization, education, and health—the subject of this volume. Each presentation benefited from comments by members of the Commission and other workshop participants from the worlds of policy, theory, and practice.

The workshops turned out to be intense and lively affairs, lasting up to three days. It became clear that experts do not always agree, even on issues that are central to growth. The same is true of the members of the Commission on a number of questions. The Commission had no wish to disguise or gloss over these uncertainties and differences. Researchers do not always know the correct "model" that might explain the world they observe; and even if they know the factors that matter, they cannot always measure them convincingly.

While researchers will continue to improve our understanding of growth, policy makers cannot wait for scholars to satisfy all of their doubts or resolve their differences. Decisions must be made with only partial knowledge of the world. One consequence is that most policy decisions, however well-informed, take on the character of experiments. They yield useful information about the way the world works, even if they do not always turn out the way policy makers had hoped. It is best to recognize this fact so that policy makers can institutionalize the process of spotting failures, learning from mistakes, and correcting policies mid-course.

The workshop on health and growth was held in October 2007. We were fortunate to benefit from the wisdom and insights of outstanding researchers and experienced practitioners. We are grateful to all the participants, who are listed below. The remainder of this preface is not an exhaustive summary of the workshop or the chapters in this volume. It instead replays some highlights of the discussion and presents some of the ideas that shaped the conclusions on health in *The Growth Report*. One strong conclusion is the vital importance of investing in the nutrition, health, and cognitive development of children in their early, preschool years. This investment is not only a matter of fairness. It also ensures that individuals can develop both cognitive and noncognitive skills, such as perseverance, motivation, self-control, self-esteem, conscientiousness, and forward-looking behavior. These skills together determine a person's lifelong earnings and health. Research by Jim Heckman, the pioneering economist in this area, suggests that the first five years of life are critical. This is one clear conclusion in a field that is otherwise often ambiguous and rapidly evolving.

The Measurement of Health

Any definition of health has its difficulties and limitations. There is no agreed-on metric. The World Health Organization has grappled with the definition and concludes that health is simply "absence of illness." This definition is pithy and can accommodate subjective perceptions and cultural differences. But it makes health hard to measure.

Whereas education can be indexed by years of schooling and road-building by kilometers of asphalt, the aggregate health of a nation is not easily measured. This in turn makes it difficult to determine its effects on growth. Accurate health statistics are a public good that only governments and intergovernmental organizations can provide. National and multilateral agencies have spent considerable sums measuring health, and they have made substantial progress tracking individual diseases. But they have enjoyed less success in compiling aggregate, summary indicators.

Health is generally captured as the absence of negative factors, such as infant mortality, or by life expectancy, which is, itself, heavily influenced by infant mortality. But the death of a child before his or her first birthday is rare even in countries afflicted by high mortality rates, and because it only happens once, it offers an incomplete measure of health.

It is, for example, entirely possible for a country's infant mortality rate to fall even as "morbidity," or illness, among the population as a whole rises. Infants, after all, are outnumbered by adults, who might suffer from chronic diseases, such as diabetes or heart disease, which evolve quite independently of threats to infant survival. If these chronic diseases worsen, even as postnatal care improves, then the infant mortality rate will give a misleading impression of the country's health trends.

Unfortunately, general ill health can't be captured in a single measure. No single number could hope to encapsulate the range of possible ailments or the varying severity of each one. As a result, general indicators of health are inevitably fuzzy and their associations with productivity tenuous. Scholars typically choose instead to refer to specific illnesses, such as hookworm, HIV/AIDS, or diabetes. The prevalence of particular morbidities is easier to measure and their economic impact easier to trace.

Progress in Health

By any measure, the average health of the world's population has improved spectacularly over the last two centuries. This is largely because of improved agriculture, which has increased the quantity of food, and a better understanding of disease transmission, which has guided public efforts to stem infectious diseases. Together, these factors have helped lower infant mortality, reduce morbidity, and extend life expectancy, allowing more people to enjoy and even outlive their three scores and ten.

Until the late eighteenth century, even the world's richer countries suffered from inadequate food production and high malnutrition. Boosts in agricultural output, particularly in the twentieth century, led to improvements in nutrition. These nutritional gains account for roughly 40 percent of the increase in life expectancy over the last 400 years according to pioneering research by Robert Fogel, a Nobel Prize–winning economic historian.

In the nineteenth century, pioneers of epidemiology discovered the transmission paths of disease. This prompted the draining of swamps to destroy mosquito breeding-grounds, thereby curbing malaria and yellow fever. It also demonstrated the need to separate water and sewerage, which controlled cholera epidemics. Such interventions on behalf of public health had dramatic effects on disease incidence and mortality.

In the early twentieth century, the United States led efforts in Latin America to establish disease surveillance systems and to suppress the "vectors," the transmitters of infectious diseases. They succeeded in reducing the number of days that traded goods had to spend in quarantine, opening up trade with tropical countries.

The elimination of hookworm in the U.S. South led to higher school enrollment, attendance, and literacy. Similar malaria control efforts in Latin America resulted in higher literacy and incomes in adulthood. Such targeted efforts at disease control allow and encourage broader investments in human capital that together contribute to improved economic performance at the household level.

Technologies that emerged after World War II—such as vaccines, the use of DDT, and effective therapies for bacterial infections, notably antibiotics—have saved lives in both developed and developing countries. But these advances have made less of an impact on health and longevity than preventive measures such as exercise, healthy eating habits, and reductions in smoking.

Macroeconomics and Health

We can say with confidence that economic growth improves health. It increases the availability of food, makes health spending affordable, and raises the demand for good health. The question is whether causality works in reverse: does health lift growth? And if so, how important is it when compared with other potential factors where the empirical evidence is more solid?

The World Health Organization's 2001 Committee on Macroeconomics and Health recommended increased spending on health as a way to promote economic growth, to raise both health status and household earnings. That committee's findings offer a starting point for a reexamination of the validity and relevance of macroeconomic evidence.

Economists and other social scientists have made considerable efforts to ferret out the effect of health investments on economic performance. Historical research, cross-sectional analysis, and innovative ways of integrating household factors into cross-country studies have pushed the methodological envelope, but the results remain inconclusive. Research is hamstrung by lack of data and imprecise measures of health. Moreover, countries that provide effective health services are also more likely to have other institutions that function well, as well as sound public management in general. This makes it hard to separate out the marginal contribution of investments in health.

Of course, improvements in health are worth the effort even if they turn out to have little effect on growth. People rank health high on their list of priorities in life. It is an end in itself, whether or not it is also a means to the further end of greater prosperity.

Do Government Investments in Health-Care Services Matter for Growth? Governments invest in health in various ways, providing public goods (for example, controlling disease vectors and promoting healthy behaviors), quasi-public goods (for example, vaccinations for communicable diseases and nutrition supplements), and subsidizing access to health care, either through insurance or direct delivery of care. There is a clear rationale for this government involvement. As infectious diseases spread from person to person, they become a public concern as well as a private one. And because illness is often a random event, it is best tackled by pooling the financial risks it poses. The question of particular concern to the Commission is how much public health spending contributes to growth.

The cross-country evidence is tenuous at best. While the lack of a meaningful health metric contributes to the problem, weak health-care institutions undermine the effectiveness of health-care investments. Chronic absenteeism among providers, poor budget execution, ineffective management, and virtually no accountability weaken public efforts and contribute to low returns on investment. If institutions cannot function, then public spending on health care will not improve health, let alone raise economic growth.

Early Investments in Health and Nutrition Improve Welfare and Earnings. Although the macroeconomic evidence is muddy and inconclusive, other lines of research into the broader implications of investments in health are yielding rich and promising insights. Findings from economics, psychology, and neuroscience all reveal the profound importance of timing. Interventions in the preschool years have a long reach, improving health, schooling, and earnings even late in life. For example, a 35-year longitudinal study in Guatemala showed that men who received a protein supplement in their first two years of childhood earned an average wage 46 percent higher than men who consumed a calorie-based supplement.

Fighting malnutrition can significantly raise the survival rates of young children and relieve the burden of illness. This translates into healthier adults who can expect to live longer lives. Both biomedical and economic research point to the striking effects of early childhood nutrition and cognitive stimulation on schooling attendance, learning, adult health, and lifelong earnings. Indeed, early life experience accounts for more of the variance in adult cognitive skills than does schooling.

In developing countries, stunted or anemic children suffer from fewer years of schooling, reduced productivity, and lower incomes in adulthood. Recent neuroscience findings link inadequate interventions in preschool years with some forms of cancer, mental illness, diabetes, and other chronic diseases in adults. Compensating adults for deficits early in life is more expensive and far less successful than targeted investments in preschoolers. These investments, on the other hand, can improve the productivity and earnings of individuals and households, with strong implications for economic growth in the aggregate over the longer term. They may also narrow inequality by breaking the intergenerational transmission of poverty.

Concluding Remarks

Historically, progress in health owed much to adequate food and public-health interventions, and those important relationships persist in the modern world. Chronic illness undermines current productivity and promises future losses in output. These deprivations can be passed on to the next generation if investments in children are not made in a targeted and timely fashion. Good health improves the capacity to learn and work, which dramatically improves income and welfare at the household level even if the effects at the aggregate level may be harder to discern. The methodological problems in capturing these gains deserve attention and further work. More attention also needs to be paid to upgrading health-care institutions, as more of the same is neither affordable nor desirable.

A. Michael Spence

Workshop Participants

Alleyne, George, Pan American Health Organization
Atlas, Scott, Stanford University
Behrman, Jere, University of Pennsylvania
Bleakley, Hoyt, University of Chicago
Canning, David, Harvard University
Chawla, Mukesh, World Bank
Ellis, Randall, Boston University
Filmer, Deon, World Bank
Fortson, Jane, University of Chicago
Gertler, Paul, University of California, Berkeley
Gottret, Pablo, World Bank
Haacker, Markus, International Monetary Fund
Hammer, Jeffrey, Princeton University
Jack, William, Georgetown University
Johnson, Simon, International Monetary Fund
Leipziger, Danny, Growth Commission Vice Chair, World Bank
Lewis, Maureen, World Bank
MacCallum, Lisa, the Nike Foundation
Manuel, Trevor, Commissioner, Minister of Finance, South Africa
Meadows, Graham, University of Sussex
Medici, Andre, Inter-American Development Bank
Merchant, Ann, World Bank
Nankani, Gobind, Global Development Network
Nowak, Dorota, World Bank

Spence, Michael, Growth Commission Chair, Stanford University

Suarez, Reuben, Pan American Health Organization

Venner, Dwight, Commissioner and Governor, Eastern Caribbean Central Bank, St. Kitts and Nevis

Weil, David, Brown University

Zagha, Roberto, World Bank

About the Editors and Contributors

Daron Acemoglu is the Charles P. Kindleberger Professor of Applied Economics at Massachusetts Institute of Technology (MIT) and winner of the 2005 John Bates Clark Medal. He is among the 20 most cited economists in the world according to IDEAS/RePEc. Acemoglu became a member of the MIT faculty in 1993. He is a member of the Economic Growth Program of the Canadian Institute of Advanced Research. He is also affiliated with the National Bureau of Economic Research, Center for Economic Performance, and Center for Economic Policy Research. His principal interests are political economy, economic development, economic growth, technology, income and wage inequality, human capital and training, and labor economics. His most recent works concentrate on the role of institutions in economic development and political economy.

Sir George Alleyne is Chancellor of the University of the West Indies, became Director of the Pan American Health Organization (PAHO) on February 1, 1995, and completed a second four-year term on January 31, 2003. In 2003 he was elected Director Emeritus of the PAHO. In February 2003, Mr. Kofi Annan, then Secretary General of the United Nations, appointed him as his special envoy for HIV/AIDS in the Caribbean. He was reconfirmed in this position by the current Secretary General, Mr. Ban Ki-moon. In October 2003 he was appointed Chancellor of the University of the West Indies. He currently holds an adjunct professorship in the Bloomberg School of Public Health, Johns Hopkins University. Sir George has received numerous awards in recognition of his work, including prestigious decorations and national honors from many countries of the Americas. In 2001 he was awarded the Order of the Caribbean Community, the highest honor that can be conferred on a Caribbean national.

Jere R. Behrman is the William R. Kenan Jr. Professor of Economics (and former Chair of the Economics Department) and Research Associate (and former Director) of the Population Studies Center at the University of Pennsylvania, where he has been on the faculty since 1965. His research interests are in empirical microeconomics, economic development, labor economics, human resources, economic demography, and household behaviors. He has published more than 300 professional articles and 32 books and monographs on these topics. He has worked as a research consultant with numerous national and international organizations, including the World Bank, the Asian Development Bank, and the Inter-American Development Bank. He has been the principal investigator or co-principal investigator on more than 50 research projects funded by organizations including the U.S. National Institutes of Health, the U.S. National Science Foundation, the Rockefeller Foundation, and the Ford Foundation. He has lectured widely in the United States and internationally and has been involved in professional research or lecturing activities in more than 40 countries in Asia, Africa, Europe, and Latin America and the Caribbean. He has received various honors, including being selected a Fulbright Fortieth Anniversary Distinguished Fellow, a Fellow of the Econometric Society, a Guggenheim Foundation Faculty Fellow, and a Ford Foundation Faculty Fellow.

Hoyt Bleakley is an Assistant Professor of Economics at the University of Chicago's Graduate School of Business. His research focuses on the childhood determinants of adult productivity. Recent work considers the impact of tropical disease eradication in both the southern United States and Latin America as well as the role of English-language skills in the economic progress of childhood immigrants in the United States. Other work measures the importance of balance sheets in amplifying crises in emerging markets. He has also taught at the University of California, San Diego, and has been a visiting scholar at the Federal Reserve Bank of Boston and the Universidad de los Andes.

David E. Bloom is Clarence James Gamble Professor of Economics and Demography at Harvard University, Chair of the Department of Population and International Health at the Harvard School of Public Health, and Director of Harvard University's Program on the Global Demography of Aging. He is also Research Associate at the National Bureau of Economic Research and Fellow of the American Academy of Arts and Sciences. He has served on the public policy faculty at Carnegie-Mellon University and on the economics faculties at Harvard University and Columbia University. He formerly served as Deputy Director of the Harvard Institute for International Development and as Chairman of Columbia University's Department of Economics.

David Canning is Professor of Economics and International Health, Department of Population and International Health, Harvard University. Prior to that he was a Professor of Economics at Queen's University, Belfast (1993–2002), and is an honorary Professor of this university; Associate

Professor, Department of Economics, Columbia University (1992–93); and lecturer in economics, Cambridge University (1989–92) and London School of Economics and Political Science (1988–89).

William Jack is Associate Professor, Department of Economics, Georgetown University. Previously he has worked at the Australian National University, the U.S. Congress, and the International Monetary Fund. He has also consulted to the World Bank and the World Health Organization. His research interests include public economics, development, and health economics.

Simon Johnson is the Ronald A. Kurtz Professor of Entrepreneurship at MIT's Sloan School of Management, a position he has held since 2004. He is also a Senior Fellow at the Peterson Institute for International Economics in Washington, DC. From March 2007 through the end of August 2008, Professor Johnson was the International Monetary Fund's Economic Counsellor (Chief Economist) and Director of its Research Department. At the International Monetary Fund, Professor Johnson led the global economic outlook team, helped to formulate innovative responses to worldwide financial turmoil, and was among the earliest to propose new forms of engagement for sovereign wealth funds. He is Co-director of a National Bureau of Economic Research project on Africa and President of the Association for Comparative Economic Studies (term of office 2008–09). Dr. Johnson is an expert on the financial sector and economic crises. Over the past 20 years he has worked on crisis prevention and mitigation, as well as issues pertaining to economic growth in advanced, emerging market, and developing countries. His work focuses on how policy makers can limit the impact of negative shocks and manage the risks faced by their countries.

Maureen Lewis is Adviser in the Development Economics Department of the World Bank. She was formerly the Chief Economist for Human Development and Adviser to the Vice President for Human Development at the World Bank. Much of her research, publications, and policy work examines financing and delivery of health care in developing and transition countries. She was formerly a Senior Fellow at the Center for Global Development for two years and prior to that managed a unit in the World Bank dedicated to economic policy and human development research and programs in Eastern Europe and Central Asia. In the early 1990s, she led the Bank's health agenda in Brazil. Before joining the World Bank, she established and led the international health policy work at The Urban Institute. She has published dozens of articles in peer-reviewed journals on health economics and health policy.

Michael Spence is Senior Fellow, the Hoover Institution, and Philip H. Knight Professor Emeritus of Management, Graduate School of Business, Stanford University. He was awarded the Nobel Memorial Prize in Economic Sciences in 2001. Mr. Spence was Philip H. Knight Professor and Dean of the Stanford Business School from 1990 to 1999. Since 1999, he has been a partner at Oak Hill Capital Partners. From 1975 to 1990, he served as Professor of Economics and Business Administration at Harvard University. Mr. Spence was awarded the John Kenneth Galbraith Prize for excellence in teaching in 1978 and the John Bates Clark Medal in 1981 for a "significant contribution to economic thought and knowledge." He was appointed Chairman of the Economics Department at Harvard in 1983 and served as Dean of the Faculty of Arts and Sciences from 1984 to 1990. At various times, he has served as a member of the editorial boards of the *American Economics Review*, *Bell Journal of Economics*, *Journal of Economic Theory*, and *Public Policy*. Professor Spence is the Chair of the Commission on Growth and Development.

Acknowledgments

The editors are most grateful for the strong support provided by the sponsors of the Commission on Growth and Development: the governments of Australia, the Netherlands, Sweden, and the United Kingdom; the William and Flora Hewlett Foundation; and The World Bank Group. Danny Leipziger, Vice President of the Poverty Reduction and Economic Management Network in the World Bank, was generous in providing resources for this effort. We are much obliged to the participants in the workshops on health and growth sponsored by the Commission, especially the chapter authors, for their numerous and diverse insights and the time they dedicated to engaging in discussions of the issues. Roberto Zagha, Secretary of the Commission, was a constant source of good ideas, encouragement, and stimulation. Roberto brings out the best in others while keeping a sharp focus on the driving issues at hand. The level of discussion and the quality of the papers that follow reflect his enthusiasm and wisdom.

A team of colleagues in the Growth Commission secretariat—Muriel Darlington, Diana Manevskaya, and Dorota Nowak—were dedicated to making every aspect of the commission's work successful. They gave us what felt like undivided attention in organizing the workshops and producing this book—one of many of the commission's activities with pressing deadlines and low tolerance for error. The whole process was only possible due to their marvelous organization and steady hard work. Cindy Fisher was pragmatic, accommodating, and rigorous in preparing the manuscript for publication. She never missed her deadlines and was very kind when we occasionally needed to shift ours. Stephen McGroarty oversaw the publication process with great skill. We thank Simon Cox of the *Economist* for his excellent work on the preface.

Michael Spence
Maureen Lewis

Abbreviations

ART	antiretroviral treatment
CINAHL	Cumulative Index to Nursing and Allied Health Literature
CPIA	Country Program and Institutional Analysis
DDT	dichloro-diphenyl-trichloroethane
GDP	gross domestic product
BMM	generalized method-of-moments
HAZ	height-for-age z score
HIV/AIDS	human immunodeficiency virus/acquired immunodeficiency syndrome
IHB	International Health Board
ILS	indirect least squares
INCAP	Institute of Nutrition for Central America and Panama
IPUMS	integrated public use micro sample
IV	instrumental variables
MIT	Massachusetts Institute of Technology
NGO	nongovernmental organization
OECD	Organisation for Economic Co-operation and Development
OLS	ordinary least squares
ORT	oral rehydration therapy
PAHO	Pan American Health Organization
RC	retrospective cohort
RSC	Rockefeller Sanitary Commission for the Eradication of Hookworm Disease
SARS	severe acute respiratory syndrome
SEA	state economic area
TFP	total factor productivity

2SLS	two-stage least squares
UN	United Nations
UNDP	United Nations Development Programme
UNICEF	United Nations Children's Fund
WAZ	weight-for-age z score
WER	Weekly Epidemiological Record
WHO	World Health Organization

CHAPTER 1
Health Investments and Economic Growth: Macroeconomic Evidence and Microeconomic Foundations

William Jack and Maureen Lewis

Improvements in health status over the last 50–100 years, as measured by a number of indicators, have been nothing short of spectacular. Vaccines, antibiotics, and other pharmaceutical developments have drastically reduced the incidence of illness and death. Economic growth has also helped: richer people are better nourished and educated, and richer countries are more able to afford the public goods (such as supply of water and sanitation and control of disease vectors such as mosquitoes) that reduce the transmission of disease.

Do improvements in health themselves help to boost economic growth? This proposition is at the heart of the report of the World Health Organization's Commission on Macroeconomics and Health (WHO 2001: i), which states, "Extending the coverage of crucial health services . . . to the

This chapter was drafted for the Commission on Growth and Development, and an earlier version was presented at the commission's workshop on health and growth, October 16, 2007. The authors thank Jeffrey Hammer, Magnus Lindelow, Mattias Lundberg, Andre Medici, Paul Schultz, Duncan Thomas, and participants at the workshop for useful comments. Ann Merchant and Erika Mae Lorenzana provided expert research assistance. The authors alone are responsible for the content of this chapter.

world's poor could save millions of lives each year, reduce poverty, spur economic development, and promote global security." According to this view, better health care may be able to accomplish what development practitioners, nongovernmental organizations (NGOs), economists, foreign aid, and diplomacy have failed to achieve. Some researchers who have found a significant link from health to growth (for example, Bloom and Canning 2003a, 2003b) have used this finding to argue for large increases in government spending on health.

Both directions of causality between health and income are likely operative, although they are difficult to measure and estimate, and a vigorous ongoing debate about which direction dominates reflects these empirical challenges. A resolution of this debate could boost the urgency of the quest for growth, inform that quest, or both. For example, a finding that economic growth reduces infant mortality could hasten the adoption of potentially growth-enhancing policy reforms. Alternatively, if better population health were found to stimulate economic growth, the full social returns to policies that directly improve health status would be higher than is now recognized, and interventions designed to improve health might be added to the armory of growth-friendly policies to be used in the quest for growth.

To help inform decision making on public policy, this review examines the routes by which improvements in health might indeed increase incomes and growth and the related evidence. Recent advances in the literature suggest that a link from health to growth may be operational, but difficult to measure, and that its effect is likely to be relatively small.

Better health may lead to income growth, but this does not necessarily mean that governments of developing countries should spend more of their budgets on health care. As Bloom and Canning (2003a: 313) point out, "The key issue is not that spending on health would be good [although some authors question even this assumption], it is whether spending on health is better than other uses of the limited funds available in developing countries." Public spending on health care might not be the best way to achieve health, let alone growth.

Thus a second goal of our review is to investigate the determinants of health itself, particularly the evidence on the impact of public expenditure policies on health. Some specific public interventions seem to be very good for health outcomes, while some broader measures seem to have little measurable effect. But overall there appears to be growing evidence that public policies only improve health when institutions are of sufficiently high quality, and that good institutions themselves are likely to have a more important *direct* effect on growth than on growth-through-health.

We caution the reader against expecting to find consensus in the empirical literature on the links from health to growth or even from health policies to health. A number of papers present unambiguous results but contradict one another. From our reading, the literature is a mix of rigorous scientific investigation and well-motivated advocacy on both sides.[1] Further, when attempting to untangle the link from health to growth, or vice versa, econometric issues of endogeneity and measurement error are particularly problematic, and the validity of even the most innovative approaches continues to be debated.

Health status is affected by food and nutrition, public health investments, lifestyle and individual medical services. In addition, other factors, notably cognitive and noncognitive educational attainment, deeply affect the predisposition to illness and the ability to ward off and manage illness in adulthood. We review the evidence surrounding all of these influences to gain some appreciation of the link between a country's investments in "health" and economic growth.

The first section of this chapter examines the links between health outcomes and economic growth at the macroeconomic level, encompassing discussion of the econometric and policy issues. Then, because the health-income literature provides little policy guidance on how to improve health, the second section reviews the microeconomic linkages between health and income and considers the crucial role that public investments outside the "health" sector have played in improving health status. The third section summarizes the weak links between investments in medical care and health status and addresses the institutional challenges within the health sector if investments in health care are to improve health. A final section concludes.

Population Health and Income: Potential Links and Evidence

This section provides an overview of the historical patterns of health improvements as background to a review of the mechanisms by which improvements in a population's health might lead to increases in income. We then present some basic evidence on the associations between trends in health and trends in national income across countries and within two large developing countries (China and India) over time, and discuss the challenges faced in interpreting these associations.

How Did We Get So Healthy?

This historical overview details the main causes of improvements in population health, many of which, such as improvements in food supply, sanitation, and control of disease vectors, lie outside the health care field.

The dramatic improvements in health status of the past 50 years—most obvious from the declines in mortality and increases in life expectancy—stem

---

1 As Dixit (2006: 23) notes in a thought-provoking discussion, conflicting research findings in the growth and development literature "can leave a user who is not an expert in a particular area in a thorough state of confusion and indecision."

mainly from improvements in nutrition, advances in public health, and education; for populations at large, higher spending on health care has had minimal impacts on mortality.

Historically, inadequate food production and the resulting malnutrition compromised adult productivity. For example, data from the United Kingdom show that, until the late eighteenth century, U.K. agricultural production could only feed 80 percent of the population. Greater output raised nutritional status, leading to longer working hours, while parallel investments in public health improved the use of the calories consumed (Fogel 2002). Fogel (1986) concludes that nutritional improvements have contributed about 40 percent to the decline in mortality since 1700, with sharp rises in nutritional status occurring in periods of abundant food, mostly in the twentieth century.

Along with better nutrition, advances in hygiene and education have played a more important role in reducing mortality than advances in medicine. McKeown, Record, and Turner (1962, 1975) examine the reasons for mortality declines in England and Wales during the nineteenth and twentieth centuries. Mortality was affected by medical measures such as immunizations, but lower exposure to infection, expanded access to piped water and sanitation, and better nutrition were the major factors explaining the rising survival rate. Reduction in death from airborne infections occurred before the introduction of effective medical treatment, and better nutrition had a large effect on the ability to ward off infection and on the probability of death. Declines in mortality from water- and food-borne diseases could be traced to improved hygiene and better nutrition, with treatment emerging as largely irrelevant.

Similarly, Fuchs (1974), in his study of infant mortality reductions in New York City between 1900 and 1930, attributed these shifts mainly to rising standards of living, education, and lower fertility, rather than to medical advances. Fogel (2002) compares morbidity levels in the post–Civil War period in the United States with those in the latter part of the twentieth century and finds that morbidity levels have fallen significantly, partly because of changes in lifestyle and partly because of other factors including medical interventions. Lleras-Muney (2005) examines the determinants of life expectancy in the United States using a synthetic cohort beginning in 1900. Her estimates indicate that each year of education increases life expectancy at age 35 by as much as 1.7 years, a very significant increase that suggests the central importance of education. Similar findings are reported in multiple studies in developing countries (Schultz 2002).

Exceptions are breakthroughs in pharmaceutical therapies after the 1940s—notably vaccines, penicillin, and other antibiotics that penicillin spawned—that changed the health landscape. Acemoglu and Johnson (chapter 4 in this volume) also point to the development of the pesticide DDT, which effectively controlled disease vectors like mosquitoes, and to the establishment of the World Health Organization, which helped to spread knowledge about, and methods for, the adoption of technologies that helped to reduce mortality. The contribution of medical advances to either morbidity or mortality is more difficult to trace and to attribute directly. This is because it is difficult to isolate the effect of individual procedures, as successful application depends on many factors.[2]

More recent evidence from Organisation for Economic Co-operation and Development (OECD) countries suggests that changes in lifestyle and nonmedical advances have had a bigger impact than medical advances and health care on longevity and well-being. Lifestyle changes such as reduced cigarette smoking and more moderate alcohol consumption have made the U.S. population healthier (Wolfe 1986).

Both in OECD countries and in China, many of the most effective therapies for infectious diseases only emerged after the improvements in public health were well established. In their examination of the declines in infectious diseases in the United States over the period 1900–73, McKinley and McKinley (1997), like other researchers, find that effective treatments emerged only after the incidence of these diseases had fallen; nonmedical factors had played important roles in reducing morbidity and mortality from those diseases. China has historically shown much better health indicators than its income might predict. Although much of this achievement was popularly attributed to the country's barefoot doctors—minimally trained medical personnel who were tasked with providing primary health services—most of the improvements in infant and child mortality occurred *before* the barefoot doctors began to be deployed in 1965; after the barefoot doctor system was abandoned, China's health status did not decline. The early health improvements can be credited to, among other things, Chairman Mao's "five pests" campaign, his exhortation to drink tea instead of (unboiled) water, and China's generally safe latrines. Figure 1.1 illustrates the lack of evidence linking barefoot doctors to health improvements.

Underlying the health improvements that countries achieved were investments informed by advances in public health science. Periodic epidemics of cholera, malaria, and other infectious diseases plagued Europe and the Americas during the nineteenth century until the science of disease transmission developed and viable interventions were discovered. Major investments in public health in the nineteenth century—in response to the work of Snow (1849) linking contaminated water with cholera—resulted in dramatic declines in mortality. Simply eliminating people's contact with sewage-contaminated water contained the cholera epidemic in London in 1854 (Crossier 2007). Similarly, the Thames embankment, which helped

---

2 Limited data for specific interventions, differences in patients' health when treated, and high variability in the medical treatment across medical facilities that complement and influence successful application of new medical technologies, among other things, make it difficult to determine the contribution of new medical procedures. Cost-effectiveness studies have shed light on some procedures, but controversy persists about the value of medical advances in terms of additional years of life. For example, Cutler (2007) examines the cost-effectiveness of therapeutic surgical care after a heart attack and concludes that it is not clear whether the benefits of revascularization are due to the procedure itself or to the other services that are associated with care at hospitals with the capacity to offer these services. Unlike the pharmaceutical and vector control innovations, the contribution of medical advances remains controversial.

Figure 1.1 Health Improvements and the Advent of Barefoot Doctors in China

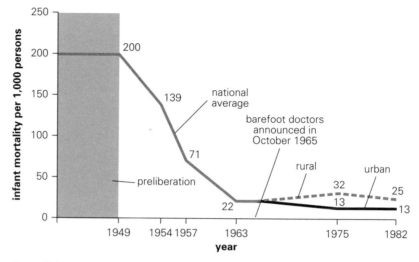

Source: Hsiao 1984.

Note: The curved arrow and associated text have been added to the original.

the river to move effluent out of London, and the draining of swamps elsewhere led to the disappearance of malaria in the United Kingdom (Kuhn and others 2003). More recently, Cutler and Miller (2005) have studied the impact of clean water on health, looking at the results of the adoption of filtration and chlorination by U.S. cities in the first quarter of the twentieth century. They attribute nearly half of the total reduction in mortality in major cities, three-quarters of the reduction in infant mortality, and two-thirds of the reduction in child mortality to improved water supply.

An important factor that facilitated the introduction of public health measures was centralized decision making with little involvement of citizens, driven by economic imperatives. Eminent domain effectively ensured that public health measures in Europe and parts of the Americas were implemented before the twentieth century. Beginning in the mid-nineteenth century in the Americas, concerns about contagious tropical illnesses such as yellow fever, cholera, and malaria prompted the region's governments to adopt the Pan American Sanitary Code, which entailed the adoption of intense disease surveillance and reporting, control of disease vectors, sanitary improvements, and significant investments in parasitology research centers across Latin America to limit quarantine and other delays to regional trade (PAHO 1999). A recent example of collective action to enhance human and economic well-being is the multicountry- and multidonor-funded Onchocerciasis (river blindness) Control Program in the Niger delta in West Africa. The program of spraying infected areas with pesticide has effectively controlled the black flies responsible for this debilitating and lethal human infection. It has enabled the recultivation of 25 million hectares of fertile agricultural land, which had been abandoned because of the prevalence of the disease (Benton 2001).

Other such public health interventions are needed across the developing world to deal with some of the same challenges that confronted European cities in earlier times. The World Bank estimates that a billion people lack access to clean water and 2.6 billion (or roughly 40 percent of the world's population) lack access to basic sanitation. Some 94 percent of diarrheal cases worldwide can be attributed to unsafe drinking water, poor sanitation, and inadequate hygiene, with 1.5 million cases resulting in death, mostly among children (World Bank 2008). The importance of these basic public health measures to promoting good health and reducing mortality remains fundamental to investments that have demonstrated links to expanding economic activity.

How Might Health Make You Rich?

The most obvious reason why healthier people might be richer is that they can work harder, longer, and more consistently than others. In turn, those who are disabled or ill can work less, placing an economic burden on the household. But can better health increase the *rate* at which income grows?

Human Capital Accumulation. A recurring theme in the literature is that health leads to income growth through its effect on human capital accumulation—and particularly through education—provided that people have sufficient food and satisfactory educational opportunities.

First, children who are healthy and adequately nourished may spend more time at school and be better learners while there, preparing themselves to earn higher incomes. Along these lines, Sachs and Malaney (2002) describe a number of channels through which malaria can compromise educational attainment, including by hampering fetal development, reducing cognitive ability, and lowering school attendance.

Second, the health status of adults affects human capital accumulation by their children. A large proportion of human capital investment decisions are made by parents on their children's behalf. But if parents die, they cannot invest in their children. Orphans do not necessarily suffer a complete withdrawal of adult support, given the social networks in many societies, but they are likely to receive less than when their parents were alive, an issue that is discussed below in the context of the economic impact of illness. Lorentzen, McMillan, and Wacziarg (2005), using an instrumental variables approach, find that the adult mortality rate affects growth less through its influence on investments in education than through its influence on fertility and physical capital investments.

Physical Capital Accumulation. A population in better health may accumulate physical capital more quickly. The most obvious route is through savings, as higher life expectancy (for example) increases the expected length of retirement. Indeed, Bloom, Canning, and Graham (2002) attribute the rapid growth of East Asia to precisely this mechanism. Alsan, Bloom, and Canning (2006) and Sachs and Malaney (2002) highlight the impact that better population health has on inflows of foreign capital, as

Figure 1.2 The Preston Curve, 2001

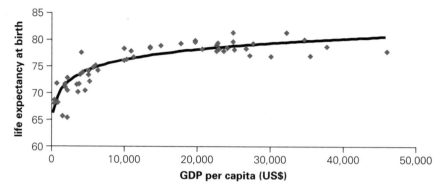

Source: World Bank, World Development Indicators.

opposed to increases in domestic savings; this effect is usually thought to operate in situations in which foreign (direct) investment and expatriates (either in the role of staff or consumers) are highly complementary. Tourism is the most commonly cited example, as the threat of communicable diseases such as SARS (severe acute respiratory syndrome) deters visitors and investment, at least in the short term, because it suggests high-risk environments (Bell and Lewis 2004).

Trends in Health and National Income

The economics and population-health professions were brought together empirically only in the last 30 years. Preston (1975) presents data on per capita income and on population health status as measured by life expectancy for a cross section of countries. More recent data confirm his finding of a concave relationship between health status and income (see figure 1.2) and show that this relationship is becoming stronger over time.

This latter fact shows that income, as measured by GDP, cannot be the sole determinant of health; if it were, countries that grew richer over time would simply have moved along the curve defined by a given year's cross-sectional data. On average, countries whose incomes have grown have achieved better health improvements than would have been predicted from the 1975 data.

The concave relationship between income and health suggests the importance of income distribution for a country's health status: in a country with highly unequal income distribution, the population at large is likely to be less healthy than would be predicted for countries with the same average income. It is commonly argued that this relationship provides a rationale for redistributing a country's income from rich to poor citizens, so as to raise average health status while keeping average income constant (ignoring the efficiency costs of redistribution). This sounds reasonable if indeed increasing the incomes of the poor will improve their health. However, if one believes that changes in health drive income growth, the same concavity properties imply that redistributing *health* from the unhealthy to the

Figure 1.3 Normalized Cross-Country Standard Deviations of Health and Income, 1960–2004

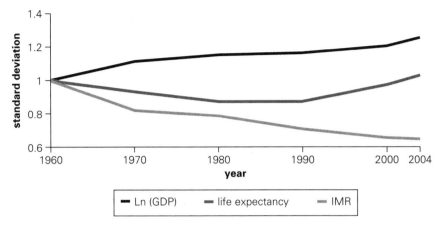

Source: Deaton 2006.

Note: The infant mortality rate (IMR) measures the number of children born who die before their first birthday per 1,000 births. The standard deviation of the under-five mortality rate shows a similar evolution and is not presented in this figure. The IMR is a significant factor in life expectancy calculations, because, particularly in countries with high death rates, a significant portion of a country's deaths occur in the first year of life.

healthy (that is, in the "wrong" direction) would increase aggregate income, with no effect on average health status. The validity, if not the desirability, of each of these interventions thus depends crucially on the direction of causality between income and health.

Although the Preston curve shows a close relationship between income and health in the cross-sectional data, longitudinal data suggest that this relationship may not hold within individual countries over time. Figure 1.3 draws on data presented by Deaton (2006) on the evolution of the cross-country distribution of national incomes and health status between 1960 and 2004. Each curve represents the standard deviation of a variable relative to its value in 1960. The figure shows that per capita incomes have steadily diverged, in keeping with the well-established evidence that incomes in poor countries have not grown fast enough to catch up with incomes in richer countries (Commission on Growth and Development 2008; Pritchett 1997). By contrast, country-level health indicators have converged—until 1990 for life expectancy and through 2004 for the infant mortality rate.[3]

Thus figure 1.3 suggests that, over time, changes in income seem to be unrelated, or even negatively related, to changes in health status: incomes have continued to diverge, while health status has converged. That is, health

---

3 The reversal of the converging trend in life expectancy in the last 15 years is likely due to the collapse of the former Soviet Union, which exhibits high adult mortality, and to the explosion of HIV/AIDS in Sub-Saharan Africa in the 1990s. HIV/AIDS, while it has implications for children and potentially for their incomes later in life—through its impact on schooling—has a more pronounced impact on adult life expectancy than on infant and child mortality.

Figure 1.4 Income Growth and Infant Mortality Rate Reductions in China and India, 1960–2000

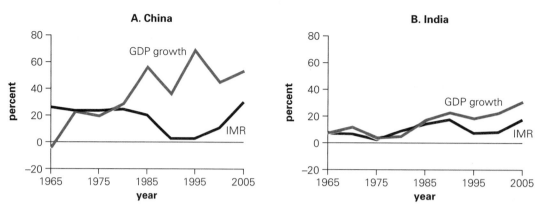

Source: World Bank data, as used by Deaton 2006; see his figure 8.

Note: Each line shows the annualized proportional change for a variable over the preceding five years. IMR is infant mortality rate.

status has improved in poor countries at a faster rate than in rich countries (albeit from a lower base), despite the fact that incomes have grown more slowly in poor countries than in rich ones.

In view of the difficulties and limitations of cross-country comparisons, we summarize the evolution of incomes and health status in two countries—China and India—since 1960. (This exercise follows Deaton 2006; Drèze and Sen 2002). Figure 1.4 suggests that both of these countries have improved their health status and per capita incomes over the last 40 years but that their experiences have differed.

In China the annualized growth rate of GDP is negatively correlated with the annualized rate of reduction of the infant mortality rate (correlation coefficient –0.45, *t* statistic), while in India the correlation is positive (correlation coefficient 0.77, *t* statistic). As Deaton (2006) notes, in China the largest gains in health *preceded* the takeoff in economic growth.

The data from India are perhaps more ambiguous: during that country's period of relatively slow economic growth from 1965 to 1985, the correlation between changes in income and health was tight, but in more recent years, as economic growth has taken off, the rate of improvement in the infant mortality rate has fallen off.

Interpreting Correlations between Health and Income: Data and Estimation Issues

Research on the links between health and growth are fraught with measurement problems, from the selection of variables and the validity of those measures to the econometric problems that emerge where there is reverse causality. Creative solutions to these challenges have met with mixed results, but from a policy perspective the bottom line is that there is a tenuous link between health and growth at the macroeconomic level. This section reviews the measurement issues, the analytic constraints, and alternative options for capturing the correlations between health and income.

Limitations of Aggregate Measures of Health and Income. Although relationships between aggregate measures of health and income can be informative, they have some limitations because both indicators are summary statistics of complex, multidimensional assessments of human activity and well-being.

Measuring "health" is tricky, and no measure aptly captures morbidity and mortality (Schultz 2005). In particular, the use of life expectancy or infant and child mortality rates as measures of health status is not without ambiguity, for both conceptual and practical reasons. First, these indicators attempt to measure aspects of health that might be related to productivity, including the extent to which individuals experience, or are at risk of, bad health, encompassing both morbidity (illness) and premature death. For example, in using life expectancy in cross-country analysis, we place too much weight on infant mortality, while that measure itself is an *imputed* variable in most contexts. Mortality is also a one-time event and remains rare even in high mortality settings. Despite the heavy reliance on mortality statistics to measure health, for all these reasons mortality is a suboptimal measure of "health."

Second, at a practical level, accurate measures of life expectancy require good vital registration data, particularly on deaths. In some developing countries, these data simply do not exist, and estimates of life expectancy are based on child mortality rates, using standard life tables to impute infant mortality levels (adjusting for guesses about mortality risks in the population where necessary). While the cross-country pattern of life expectancy *levels* is likely to be reasonably accurate, data on *changes* in life expectancy may well embody large errors, due to the variety of (unmeasured) causes of such changes.

Third, interventions that affect morbidity but not mortality may well have important effects on productivity that will not be attributed to changes in health status if the latter are measured by life expectancy or infant and child mortality rates. A primary example of such an intervention is the control of the *vivax* strain of malaria, which causes relatively few deaths but high morbidity rates, compared with the more lethal *falciparum* strain. Controlling *vivax* malaria could significantly boost productivity, both directly as adults suffer fewer and less severe attacks and indirectly through increases in the return to, and hence the level of, schooling for children (Bleakley 2006b). Alternative measures of morbidity such as self-reported health status or activities of daily living are not only rarely available but tend to be less reliable than objectively collected data, and they are hard to compare across countries.

Econometric Approaches. Interpreting the observed correlations between country-level health status and income is challenging. First, it is very likely that higher incomes help to improve health status. Second, there may be other factors that affect *both* income and health in a country (Deaton 2006); for example, these might include the country's climate and its disease environment. For both of these reasons, a correlation between income and health might be observed even if there is no direct causal relationship from health to income.

These identification problems are at the root of the lively debate among economists and public health researchers and are well recognized. For example, Bleakley (2007: 73, 74) notes, "Simple correlations of public health and economic outcomes are unlikely to measure the causal effect [of health on income] since public health is endogenous. Indeed, it is likely a normal good." Similarly, in a paper focusing on the impact of malaria, Malaney, Spielman, and Sachs (2004: 143) acknowledge concerns over endogeneity and omitted variables: "The causal effect of malaria on poverty cannot readily be isolated from the effect of poverty on malaria. A second econometric problem lies in the effect of such confounding factors as climate that may drive both poverty and malaria."

Researchers have used various procedures to try to overcome these and other estimation problems. Some studies focus on the relationships between measures of population health (such as life expectancy) and national income (such as GDP) and use econometric techniques to correct for endogeneity and omitted-variable biases; we refer to these as macro approaches in the discussion that follows. At the other extreme, micro approaches examine the link for individuals between health improvements and incomes, with the goal of minimizing identification problems by careful choice of setting. A third strand of the literature combines the macro and micro approaches within a growth-accounting framework, scaling up micro-level measures of the effects of individual health improvements on incomes to yield macro-level estimates of the impact of changes in population health on national income. The following subsections briefly review the findings of studies using the macro and growth-accounting techniques. Subsequently, we explore the more micro approaches.

Findings of Macroeconomic Studies

If we look at a wide enough range of countries, we find that people in richer countries are on average healthier: they live longer and fall ill less often. A cross-country regression quantifies this correlation. One of the first contributions to this literature is the work of Pritchett and Summers (1996), who conclude that "wealthier was healthier"—that is, the causality ran from income to health.

Subsequent work focused on the link between health and *changes* in income: healthier countries might be richer, but do they grow more quickly? Gallup and Sachs (2001) address this question and find a strong correlation between the level of population health and income growth. Of course, there are obvious endogeneity and omitted-variable concerns with this kind of exercise, but it offers the tantalizing prospect that a country can raise its income by improving its health.

A range of papers subsequently refined and extended the Gallup and Sachs methodology. Bloom, Canning, and Sevilla (2004) report the results of 13 studies that all employ cross-country regressions and all show large effects of health on growth. To try to correct for possible third factors that affect both the level of health and the growth of income, Bloom, Canning, and Sevilla (2004) assess the correlation between changes in health status and changes in income across countries; they find similar results.

The problem of endogeneity affects virtually all of the cross-country studies in this genre, because differences in the levels and growth rates of income can plausibly affect the levels and changes in health status. The methodological response is to use a proxy indicator for health status (or for changes therein), which the researcher believes does not *directly* affect the level or growth of income. Any observed correlation between such an "instrumental variable" and income is then evidence of a causal link from health to income.[4]

Gallup and Sachs (2001) use geography as an instrumental variable for health status. The basic epidemiology and biology of infectious diseases mean that at any given level of income these diseases are likely to be more prevalent in tropical regions. An impact of geography (distance from the equator) on incomes might then constitute evidence of an impact of health on incomes. This approach has been questioned in a series of papers (Acemoglu, Johnson, and Robinson 2002; Easterly and Levine 2003; Rodrik, Subramanian, and Trebbi 2002) that challenge the assumption made by Gallup and Sachs that geography does not affect growth either directly or through its impact on a third factor that is itself important for growth. In particular, these critics illustrate that, once the effect of geography on a country's *choice of institutions* is accounted for, geography has little independent impact on incomes. Broadly speaking, tropical equatorial countries have tended to adopt institutions that are less conducive to economic growth than have other countries, and it is the choice of institutions that induces a correlation between health and income. The stark implication of their findings is that improving health status (by, say, expanding the use of bed nets to reduce the incidence of malaria) would have little impact on overall growth and that institutional reform is what is needed to increase income.

Sachs (2003) admits the possibility that geography affects institutional quality, but takes issue with the finding that this is the *only* effect that geography has. To this end, he conducts a series of cross-country regressions aimed at distinguishing the effect of malaria prevalence—which is highly correlated with geography—from that of institutional quality. Instead of using a simple measure of geography (distance from the equator) as a proxy for health outcomes, which are arguably correlated with income, he constructs two instruments: one for malaria risk, which he calls "malaria

---

4 Bloom, Canning, and Sevilla (2004) use lagged values of health-related inputs and economic output (and their lagged growth rates) as instruments. However, Weil (2005) questions the validity of this strategy and claims that "the identifying assumption required . . . is not explicitly stated or defended." Mankiw (1995: 303–04) goes as far as to suggest that "cross-country data can never establish, for instance, the direction of causality between investment [or health] and growth." He notes the implausibility of lagged variables being good instruments, highlights the issue of multicollinearity—"those countries that do things right do most things right, and those countries that do things wrong do most things wrong"—and illustrates how lack of independence and measurement errors (both of which are acute in cross-country regressions) can bias results.

ecology" and which is based on climatological conditions and vector preva-lence, and one for institutional quality, which is based on settler mortality and the share of a country's population living in temperate zones. In all his specifications he finds that both institutional quality *and* malaria risk are statistically significant determinants of income. But even this approach does not escape methodological criticism. In particular, the measured impact of malaria ecology on growth is unbiased only if we believe that malaria ecol-ogy does not affect institutional quality.

Aside from the econometric issues that arise when conducting cross-country regressions, one should not rely too heavily on results that selectively exclude some countries. Bloom and Canning (2003b) illustrate this point. They analyze how the demographic changes in East Asia that were brought about by health improvements led to increased savings and growth. They then reflect on the experience of Latin America, which had "broadly similar demographic and health conditions," and note, "East Asia's economy grew explosively, while economic growth in Latin America was stagnant. Latin America's policy environment—with poor labor market policies, a lack of openness to world markets, and an inadequate education system—was quite different from East Asia's and did not offer the same favorable conditions." While it may be that the interaction of good policies with good health is what matters, the comparison between East Asia and Latin America sug-gests that it is, to first order, simply good *policy* that matters.

Several recent papers have attempted to identify the impact of health on income and growth by modeling innovations in the health environment that can plausibly be taken as exogenous. For example, Acemoglu and Robinson (2008) investigate whether advances in the health sciences have affected national income. They analyze the considerable technical prog-ress in drug therapies, vaccines, insecticides, and the dissemination of scien-tific knowledge through international organizations that occurred in the twentieth century and find that these advances did not cause a rise in per cap-ita income. For their study, the authors construct a measure of how much a country could expect to gain from these technological and institutional inno-vations—countries with a high incidence of now curable or avoidable diseases would be predicted to have greater gains in terms of reduced mortality—and use this measure as an instrumental variable for actual changes in population health. The idea is that the instrument is correlated with actual improvements in health, but not directly with changes in income. They find that the advances in medicine significantly raised the growth rate of population and that income (as measured by GDP) also increased. Since the increase in income did not match the increase in population, real per capita income fell, despite the health improvements. This effect is essentially a general equilibrium phenomenon: labor supply rose, while other factors (land, capital) did not adjust, thereby reducing per capita output.

Their result mirrors that obtained by Young (2005), who uses micro data to calibrate a neoclassical growth model with fertility effects, in order to estimate the impact of the HIV/AIDS epidemic in South Africa. Young finds that, because of the negative effect of the epidemic on population, capital-labor ratios increase enough to offset any plausible reduction in the rate of intergenerational human capital transmission associated with parental deaths.

Commenting on a paper by Acemoglu and Johnson (see chapter 4 of this volume), Bleakley (2006a) notes that these authors find no impact of health changes on aggregate GDP. He emphasizes that labor market conditions, in particular the extent of unemployment and underemployment, are crucial in determining the impact of health improvements on measured GDP. Suggesting that a model assuming that capital is fixed is inappropriate, Bleakley notes that in reality the capital stock should have responded over the 40 years covered by these authors' analysis and that land productivity too is likely to have improved over the period (due to increased urbanization and the green revolution in agriculture).

Using Growth Accounting to Assess the Impact of Health on Economic Returns

Another group of studies attempts to overcome the shortcomings of the macroeconomic evidence by adding microeconomic elements. Their use of more refined techniques and reliance on measures that better capture the economic effects of health and nutrition investments arguably provide a firmer foundation than the macro studies for drawing conclusions about the link between health and growth.

Shastry and Weil (2003) and Weil (2005) use a different methodology to estimate the share of cross-country variation in income that can be associated with differences in health status. Combining microeconomic estimates of the impact of health on productivity with a macroeconomic accounting model, they decompose aggregate country output into a (residual) productivity term plus the return to certain factors, including physical capital, educational human capital, and health human capital. Measures of output, physical capital, and educational capital (proxied by years of schooling) are readily available for some countries, although admittedly a subset, particularly for education; the challenge is to construct a measure of health that is relevant to productivity.

Weil's (2005) approach to accounting for the effect of health on economic performance is to estimate the returns (in terms of higher wages) to a number of health indicators, including adult height, adult survival rate, and age of menarche, using instruments for differences in health inputs, birth weight differences between twins (see, for example, Behrman and Rosenzweig 2004), and historical data on caloric intake (see Fogel 1997). He finds that a 10 percent increase in the adult survival rate would lead to an increase in labor input per worker of 6.7 percent and in GDP per worker of about 4.4 percent. Notably, this estimate of the increase in GDP per worker is much smaller than other such estimates in the literature.[5] Weil

---

5 Indeed it lies *below* the lower bound of the 95 percent confidence interval for the same measure as estimated by Bloom and Canning (2005) using a cross-country regression with lagged variables as instruments.

calculates that about 9.9 percent of the variance of log GDP per worker is attributable to health and nutrition gaps between countries. He concludes, "My estimates do not match the characterization of ill health as a major stumbling block to economic development, as described in the WHO [World Health Organization] report on macroeconomics and health."

When general equilibrium effects associated with fertility and population changes are incorporated into Weil's analysis—which, as Acemoglu and Robinson (chapter 4 of this volume) point out, implicitly assumes a fixed population size—the estimated impact of health on per capita income may be somewhat smaller. However, the aggregation methodology does not allow for certain behavioral responses to improved health, such as changes in savings rates or educational choices, which could possibly increase incomes in the long term. In a more recent paper, Ashraf, Lester, and Weil (2007) incorporate these additional channels by which health changes might affect growth, but they still find only modest income gains.

The conclusions from these combined micro-macro studies suggest some limitations. As discussed below regarding microeconomic studies (for example, Bleakley in chapter 5 of this volume), health improvements can improve economic performance but are unlikely to explain why some countries lag far behind others in material well-being. Moreover, because the most significant health improvements occur early in a person's life, the associated income effects take a long time to come to fruition.

The Links between Individual Health and Productivity: Microeconomic Evidence on Health and Growth

An alternative approach to studying links between health and income is to examine individual and household investments and their effects on household income. The advantage of this approach, given data of sufficient quality, is that we might have more confidence in attributing certain impacts to particular health or other variables.

The disadvantages of a microeconomic approach are that the results may not be easily applicable to other circumstances and that what may be true at the micro level may not apply for the population at large because of external or general equilibrium effects. For example, if the labor market rewards individuals solely according to their health rank (healthier people get more job offers), then improvements in one person's health will translate into increases in his or her income, matched by reductions in the income of others, and there will be no impact on aggregate income. More generally, as in Acemoglu and Robinson (2008), if workers use other factors of production that are in relatively fixed supply, such as land and capital, then health improvements that increase the supply of labor could conceivably reduce average output per worker. Micro-level studies cannot pick up such effects.

Despite these shortcomings, micro approaches provide important insights into the potential impact of health on economic well-being. Below we focus on two broad sources of health-related variation across individuals and see how these translate into differences in economic productivity. The first source of differences among individuals is in the basic inputs to a healthy and productive life; we report on the economic implications of these differences and on the results of interventions to improve nutrition and caloric intake, on the one hand, and to enhance early childhood development, on the other. The second source of differences is in the incidence of illnesses and the access to and use of medical treatments; we report the findings of select studies on the negative impacts of HIV and malaria on productivity and the economic impacts of treatments such as deworming tablets and antiretroviral therapy.

Impact of Interventions Affecting Early Childhood Development

Mounting evidence from economics, psychology, and neuroscience indicates that early investments in young children profoundly affect their long-term physical and mental health, earnings, and well-being. Early experience shapes brain architecture (Knudsen and others 2006), and early childhood development has a long reach that affects physical and mental health and well-being later in life (Drukker and Tassenaar 1997; Fogel 1994; Mustard 2006). Knudsen (2004) has shown that there are sensitive periods for neurological development early in life that influence long-term memory. Thus the critical period for intervention is in the preschool years. Recent work has produced considerable evidence on the issue.

Victora and others (2008) summarize the results and long-term implications of maternal undernutrition from five developing-country cohort studies and review the literature on the same topic. They find that undernutrition can cause structural damage to the brain and that maternal and child undernutrition result in shorter adults, less schooling, lower productivity, and lower birth weights among their offspring. There is also a link with adult cancer, lung disease, and mental illness, all of which compromise productivity and earnings.

Thomas and Frankenberg (2002) provide a useful review of microeconomic studies of the impact of nutrition on economic outcomes at the individual level. They summarize their findings as indicating that "while the establishment of this link [from health to income] is not straightforward, the weight of evidence points to nutrition, and possibly other dimensions of health, as significant determinants of economic productivity." Walker and others (2007), in a meta-study of risk factors for young children, note that stunted children consistently show cognitive and educational deficits, although the size of the deficit varies across settings. They argue for intervention to prevent stunting, inadequate cognitive stimulation, iodine deficiency, and iron deficiency anemia.

Heckman (2007) emphasizes the importance of noncognitive skills in preparing children for school, adulthood, and the workplace, and his research suggests that both the cognitive and social-emotional abilities of individuals as children explain many features of their later economic and social behavior. Gaps in cognitive ability are established early, and in the United

States they explain much of the differential in individuals' educational performance across income levels (Cunha and others 2006).

Grantham-McGregor and others (2007) summarize the scientific and behavioral evidence from developing countries and point to poverty, malnutrition, poor health, and unstimulating home environments as compromising the cognitive, motor, and social-emotional development of children. Their meta-study finds that both poverty and childhood stunting (due to persistent undernutrition) correlate with poor school performance, lower income in adulthood, higher fertility, and inadequate care of their own offspring.

Longitudinal studies show the relationship between early childhood development and language, intelligence, and criminality. Black and others (2008) illustrate how low birth weights significantly affect longer-run outcomes such as adult height, intelligence quotient, earnings, and education. Verbal exposure by reading and talking has significant effects on children's verbal skills and language at later stages of development (Mustard 2006: 33). Many studies (cited in Mustard 2006: 37) have shown that children with poor verbal skill development during their first three years of life do poorly in language and literacy in school.

Both stunting and poverty are associated with declines in years of schooling. In Brazil, low-income, stunted children receive more than four fewer years of schooling on average and, once they become adults, earn an estimated 30 percent less income than the average worker (Grantham-McGregor and others 2007).[6] Thomas and Strauss (1997) show almost a 20 percent reduction in returns to schooling among self-employed males in Brazil when height is added to the wage function.

Studies of adult literacy in the United States under the U.S. Department of Education National Education Assessment Program have shown that children with the lowest physical and mental health also perform at the bottom of the distribution in standardized tests. Figure 1.5, from Grantham-McGregor and others (2007), shows the cognitive deficits resulting from being in the lowest wealth quintile in the first three years of life. On the basis of income, the standard deviations in cognitive and schooling deficits of children (z scores) in the poorest 20 percent of households are significant. The five countries featured represent three continents and both low- and middle-income groups, suggesting that culture and location are less important than biology in determining these deficits.

What of the impact of interventions? Cuba, with its extensive programs for pregnant women and young children, has achieved significantly better performance on literacy assessments, scoring two standard deviations higher than any other Latin American country (Carnoy and Marshall 2005, as cited in Mustard 2006: 39).

Fogel (2002) and Alderman, Behrman, and Hoddinott (2003) show the importance of specific nutrition interventions in bolstering cognitive

---

6 Stunted children with limited cognitive skills are more likely to drop out and to learn less when they do stay in school (Grantham-McGregor and others 2007).

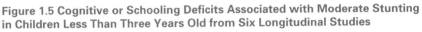

Figure 1.5 Cognitive or Schooling Deficits Associated with Moderate Stunting in Children Less Than Three Years Old from Six Longitudinal Studies

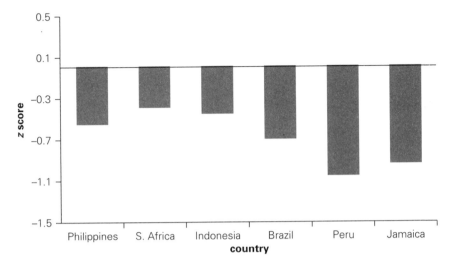

Source: Grantham-McGregor and others 2007.

development, physical stature and strength, earlier school enrollment and more regular school attendance, greater schooling and learning, increased adult productivity, and healthier offspring.

A recent 35-year longitudinal study of the long-term impacts of nutrition intervention during early childhood provides striking results (Behrman in chapter 6 of this volume; Melgar and others 2008). Two nutrition supplements were randomly assigned to low-income children in rural Guatemala; children who consumed the protein-rich supplement achieved dramatically better educational performance and labor force earnings. Women who received the protein-rich supplement during their first three years of life attained 1.17 more years of schooling, their infants' birth weight was 179 grams heavier, and their children were a third taller than those of women who consumed the calorie-based supplement as children. Men who consumed the high-protein supplement in the first two years of their childhood earned an average wage 46 percent above that of men who consumed the calorie-based supplement.

Thus the evidence on the value of interventions in the preschool years is striking. Indeed, recent evidence (see figures 1.6 and 1.7) suggests that the economic rate of return to preschool attendance dwarfs the returns to university or job training (Carneiro and Heckman 2003) and that the lack of attention to early childhood development has high long-run costs (Heckman 2007).

Investments in individual children before the age of three produce more significant impacts than any other social or health investments and at a lower marginal cost (Carneiro and Heckman 2003). Only investments in public health improvements may be more important, but these tend to be complements to, rather than substitutes for, interventions targeted to young children.

Figure 1.6 Returns to Different Levels of Education Based on Family Background

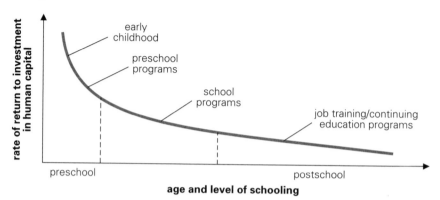

Source: Adapted from Cunha and others 2006.

Figure 1.7 Returns to Different Levels of Education and Family Background

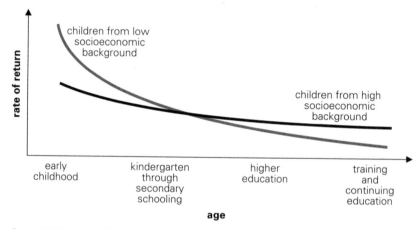

Source: Wößmann and Schütz 2006.

To sum up, interventions affecting early childhood development produce long-term benefits for human capital and productivity. The microeconomic studies reviewed above suggest that prenatal care, food supplements for malnourished children, micronutrients, and preschool for disadvantaged children, among other such investments, help to raise the potential for long-term academic and workplace success and lifelong well-being. These results are among the most robust in terms of the direct impacts on individuals and long-term implications for enhanced health status, productivity, and income. Perhaps even more important is the potential impact on the next generation. Indeed, these findings suggest that the cycle of poverty, morbidity, and early mortality can be broken by interventions in early childhood.

Unfortunately, early childhood investments have not received enough attention or resources. Developed and developing countries alike now have a major opportunity to enhance human capital by turning their attention to such investments.

Impact of Illness on Income

Investments in young children and better nutrition for malnourished children are likely to make people healthier and less likely to fall ill. But what happens to productivity when people do fall ill? A broad literature addresses this issue, using the so-called cost-of-illness approach to measure the impact of health on income. Some studies focus on the immediate impacts of illness, including reduced labor supply and the lower productivity of sick people while on the job, and others include possibly long-term effects due to protracted separations from the labor force and disengagement from economic activities.

Two studies by Bleakley (chapter 5 of this volume) examine the effects of disease-eradication campaigns on health and economic outcomes; his results suggest that improving health could be important for growth on the margin but is unlikely to be a panacea. In his 2007 study of the impact of hookworm eradication efforts under the Rockefeller Sanitary Commission in the American South in the early twentieth century, Bleakley measures the infection rates that prevailed before the intervention; on average, 40 percent of school-age children were infected. Like Acemoglu and Johnson (chapter 4 of this volume), he uses data on infection rates by location, which reflect the geographic variation in potential benefits from hookworm eradication, to identify the impact of changes in the health environment on economic outcomes.

Bleakley finds that areas with higher preexisting infection rates saw greater increases in school enrollment, attendance, and literacy after the intervention. For example, he finds that school attendance before 1910 was negatively correlated with 1913 infection rates, but that by 1920 the 1913 infection rates did not predict attendance. That is, those areas that had more to gain from hookworm eradication saw their school enrollment rates increase more. Bleakley finds similar results for literacy. Other changes in the economic environment could have led to similar trends over this period, but he argues that, if so, these influences would have affected adults in different areas in similar ways. However, he finds no similar pattern among adults across the affected areas who, by the nature of the disease, had virtually no preexisting infection.

Bleakley (2006b) undertakes a similar exercise, focusing on the malaria eradication campaigns in the United States circa 1920 and in Brazil, Colombia, and Mexico circa 1955. Preexisting prevalence rates across regions, combined with a paced eradication campaign across the U.S. South, which provide exogenous variation, permit him to identify the impact of childhood exposure to malaria on future adult literacy and incomes. He finds that, among individuals born well before the relevant eradication campaign, those born in more malarial regions had lower wages and lower literacy rates later in life, while among individuals born well after the campaigns, malaria prevalence before the eradication campaign had little effect on future wages and literacy. He concludes, "Persistent childhood malaria infection reduces adult income by 40 to 60 percent."

Bleakley is able to differentiate the impact of morbidity from that of mortality on future income. He finds that eradication of *vivax* malaria (which causes high morbidity, but relatively few deaths) leads to significant increases in human capital formation and future income, but that eradication of *falciparum* malaria (which is often fatal) produces no such gains. To explain this result, he argues that, although reductions in mortality rates increase the marginal benefit of human capital acquisition (because people who survive have more years in which to earn a return on human capital investments), this might have little impact on the level of investment if marginal costs are rising steeply. By contrast, a reduction in morbidity makes it easier to attend school and to learn while there, thereby flattening the marginal cost curve and leading to significant increases in human capital acquisition.

Bleakley uses his results to extrapolate across countries and estimates that malaria may account for about 10–16 percent of the income gap between the United States and Latin America. This suggests that eradicating malaria could modestly narrow the income gap by inducing higher growth in Latin America. He concludes, "While reducing malaria could bring substantial income gains to some countries, the estimated effect is approximately an order of magnitude too small to be useful in explaining the global income distribution" (Bleakley 2006b: 26).

Several other studies of the effects of malaria eradication programs find that the control of disease vector environments (for example, swamps) has a profound effect on health status and on education and productivity. Cutler and others (2007) examine the impact of a malaria eradication program across Indian states during the 1950s and find that the program increased literacy and primary school completion rates by 10 percentage points, accounting for about half the observed gains in these measures over the period spanning the intervention in malarial regions. Barecca (2007), Hong (2007), and Lucas (2005) all find significant effects of either exposure to malaria or its eradication on a variety of economic outcomes such as schooling, literacy, labor force participation, and wealth. These findings call to mind the broad-ranging positive results of the West African Onchocerciasis Control Program, discussed above.

The recent expansion in the availability of antiretroviral drugs in Sub-Saharan Africa has enabled researchers to examine the impact of HIV/AIDS treatment on labor market outcomes. The effects on labor supply and income seem to be considerable. In a study in western Kenya, Thirumurthy, Graff Zivin, and Goldstein (2005) find that, within six months of starting treatment, a patient is 20 percent more likely to participate in the labor force and has a 35 percent increase in weekly hours worked. Larson and others (2008) study a similar expansion of antiretroviral treatment (ART) in Kericho, a tea-growing region of western Kenya. They find that in the nine months before starting ART, HIV-positive individuals worked significantly fewer days plucking tea each month than their comparators without HIV, but that, after starting ART, the individuals undergoing treatment quickly increased the number of days they spent on this work (to 6.8, 11.8, and

14.3 days a month at one, six, and 12 full months on ART, respectively), while the labor supply of their comparators remained constant at 17–18 days a month. Also, during the first six months on ART, the individuals on treatment earned on average 25 percent less than their comparators, but during the next six months of therapy they raised their earnings to 89 percent of those of their comparators.

Health care can work to improve children's school attendance as well as adults' labor supply. Miguel and Kremer (2004) provide something of a benchmark analysis of the link between health care and schooling by examining the impact of randomly assigned deworming treatment across schools in western Kenya. They find that the intervention reduced student absenteeism by a quarter, with the larger gains among the youngest students and among girls compared with boys. Despite the impressive gains in school attendance, however, their study found no effect on educational outcomes as measured by test scores. This may be because school attendance was not enough to ensure good academic performance: complementary inputs such as teachers and facilities may have been sufficiently poor, or sufficiently overstretched, that children's additional days at school had little impact on learning.[7]

Another route by which health affects schooling is orphanhood. This has received a great deal of attention in the literature on the economic effects of AIDS. If orphans receive less education, then the intergenerational transmission of human capital can be interrupted, with important, and potentially disastrous, long-term effects (Bell, Devarajan, and Gersbach 2003). Case, Paxson, and Ableidinger (2002) use demographic and health surveys across 10 Sub-Saharan countries to examine the impact of orphanhood and find that orphans are significantly less likely than other children to be enrolled in school. In this study, however, the repeated cross-sectional nature of the data means that the interpretation of the results is not without ambiguity. Gertler, Levine, and Ames (2004) use panel data from Indonesia and find that a parental death doubles the probability that a child will drop out of school the same year. Neither of these two studies finds a gender effect, either at the parent or child level. Other studies find little impact of parental death on schooling, possibly because members of extended families take on the parenting function (Ainsworth, Beegle, and Koda 2002; Kamali and others 1996; Lloyd and Blanc 1996).[8]

Consistent with this view, Fortson (2006: 26) reports that children in areas in southern Africa with high HIV prevalence are "less likely to attend school, [are] less likely to complete primary school, and progress more slowly through school." Fortson shows that more than half of this

---

7   Miguel and Kremer (2004) suggest that the classroom overcrowding that resulted from lower infection rates could have offset any positive effect from lower absenteeism.

8   Evans and Miguel (2003), as discussed in Miguel (2005), use data from the randomized deworming project in western Kenya to address some of the identification issues that trouble cross-sectional and panel data studies. Their results on the impact of parental death on schooling mirror those of Case, Paxson, and Ableidinger (2002) and Gertler, Levine, and Ames (2004): parental death seems to reduce schooling, and there is little difference by gender.

impact on schooling can be attributed to the expectation of a shorter life of the parent and not to orphanhood itself; all children do badly when adults expect to die sooner. Reductions in adult mortality might lead to greater investment in children's education, because of higher demand either by parents or by children themselves, who expect to reap the future returns for longer.

Another important dimension of poor health is the economic impact it has on other people. Thirumurthy, Graff Zivin, and Goldstein (2005), studying the impact of HIV/AIDS treatment in Kenya, find that the labor supply of other household members changes: young boys and women in the household work considerably less after the patient in their family starts treatment, although girls and men in the household do not change their labor supply. The authors highlight the important potential implications for schooling outcomes. Beegle, De Weerdt, and Dercon (2006) study the impact of mortality from AIDS on the economic well-being of surviving household members, in both the short and long term, in a 13-year cohort of individuals in Tanzania. The authors find that households who have experienced an adult death due to AIDS see a reduction in their consumption of 7 percent after five years, while households not so affected see an increase in their consumption of 12 percent over the same period. Thus, vis-à-vis the average household, households who experience an adult death due to AIDS suffer a 19 percent fall in consumption after five years. There is some evidence that such losses are persistent, although they are estimated imprecisely, and the possibility that they are reversed in the long term cannot be rejected. An interesting finding is that losing a *female* adult to AIDS leads to a particularly severe fall in consumption.

Health-Related Interventions and Health: Evidence and Policy Implications

The above review of the literature suggests that the macro link from health to growth is still not beyond dispute, although our interpretation is that the link, if it exists, is relatively small. However, individuals and households can improve productivity and boost their incomes with specific health-related investments.

What this means for policy choices is not immediately clear. Improving life expectancy by a year might increase a country's income by some amount, but *how* such a health improvement is to be achieved is the subject of a whole separate literature. However, we need to examine whether we care about health only for its own sake or also for its potential role in improving incomes.

Experience shows that it will not be that easy to spend our way to better health and thence, if there is a causal link, to higher growth: just as growth-inducing policy interventions are elusive, so too can health-improving strategies be difficult to identify and politically unpopular.[9] All too often the link from spending on health care to health outcomes is weak (Filmer, Hammer, and Pritchett 2000). The question is why that is the case and what interventions and policies can remedy the situation.

Market Failures and the Financing and Delivery of Health Care

As well as investing in public goods that improve health and hygiene, all governments take an active role in financing and providing health care, which has the attributes of a private good, given the significant failures in private markets for both health care and insurance. Economists have long understood the limitations of unfettered private markets in delivering health care. First, an agency problem can exist between the provider and the patient: the patient, being at an informational disadvantage, might not know the cause of illness or what health intervention, if any, is appropriate, and she is at the mercy of the provider. Of course, similar problems exist in many service markets, from auto repair to accounting services, many of which appear to operate reasonably well.

The second feature of medical care markets that can restrict their efficiency is individuals' need for insurance against the possibility of random catastrophic events. Such events can expose individuals to significant risks, but adverse selection might limit the extent to which private markets can spread those risks. Governments sometimes respond by financing or delivering medical care themselves (as in the U.K. National Health Service), in order to maintain coverage of a broad pool of individuals. This desire to provide a safety net explains the significant presence of public spending on health in most developing countries and, especially, in countries in transition from communism, where governments continue to dominate health care delivery.

Some countries couple more or less universal public insurance with private provision of medical care. Examples include the U.S. insurance programs for the elderly (Medicare) and the poor (Medicaid) and the Australian, French, and German health care systems. In much of the developing world, universal health care translates into government financing and provision from mandatory wage taxes or general revenue that underwrite health care costs. Parallel out-of-pocket costs and private insurance finance private health care. Transition countries, with their history of generous government financing and provision, now combine public provision and finance with some private sector activity and informal, under-the-table payments to public providers.

---

9 Indeed, while the technical and scientific knowledge exists to solve many health problems, the fact that these solutions are often not widely adopted suggests that they are not simple to implement (World Bank 2005). For example, oral rehydration therapy (ORT) is a simple and cheap way to reduce diarrhea, which kills more than 4 million children a year. But ORT fails to reach needy families in some developing and transition countries for the same reasons that most redistributive policies are not fully effective: political tradeoffs, vested interests, corruption, and a general lack of resources.

Relatively open-ended public insurance coverage, in conjunction with strong profit motives in the private sector, can often lead to inefficient levels of care, such as overprescription of drugs and unnecessary procedures. Not facing the (marginal) cost of their decisions regarding the use of services, physicians order and patients opt for excess testing, treatment, and other benefits. Even if there is no agency problem between provider and patient, insurance leads to overconsumption. To control costs, these moral hazard effects have led to the introduction of provider payment arrangements that reward performance and discourage overspending (for example, prospective payments systems), rationing of care, and other cost-control measures.

Physician agency, adverse selection, and moral hazard together suggest that health care services will be provided excessively to people with insurance and deficiently to people without. In practice, however, the failures of the medical care market are more nuanced. While spending might be excessive in some countries, the actual delivery of useful services does not always follow suit: far from spending and getting too much, society spends too much and gets too little. Similarly, the theory of adverse selection implies that the bad (risks) will drive out the good (risks), but policy makers usually express exactly the opposite concern: that people with high risks will not be able to afford insurance. Publicly financed insurance is then likely to appear expensive, precisely because it covers relatively expensive, high risk individuals.

Cross-Country Evidence on Health Care Spending and Health in Developing and Transition Countries

Cross-country evidence on the link between health care spending and health status is not encouraging. Both market *and* government failures combine to complicate the design of health policy, in general, and the financing and delivery of health care, in particular. Indeed, considerable debate continues over what effect, if any, public spending on health care has on health in developing and transition countries. At first, this ambiguity seems surprising: surely spending on widgets should produce widgets?

The reasons why public spending on health care might not improve health, as set out by Filmer, Hammer, and Pritchett (2000), are economically straightforward. First, if there is a functioning private market for health care, public spending may simply replace private activities, rather than adding to the aggregate supply of health care. Second, public purchase of health care services does not necessarily assure their delivery to patients: doctors who are paid but do not show up to work, drugs that are procured but are siphoned off, and diagnostic equipment that lies idle for lack of maintenance or complementary inputs, such as electricity or skilled labor, all contribute to health spending, but not to health. Third, the technical efficacy of some health care spending (on garlic as a cure for AIDS, for example) is very low or even zero, so that even if some publicly financed services are delivered to patients, they might have little effect.

One way to examine the impact of public spending on health is to employ cross-country regression techniques, as in the health-income literature reviewed above. In this case, though, we can be somewhat more confident about the use of cross-country comparisons, because problems of endogeneity seem to be less severe: it is unlikely that better population health would, in itself, lead to greater public spending on health.

Filmer and Pritchett (1999) regress under-five mortality on a variety of variables, including public health spending, and find that virtually all the cross-country variation is attributable to average per capita income, its distribution, female education, ethnolinguistic diversity, and religious and regional dummy variables. That is, health spending is more or less uncorrelated with health outcomes: independent variation in public health spending explains a paltry one-seventh of 1 percent of the variation in child mortality.

Wagstaff and Claeson (2004) examine how these results are affected by good governance. They find that health spending does reduce under-five mortality as long as the quality of governance, as measured by the CPIA (country program and institutional analysis) index, is high.[10] Flawed institutions would be expected to produce limited and poor-quality health services. But Lewis (2006) finds no association between the effectiveness of health spending and proxy measures for the effectiveness of institutions in the health sector—either the government effectiveness or the corruption measures of Kaufmann, Kraay, and Mastruzzi (2005).

One channel through which public spending may affect health—and one that, implicitly or otherwise, motivates some calls for greater spending—is its impact on the poor. Bidani and Ravallion (1997) find that public health spending significantly affects the health of the poor, but (consistent with Filmer and Pritchett 1999) not aggregate health.

In more recent work, Boone and Zhan (2006) investigate the determinants of child mortality using survey data on 278,000 children in 45 low-income countries. Their results provide some nuances to those of Filmer, Hammer, and Pritchett (2000). Somewhat controversially, they find that the prevalence of common diseases and the supply of infrastructure such as water and sanitation are *not* good predictors of child mortality, but that parents' education and a mother's propensity to seek out modern medical care are. Here the simulated effects they report appear large: for example, they find that if all mothers and fathers in the 45 countries had years of schooling equal to those of parents in Egypt, child mortality in these countries would fall by 19 percent. They also report that halving the prevalence of diarrhea, fever, and cough would reduce child mortality by only 3 percent.[11]

In keeping with the results of country-level studies, Boone and Zhan (2006) conclude that educated parents demand health services and that these services will be forthcoming from the private market. Educated parents

---

10 This is good news as much for health spending as for the CPIA index as a measure of governance. "Good" public spending should lead to improved health outcomes (unless it simply crowds out private spending), so the fact that countries with high CPIA scores show a positive link from spending to health is consistent with the CPIA measuring something relevant.

11 These numbers are, however, difficult to apply to decision making, as the costs of the two hypothetical interventions are not reported.

may well be better able to obtain a supply of quality medical care from the private market. They might even be better able, or better motivated, to ensure good governance procedures within the public sector, thereby improving both the quality of publicly delivered medical care and the reliability and adequacy of public infrastructure.

In the OECD countries the evidence on the impact of health spending on health status is tenuous. Bunker, Frazier, and Mosteller (1994) suggest that the main effect of health care is on the quality of life and well-being, as measured by increases in activity and mobility. This indirect evidence suggests that health care plays a key role by providing information (about lifestyle and prevention) and reducing morbidity.

Country-Level Evidence on the Effectiveness of Health Care Spending: The Importance of Institutions

Examining why the link between health spending and health status is so tenuous is easiest at the country and health facility level, where institutional issues can be fully explored. Limited data and research on the subject complicate the design of effective policies, but evidence is beginning to emerge on the nature of health institutions in developing and transition countries and the kinds of services that they support. Our reading of the literature suggests that the most severe constraints in improving health through the delivery of health care in developing countries are institutional in nature and include the establishment and enforcement of basic performance incentives and cost containment. This section discusses some recent evidence on these topics and their relevance for institutional strengthening to improve health care service delivery.

Access to health care has improved markedly in the last two decades, but the quality of public health care services has been examined only recently. For the most part it has been found wanting. Recent evidence suggests that ineffective incentives and lack of accountability undermine the public provision of health services, leading to underperformance and substandard care (Lewis 2006). This may help to explain why public spending shows minimal effects on health status. Jack and Lewis (2004) attribute the shortcomings to government failure, effectively "government interventions that have gone wrong."

Institutions in health care are important but understudied. The lack of sound institutions undermines health investments and leads to ambiguous evidence on the relationship between health care services and health status. Accepted indicators of health care performance such as hospital infection rates, utilization statistics, or surgery survival rates are rarely collected even where required, for lack of some combination of oversight, regulation, and enforcement. This applies in middle-income countries as well as poorer ones. Indirect indicators of poor performance that are increasingly relied on in the absence of more direct measures include provider absenteeism, lack of basic medical supplies and drugs, poor management of purchases, corruption in selling public positions, leakage of funds, and under-the-table payments by patients, all of which highlight the nature of the performance lapses that undermine effective service delivery (Lewis 2006).

Figure 1.8 Absentee Rates among Health Workers in Select Countries, 1989–2003

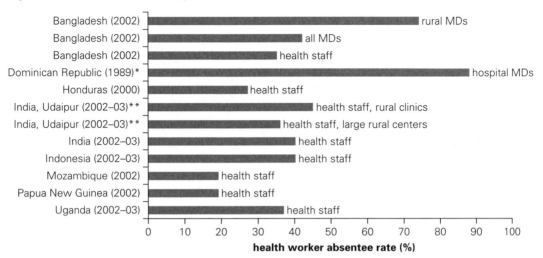

Sources: Banerjee, Deaton, and Duflo 2005; Chaudhury and Hammer 2004; Chaudhury and others 2005; Lewis 2006; Lewis, La Forgia, and Sulvetta 1996; Lindelow, Kushnarova, and Kaiser 2006.

*Santo Domingo Hospital, Dominican Republic.
**Udaipur District, Rajasthan, India.

An extraordinarily important factor in public health care is simply whether workers show up for work. Chaudhury and Hammer (2004) report shockingly high rates of absenteeism among doctors in rural Bangladesh: 40 percent of doctors in large clinics and fully 74 percent of doctors in small (single-doctor) clinics. Chaudhury and others (2005) report figures on the absenteeism of health workers and teachers across six developing countries (Bangladesh, Ecuador, India, Indonesia, Peru, and Uganda). Figure 1.8 summarizes evidence from these studies and others that show similarly high rates of absence using different methods including surprise visits, time-in-motion studies, and clinical observations. Absenteeism has been captured in qualitative work as well (DiTella and Savedoff 2001).

Results from a range of countries—India, Tanzania, and Brazil—are instructive. A study in India finds that the public sector provides medical practitioners with attenuated incentives for good performance: Das and Hammer (2007) report the results of observing more than 4,000 doctor-patient interactions in Delhi and comparing clinical practices with what the doctor knew to be appropriate behavior.[12] They find that "public doctors exert much less effort than their private counterparts" (Das and Hammer 2007: 8). In addition, better-trained doctors do not necessarily provide better service: Das and Hammer find that, although providers without medical degrees are less competent (that is, they know less about what *should* be done in clinical situations), providers with medical degrees exert significantly less effort. Indeed, "clearly incentives are strong for MBBS [that is,

---

12 Vignettes are case studies that assess adherence to clinical protocols.

degree-holding] doctors to do less than they know, and [the incentives are] stronger still in the public sector."

In Tanzania, using vignettes and direct clinical observation, Leonard and Masatu (2006) show that NGO physicians consistently provide more accurate diagnoses and better treatment than their public sector colleagues. The main differences are that NGOs charge more and exhibit better management, incentives, and accountability. These authors' results suggest that performance is better where facility directors have greater authority, particularly the ability to hire and fire staff and adjust compensation. Leonard and Masatu (2007) indicate that in rural Tanzania a physician's training has little effect on performance once the ownership of the provider is taken into account: what counts is not what you know but what you do, and the two are unrelated where incentives are not in place to encourage the application of medical knowledge.

In Brazil, a recent experiment in hospital autonomy in 12 general public hospitals in the state of São Paulo led to significantly higher productivity of staff, more care, lower infection rates, reduced mortality, and lower costs when compared to a set of 12 traditionally managed general public hospitals of the same size in other similar locations. The ability to contract and terminate staff and to initiate efficiency measures provided powerful incentives for better hospital performance. Hospital directors who did not improve under the pilot project had their appointments terminated. Monthly tracking of performance led to impressive improvements in both quality and efficiency in hospitals where the ability to terminate both staff and management appointments provided accountability to the state funding agency (La Forgia and Couttolenc 2008).

The evidence from India, Tanzania, and Brazil highlights the critical roles of incentives, supervision, and accountability in raising performance and ensuring that expenditures will have positive returns in enhancing the health status of patients. Lewis (2006) summarizes a wealth of complementary evidence on issues of financing and delivery of care, identifying shortcomings and their measurement and emphasizing the importance of incentives and accountability if health institutions are to contribute effectively to improving health status and individual well-being.

One response to poor performance in public facilities is to shift the focus to private actors, but as Das and Hammer (2007) illustrate, this is by no means a panacea in service delivery, for the reasons discussed above. At the same time, adverse selection problems in the insurance market can lead to a breakdown in private insurance coverage as the unhealthy and the poor are excluded. In this case, some form of mandatory insurance coverage, even if privately provided and financed, may be necessary to avert an adverse selection spiral. This is the approach taken in Chile, Colombia, Switzerland, and, more recently, the U.S. state of Massachusetts. In all of these cases, and others, the government requires the private purchase of insurance by people earning middle and upper incomes, while subsidizing coverage for the poor, who would otherwise be unable to comply with the insurance mandate.

To sum up, if health care spending is to improve health status, institutions matter. The systemic problems are increasingly well understood, but without shifts in the institutions and the incentives for performance embedded in them, the link between spending and outcomes is likely to remain weak.

Conclusions

The impacts of a population's health on national income are hotly debated, and they probably vary depending on the health indicator used and the countries included in the analysis. Some cross-country regressions using instrumental variables find quite large impacts of health on income, but few other analytical approaches yield similar results. Part of the problem in resolving the debate lies in the fact that comparisons of health and non-health interventions in nonexperimental environments are besieged by identification problems, while (quasi) experimental settings that would allow such comparisons are especially rare. It is difficult enough to estimate the impact of a health *or* growth intervention compared with the status quo, but comparing health *and* growth interventions has proven especially intractable, particularly in light of the vast array of interventions that are feasible in both areas.

The two empirical approaches to this dilemma have been, first, to estimate the effects of arguably exogenous innovations in population health status on incomes at the macro level and, second, to focus at the micro level on the impact of specific health interventions on economic outcomes.

At the macroeconomic level, our tentative conclusion is that the effect of health on income is small if it exists at all and that the results are ambiguous, largely because of the methodological challenges discussed above. National public health investments such as environmental cleanup or vaccinations show an impact on overall health status and are associated with improved investment opportunities that contribute to growth. At the microeconomic level, clear causal relationships have been documented from health to earning potential and income.

Although the macroeconomic analyses seek to provide information on the impacts of improved health on aggregate incomes, they cannot really tell us whether an extra dollar of public funding should be allocated to the health sector or to an alternative or which interventions provide the biggest bang to health *and* income for the buck. Our understanding is that some health policies and investments, particularly those with pure public-good attributes, can plausibly have important impacts on incomes, but that at the macroeconomic level health and incomes are at least as likely to be jointly determined by such intangible features as institutional quality, corruption, and public sector accountability.

Nevertheless, microeconomic studies provide solid guidance on marginal benefits and on some of the tradeoffs across investments at the individual and household levels. Factors that foster greater productivity and higher wages are nutrition, early childhood education (both cognitive and noncognitive), education more generally, and mother's education in particular. Public health investments that eliminate pathogens raise health status and expand access to agricultural land, which translate into enhanced learning and rising agricultural yields, respectively, and serve to raise productivity, labor supply, and earnings. Much remains to be done, however, on ensuring the benefits of medical interventions and investing to improve their effectiveness and impact.

The lack of clarity about the macroeconomic link from health to economic growth is not a reason to refocus public investment away from the health sector. The link from growth to health itself takes many forms, and it would seem to be a mistake to put all our eggs in the growth basket if we care about health for its own sake. The more pressing problem is to improve the link from health spending to health outcomes: scarce resources allocated to the health sector that have little impact on health are very unlikely to have the knock-on effect on incomes that some scholars and advocates seek. Institutions matter and need to be considered and invested in if health care spending is to pay off. Even if it turns out that there is little effect on growth, the improvements in health status will be worth the effort.

References

Acemoglu, Daron, and Simon H. Johnson. 2006. "Disease and Development: The Effect of Life Expectancy on Economic Growth." NBER Working Paper W12269, National Bureau of Economic Research, Cambridge, MA. http://ssrn.com/abstract=906747.

Acemoglu, Daron, Simon H. Johnson, and James Robinson. 2002. "Reversal of Fortune: Geography and Institutions in the Making of the Modern World Income Distribution." *Quarterly Journal of Economics* 117 (4): 1231–94.

Acemoglu, Daron, and James Robinson. 2008. "Persistence of Power, Elites, and Institutions," *American Economic Review* 98 (1): 267–93.

Ainsworth, Martha, Kathleen Beegle, and Godike Koda. 2002. "The Impact of Adult Mortality on Primary School Enrollment in Northwestern Tanzania." UNAIDS Africa Development Forum Paper, World Bank, Washington, DC.

Alderman, Harold, Jere R. Behrman, and John Hoddinott. 2003. "Nutrition, Malnutrition, and Economic Growth." In *Health and Economic Growth,* ed. Guillem López-Casasnovas, Berta Rivera, and Luis Currais, ch. 7. Cambridge, MA: MIT Press.

Alsan, Marcella, David Bloom, and David Canning. 2006. "The Effect of Population Health on Foreign Direct Investment Inflows to Low- and Middle-Income Countries." *World Development* 34 (4): 613–30.

Ashraf, Quamrul, Ashley Lester, and David Weil. 2007. "When Does Improving Health Raise GDP?" Working Paper 2008-7, Brown University, Department of Economics, Providence, RI.

Banerjee, Abhijit, Angus Deaton, and Esther Duflo. 2004. "Wealth, Health, and Health Services in Rural Rajasthan." *American Economic Review* 94 (2): 326–30.

Barecca, Alan. 2007. "The Long-Term Economic Impact of *in utero* and Postnatal Exposure to Malaria." University of California, Davis. http://economics. missouri.edu/seminars/files/2008/021208.pdf.

Beegle, Kathleen, Joachim De Weerdt, and Stefan Dercon. 2006. "Adult Mortality and Consumption Growth in the Age of HIV/AIDS." Policy Research Working Paper 4082, World Bank, Washington DC.

Behrman, Jere R., and Mark Rosenzweig. 2004. "Parental Allocations to Children: New Evidence on Bequest Differences among Siblings." *Review of Economics and Statistics* 86 (2): 447–64.

Bell, Clive, and Maureen Lewis. 2004. "The Economic Implications of Epidemics Old and New." *World Economics* 5 (4): 137–74.

Bell, Clive, Shanta Devarajan, and Hans Gersbach. 2003. "The Long-Run Economic Costs of AIDS: Theory and an Application to South Africa." Policy Research Working Paper 3152, World Bank, Washington, DC.

Benton, Bruce. 2001. "The Onchocerciasis (River Blindness) Program's Visionary Partnerships." Africa Region Findings 174, World Bank, Washington, DC. http://www.worldbank.org/afr/findings/english/find174.htm.

Bidani, Benu, and Martin Ravallion. 1997. "Decomposing Social Indicators Using Distributional Data." *Journal of Econometrics* 77 (1): 125–39.

Black, Robert, Lindsay Allen, Zulfiqar Bhutta, Laura Caulfield, Mercedes de Onis, Majid Ezzati, Colin Mathers, and Juan Rivera. 2008. "Maternal and Child Undernutrition: Global and Regional Exposures and Health Consequences." *Lancet* 371 (9608): 5–22.

Bleakley, Hoyt. 2006a. "Disease and Development: Comments on Acemoglu and Johnson (2006)." Remarks delivered at the NBER Summer Institute on Economic Fluctuations and Growth, July 16. http://home.uchicago. edu/~bleakley/Bleakley_Comments_Acemoglu_Johnson.pdf.

———. 2006b. "Malaria in the Americas: A Retrospective Analysis of Childhood Exposure." Documentos CEDE 003185, Universidad de los Andes, Centro de Estudios sobre Desarrollo Económico, Bogotá.

———. 2007. "Disease and Development: Evidence from Hookworm Eradication in the American South." *Quarterly Journal of Economics* 122 (1): 73–117.

Bloom, David, and David Canning. 2003a. "Health as Human Capital and Its Impact on Economic Performance." *Geneva Papers on Risk and Insurance* 28 (2): 304–15.

———. 2003b. "The Health and Poverty of Nations: From Theory to Practice." *Journal of Human Development* 4 (1): 47–71.

———. 2005. "Health and Economic Growth: Reconciling the Micro and Macro Evidence." Unpublished document, Harvard School of Public Health, Cambridge, MA.

Bloom, David, David Canning, and Bryan Graham. 2002. "Longevity and Life Cycle Savings." NBER Working Paper 8808, National Bureau of Economic Research, Cambridge, MA. http://www.nber.org/papers/w8808.

Bloom, David, David Canning, and Jaypee Sevilla. 2004. "The Effect of Health on Economic Growth: A Production Function Approach." *World Development* 32 (1): 1–13.

Boone, Peter, and Zhaoguo Zhan. 2006. "Lowering Child Mortality in Poor Countries: The Power of Knowledgeable Parents." CEP Discussion Paper 751, London School of Economics, Centre for Economic Policy Research, London.

Bunker, John P., Howard S. Frazier, and Frederick Mosteller. 1994. "Improving Health: Measuring Effects of Medical Care." *The Milbank Quarterly* 72 (2): 225–58.

Carneiro, Pedro Manuel, and James J. Heckman. 2003. "Human Capital Policy." NBER Working Paper W9495, National Bureau of Economic Research, Boston, MA.

Carnoy, Martin, and Jeffrey Marshall. 2004. "Comparing Cuba Students' Academic Performance with the Rest of Latin America." Unpublished manuscript.

Case, Anne C., Christina H. Paxson, and Joseph D. Ableidinger. 2002. "Orphans in Africa." NBER Working Paper W9213, National Bureau of Economic Research, Cambridge, MA. http://ssrn.com/abstract=332257.

Chaudhury, Nazmul, and Jeffrey Hammer. 2004. "Ghost Doctors: Absenteeism in Bangladeshi Health Facilities." *World Bank Economic Review* 12 (3): 423–41.

Chaudhury, Nazmul, Jeffrey Hammer, Karthik Muralidharan, and F. Halsey Rogers. 2005. "Missing in Action: Teacher and Health Worker Absence in Developing Countries." *Journal of Economic Perspectives* 20 (1): 91–116.

Commission on Growth and Development. 2008. *The Growth Report: Strategies for Sustained Growth and Inclusive Development.* Washington, DC: Commission on Growth and Development, World Bank. http://www.growthcommission. org/index.php?option=com_content&task=view&id=96&Itemid=169.

Crossier, Scott. 2007. "John Snow: The London Cholera Epidemic of 1854." Center for Spatially Integrated Science, University of California, Santa Barbara.

Cunha, Flavio, James J. Heckman, Lance J. Lochner, and Dimitriy V. Masterov. 2006. "Interpreting the Evidence on Life Cycle Skill Formation." In *Handbook of the Economics of Education,* ed. Eric A. Hanushek and Finis Welch, 697–812. Amsterdam, the Netherlands: North-Holland.

Cutler, David. 2007. "The Lifetime Costs and Benefits of Medical Technology." NBER Working Paper 13478, National Bureau of Economic Research, Boston, MA.

Cutler, David, Winnie Fung, Michael Kremer, and Monica Singhal. 2007. "Mosquitoes: The Long-Term Effects of Malaria Eradication in India." Unpublished working paper, Harvard University, Cambridge, MA.

Cutler, David, and Grant Miller. 2005. "The Role of Public Health Improvements in Health Advances: The Twentieth Century United States." *Demography* 42 (1): 1–22.

Das, Jishnu, and Jeffrey Hammer. 2007. "Money for Nothing: The Dire Straits of Medical Practice in Delhi, India." *Journal of Development Economics* 83 (1): 1–36.

Deaton, Angus. 2006. "Global Patterns of Income and Health: Facts, Interpretations, and Policies." NBER Working Paper W12735, National Bureau of Economic Research, Cambridge, MA. http://ssrn.com/abstract=948648.

DiTella, Rafael, and William Savedoff, eds. 2001. *Diagnosis Corruption: Fraud in Latin America's Public Hospitals.* Washington, DC: Inter-American Development Bank.

Dixit, Avinash. 2006. "Evaluating Recipes for Development Success." Policy Research Working Paper 3859, World Bank, Washington, DC.

Drèze, Jean, and Amartya Sen. 2002. *India: Development and Participation.* Oxford: Oxford University Press.

Drukker, Jan W., and Vincent Tassenaar. 1997. "Paradoxes of Modernization and Material Well-Being in the Netherlands during the 19th Century." In *Health and Welfare during Industrialization,* ed. Richard H. Steckel and Roderick Floud, 331–79. Chicago: Chicago University Press.

Easterly, William, and Ross Levine. 2003. "Tropics, Germs, and Crops: How Endowments Influence Economic Development." *Journal of Monetary Economics* 50 (1): 3–39.

Evans, David, and Edward Miguel. 2003. "Will the Sun Come out Tomorrow? Orphans and Schooling." Unpublished working paper, University of California, Berkeley.

Filmer, Deon, Jeffrey Hammer, and Lant Pritchett. 2000. "Weak Links in the Chain: A Diagnosis of Health Policy in Poor Countries." *World Bank Research Observer* 15 (2): 199–224.

Filmer, Deon, and Lant Pritchett. 1999. "The Impact of Public Spending on Health: Does Money Matter?" *Social Science and Medicine* 49 (1): 1309–23.

Fogel, Robert W. 1986. "Nutrition and the Decline in Mortality since 1700: Some Additional Preliminary Findings." NBER Working Paper 1802, National Bureau of Economic Research, Boston, MA.

_____. 1994. "Economic Growth, Population Theory, and Physiology: The Bearing of Long-Term Processes on the Making of Economic Policy." *American Economic Review* 84 (June): 369–95.

_____. 1997. "New Findings on Secular Trends in Nutrition and Mortality: Some Implications for Population Theory." In *Handbook of Population and Family Economics.* Vol. 1A, ed. Mark Rosenzweig and Oded Stark. Amsterdam: Elsevier.

_____. 2002. "Nutrition, Physiological Capital, and Economic Growth. Lecture." Pan American Health Organization and the Inter-American Development Bank, Washington, DC.

Fortson, Jane. 2006. "Mortality, Risk, and Human Capital Investment: The Impact of HIV/AIDS in Sub-Saharan Africa." Unpublished paper, University of Chicago.

Fuchs, Victor R. 1974. *Who Shall Live? Health, Economics, and Social Choice.* New York: Basic Books.

Gallup, John Luke, and Jeffrey Sachs. 2001. "The Economic Burden of Malaria." *American Journal of Tropical Medical Hygiene* 64 (1-2): S1–S11.

Gertler, Paul, David Levine, and Minnie Ames. 2004. "Schooling and Parental Death." *Review of Economics and Statistics* 86 (1): 211–25.

Grantham-McGregor, Margaret, Yin Bun Cheung, Santiago Cueto, Paul Glewwe, Linda Richter, and Barbara Strupp. 2007. "Development Potential in the First Five Years for Children in Developing Countries." *Lancet* 369 (9555): 60–70.

Heckman, James. 2007. "Investing in Disadvantaged Young Children Is Good Economics and Good Public Policy." Testimony before the Joint Economic Committee, Washington, DC, June 27.

Hong, Sok Chul. 2007. "A Longitudinal Analysis of the Burden of Malaria on Health and Economic Productivity: The American Case." Unpublished paper, University of Chicago.

Hsiao, William C. 1984. "Transformation of Health Care in China." *New England Journal of Medicine* 310 (14): 932–36.

Jack, William, and Maureen Lewis. 2004. "Falling Short of Expectations: Public Health Interventions in Developing and Transition Economies." *Social Science and Medicine* 58 (2): 223–25.

Kamali, A., J. A. Seeley, A. J. Nunn, J. F. Kengeya-Kayondo, A. Ruberantwari, and D. W. Mulder. 1996. "The Orphan Problem: Experience of a Sub-Saharan Africa Rural Population in the AIDS Epidemic." *AIDS Care* 8 (5): 509–15.

Kaufmann, Daniel, Art Kraay, and Massimo Mastruzzi. 2005. "Governance Matters IV: Governance Indicators for 1996–2004." Policy Research Working Paper 3630, World Bank, Washington, DC. http://ssrn.com/abstract=718081 or DOI: 10.2139/ssrn.718081.

Knudsen, Eric I. 2004. "Sensitive Periods in the Development of the Brain and Behavior." *Journal of Cognitive Neuroscience* 16 (8): 1412–25.

Knudsen, Eric I., James J. Heckman, Judy L. Cameron, and Jack P. Shonkoff. 2006. "Economic, Neurobiological, and Behavioral Perspectives on Building America's Future Workforce." *PNAS (Proceedings of the National Academy of Sciences)* 103 (27): 10155–62.

Kuhn, Katrin Gaardbo, Diarmid H. Campbell-Lendrum, Ben Armstrong, and Clive R. Davies. 2003. "Malaria in Britain: Past, Present, and Future." *PNAS (Proceedings of the National Academy of Sciences)* 100 (17): 9997–10001. http://www.pnas.org/content/100/17/9997.full.

La Forgia, Gerard M., and Bernard F. Couttolenc. 2008. *Hospital Performance in Brazil: The Search for Excellence.* Washington, DC: World Bank.

Larson, Bruce A., Matthew P. Fox, Sydney Rosen, Margaret Bii, Carolyne Sigei, Douglas Shaffer, Fredrick Sawe, Monique Wasunna, and Jonathan L. Simon. 2008. "Early Effects of Antiretroviral Therapy on Work Performance: Preliminary Results from a Cohort Study of Kenyan Agricultural Workers." *AIDS* 22 (3): 421–25.

Leonard, Kenneth, and Melkiory Masatu. 2006. "The Use of Direct Clinician Observation and Vignettes for Health Services Quality Evaluation in Developing Countries." *Social Science and Medicine* 61 (9): 1944–51.

———. 2007. "Variation in the Quality of Care Accessible to Rural Communities in Tanzania." *Health Affairs* 26 (3): w380–w392.

Lewis, Maureen. 2006. *Governance and Corruption in Public Health Care Systems.* Center for Global Development Working Paper 78, Center for Global Development. http://ssrn.com/abstract=984046.

Lewis, Maureen, Gerald La Forgia, and Margaret Sulvetta. 1996. "Measuring Public Hospital Costs: Empirical Evidence from the Dominican Republic." *Social Science and Medicine* 43 (2): 221–34.

Lindelow, Magnus, Inna Kushnarova, and Kai Kaiser. 2006. "Measuring Corruption in the Health Sector: What Can We Learn from Public Expenditure Tracking and Service Delivery Surveys in Developing Countries?" In *Global Corruption Report 2006: Special Focus on Corruption and Health.* Transparency International. London: Pluto Press.

Lleras-Muney, Adriana. 2005. "The Relationship between Education and Adult Mortality in the United States." *Review of Economic Studies* 72 (1): 189–221.

Lloyd, Cynthia B., and Ann K. Blanc. 1996. "Children's Schooling in Sub-Saharan Africa: The Role of Fathers, Mothers, and Others." *Population and Development Review* 22 (2): 265–98.

Lorentzen, Peter, John McMillan, and Romain Wacziarg. 2005. "Death and Development." NBER Working Paper 11620, National Bureau of Economic Research, Boston, MA.

Lucas, Adrienne. 2005. "Economic Effects of Malaria Eradication: Evidence from the Malarial Periphery." Unpublished paper, Brown University, Providence, RI.

Malaney, Pia, Andrew Spielman, and Jeffrey Sachs. 2004. "The Malaria Gap." *American Journal of Tropical Medicine and Hygiene* 71 (suppl 2): 141–46.

Mankiw, N. Gregory. 1995. "The Growth of Nations." *Brookings Papers on Economic Activity* 1: 275–326.

McKeown, Thomas, R. G. Record, and R. D. Turner. 1962. "Reasons for the Decline of Mortality in England and Wales during the Nineteenth Century." *Population Studies* 16 (2): 94–122.

————. 1975. "An Interpretation of the Decline of Mortality in England and Wales during the Twentieth Century." *Population Studies* 29 (3): 391–421.

McKinley, John, and Sonja J. McKinley. 1997. "The Questionable Contribution of Medical Measures to the Decline of Mortality in the United States in the Twentieth Century." *Millbank Memorial Fund Quarterly/Health and Society* 55 (3): 404–28.

Melgar, Paúl, Luis Fernando Ramírez, Scott McNiven, Rosa Mery Mejía, Ann DiGirolamo, John Hoddinott, and John A. Maluccio. 2008. "Resource Flows among Three Generations in Guatemala Study (2007–08): Definitions, Tracking, Data Collection, Coverage, and Attrition." Working Paper Series 0803, Middlebury College, Department of Economics, Middlebury, VT.

Miguel, Edward. 2005. "Health, Education, and Economic Development." In *Health and Economic Growth: Findings and Policy Implications*, ed. Guillem López-Casasnovas, Berta Rivera, and Luis Currais, pp. 143–68. Cambridge, MA: MIT Press.

Miguel, Edward, and Michael Kremer. 2004. "Worms: Identifying Impacts on Education and Health in the Presence of Treatment Externalities." *Econometrica* 72 (1): 159–217.

Mustard, J. Fraser. 2006. *Early Child Development and Experience-Based Brain Development: The Scientific Underpinnings of the Importance of Early Child Development in a Globalized World.* Washington, DC: Brookings Institution. http://www.brookings.edu/views/papers/200602mustard.htm.

PAHO (Pan American Health Organization). 1999. *The Pan American Sanitary Code: Toward a Hemispheric Health Policy.* Washington, DC: World Health Organization, Pan American Health Organization.

Preston, Samuel H. 1975. "The Changing Relation between Mortality and Level of Economic Development." *Population Studies* 29 (2): 231–48.

Pritchett, Lant. 1997. "Divergence, Big Time." *Journal of Economic Perspectives* 11 (3): 3–17.

Pritchett, Lant, and Lawrence H. Summers. 1996. "Wealthier Is Healthier." *Journal of Human Resource*s 31 (4): 841–68.

Rodrik, Dani, Arvind Subramanian, and Francesco Trebbi. 2002. "Institutions Rule: The Primacy of Institutions over Geography and Integration in Economic Development." NBER Working Paper 9305, National Bureau of Economic Research, Boston, MA.

Sachs, Jeffrey D. 2003. "Institutions Don't Rule: Direct Effect of Geography on Per Capita Income." NBER Working Paper 9490, National Bureau of Economic Research, Boston, MA.

Sachs, Jeffrey D., and Pia Malaney. 2002. "The Economic and Social Burden of Malaria." *Nature* 415 (February 7): 680–85.

Schultz, Paul. 2002. "Why Governments Should Invest More to Educate Girls." *World Development* 30 (2): 207–25.

———. 2005. "Productivity Benefits of Health: Evidence from Low-Income Countries." In *Health and Economic Growth*, ed. Guillem López-Casasnovas, Berta Rivera, and Luis Currais. Cambridge, MA: MIT Press.

Shastry, Gauri Kartini, and David Weil. 2003. "How Much of Cross-Country Income Variation Is Explained by Health?" *Journal of the European Economic Association* 1 (2-3): 387–96.

Snow, John. 1849. *On the Mode of Communication of Cholera*. London: John Churchill.

Thirumurthy, Harsha, Joshua Graff Zivin, and Markus Goldstein. 2005. "The Economic Impact of AIDS Treatment: Labor Supply in Western Kenya." NBER Working Paper 11871, National Bureau of Economic Research, Cambridge, MA.

Thomas, Duncan, and Elizabeth Frankenberg. 2002. "Health, Nutrition, and Prosperity: A Microeconomic Perspective." *Bulletin of the World Health Organization* 80 (2): 106–13.

Thomas, Duncan, and John Strauss. 1997. "Health and Wages: Evidence on Men and Women in Urban Brazil." *Journal of Econometrics* 77 (1): 159–86.

Victora, Cesar, Linda Adair, Caroline Fall, Pedro Hallal, Reynaldo Martorell, Linda Richter, and Harshpal Singh Sachdev. 2008. "Maternal and Child Undernutrition: Consequences for Adult Health and Human Capital." *Lancet* 371 (9609): 340–57.

Wagstaff, Adam, and Mariam Claeson. 2004. *Rising to the Challenge: The Millennium Development Goals for Health*. Washington, DC: World Bank.

Walker, Susan P., Theodore Wachs, Julie Meeks Gardner, Betsy Lozoff, Gail Wasserman, Ernesto Pollitt, and Julie Carter. 2007. "Child Development: Risk Factors for Adverse Outcomes in Developing Countries." *Lancet* 369 (9556): 145–57.

Weil, David N. 2005. "Accounting for the Effect of Health on Economic Growth." NBER Working Paper 11455, National Bureau of Economic Research, Boston, MA.

WHO (World Health Organization). 2001. *Report of the Commission on Macroeconomics and Health*. Geneva: WHO. whqlibdoc.who.int/publications/2001/924154550x.pdf.

Wößmann, Ludger, and Gabriela Schütz. 2006. *Efficiency and Equity in European Education and Training Systems: Analytical Report for the European Commission*. Munich: European Expert Network on Economics of Education.

Wolfe, Barbara. 1986. "Health Status and Medical Expenditures: Is There a Link?" *Social Science and Medicine* 22 (10): 993–99.

World Bank. 2005. *World Development Report 2004: Making Services Work for Poor People*. Washington, DC: World Bank.

———. 2008. *Global Monitoring Report: MDGs and the Environment*. Washington, DC: World Bank.

Young, Alwyn. 2005. "The Gift of the Dying: The Tragedy of AIDS and the Welfare of Future African Generations." *Quarterly Journal of Economics* 120 (2): 423–66.

CHAPTER 2
Health and Economic Growth: Policy Reports and the Making of Policy

Sir George Alleyne

I have been involved in health policy for a large part of my working life, and in this chapter my main concern is with how reports on health policy issues can persuade policy makers to take action. In particular, how is public policy made in the health area? What are its ingredients? And what convinces policy makers to focus on health rather than on some other national concern?

I often recall a conversation with a cabinet minister. When he and his colleagues would discuss the allocation of resources, the minister of agriculture would say, "If we buy this much fertilizer and plant this much acreage, we can produce this much, and if the world market price is this much, our income will be this much." And the minister of transport would say, "But we can't get our products to the port because the roads are in terrible condition, and if we invest in roads our export earnings will go up by this much." Then the minister of health would speak up and say, "Health is a human right." And in the councils and budgets of his government, like many other governments, the health sector would normally get short shrift. Ministers in other sectors know that, when budgets are discussed, health ministers are usually not much good at persuading finance ministers to spend money.

Clearly health is important. The largest poll in the world found that, across the world, health is what people value most—more than a happy family life, more than employment, and more than living in peace.[1] The intrinsic, or constitutive, value of health is an important topic that has engaged the minds of many people. Those who would argue for the use of some metric like Jeremy Bentham's Felicific Calculus (Bentham 1780) would say, "We should be involved in promoting health, because health in itself is a good thing."

But we can also look at health as an instrument for human development. From the point of view of practical policy making and budgeting, this is much the more promising approach. Here I briefly offer what I consider to be four phases of the development of interest in the instrumental aspect of health, before discussing some current concerns in the application of policy analysis to policy making.

The Instrumental Aspect of Health: Four Phases of Evolution

Initially, the relationship between health and economic growth was perceived in terms of the *effect of disease on labor productivity*, especially at the individual level. Thus the implications for policy centered on disease reduction. Next to evolve was the *historical retrospective* approach, drawing associations between health status and economic progress over time at the country or regional level. The *human capital* approach emerged in the 1990s, treating health, like education, as a productive asset contributing to growth. The relationship between *macroeconomics and health* was the subject of an influential commission, chaired by Jeffrey Sachs, which reported to the World Health Organization in 2001 (Commission on Macroeconomics and Health 2001b). The commission identified channels through which health affects economic growth and some of the policy levers that governments can use for improving health and, thereby, a country's broader development prospects (Lewis 1955).

Disease and Individual Productivity

Some of the early literature on the relationship between health and economic growth in this country concerned hookworm. In the Southern United States in the 1930s, hookworm was called "the germ of laziness," because the Southerners were seen as lazy and their productivity was low until hookworm was eliminated (Ettling 1981). When Arthur Lewis wrote about illness and development, he spoke about hookworm as a cause of anemia and thus as a drain on productivity (Lewis 1955).

A very early example of this literature comes from a bauxite mine in Guyana. In 1924 Dr. Giglioli, who was probably one of the greatest

---

1   Gallup International Millennium Survey, http://www.gallup-international.com/. At the turn of the millennium, 50,000 people in 60 countries were asked to rate "the most important things in life." "Good health" topped the list for 44 percent of the respondents, followed by "happy family life" (38 percent), "employment" (27 percent), and "live in a country without war" (17 percent).

scientists to live in the Caribbean, received this letter from his manager (Giglioli 2006):

> Dr. G. Giglioli   11.2.1924
> Relative to our conversation in regards to the benefits derived from the elimination of hookworm at Akyma, I would like to call your attention to the following facts: In the beginning of 1923, ninety-six miners on the ore face were mining 342 tons of bauxite per working day, whereas on the 1st of February 1924, 76 miners at the ore face are mining 540 tons of bauxite per working day. In September 1923, you tried the carbon-tetrachloride treatment on these miners.

Carbon-tetrachloride is now known to be toxic to the liver, but at that time Dr. Giglioli gave the miners carbon-tetrachloride to eliminate the hookworm and then measured their output afterward. It is obvious that the amount of ore they mined per worker went up (see figure 2.1).

The mine manager was impressed and continued:

> I cannot say I attribute this increase in the output of ore per man per day entirely to the treatment which you gave for hookworm, but I do think that, to a great extent, the elimination of this disease has had something to do with our increased output and our reduction of costs. For the five months previous to September 1923, the increase in tonnage per man per day was nil, whereas during the five months following September 1923, our increase in tonnage has amounted to 1 3/4 tons per man per day.
>
> (Signed) B. Barnes, Manager

Although nowadays we have a better hookworm treatment than carbon-tetrachloride, the thesis is still the same: eliminating infectious disease can raise labor productivity.

For a long time we have known of studies on the economic effects of malaria. Gladys Conly (1975) was one of the first to point out, in Paraguay, that productivity would rise if malaria were eradicated. Ram and Schultz (1979) showed that improvement in health led to increased output growth and that agricultural productivity was higher in those areas of India in which the prevalence of malaria was low. And in St. Lucia, the economist Burton Weisbrod and his colleagues (1973) looked at what would happen to the economy if schistosomiasis could be eradicated.

Figure 2.1 Tons of Ore Mined per Worker per Day, 1923

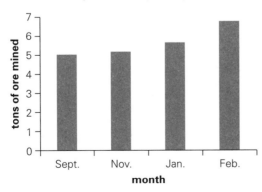

Source: Giglioli 2006.

Historical Retrospective Approach

By the 1940s and 1950s, it was broadly recognized that disease impairs a country's economic growth because it decreases the expectancy of a healthy life, because it has demographic effects—keeping fertility high in response to high child mortality—and because it lowers the returns to economic activity.

I attribute much of the development of the historical retrospective approach to Robert W. Fogel (1986), several of whose works have shown how much of a country's or region's economic growth would depend on the extent to which there was proper nutrition and improved health.

Suchit Arora (2001) took the same approach, looking back over almost 100 years to see whether health had improved and whether, because of improved health, countries' economies had grown.

Human Capital

The 1960s saw the emergence of the human capital approach. In 1962 Selma Mushkin wrote in a landmark article in the *Journal of Political Economy,* "Health is an investment" (Mushkin 1962). This was the first time that I understood clearly the extent to which improving health could be an investment.

At the time that Selma Mushkin was writing, there was still a certain amount of debate as to whether improvement in human capital, as contributed by investment in health, was important for economic growth. A purple passage by one pair of authors said, "Once one leaves the *terra firma* of material capital and branches out in the upper ether of human capital, there is endless difficulty in finding a resting place" (Bauer and Yamey 1957).

But by the 1990s, the effects of health on wealth were being clearly documented. Smith (1999), for example, pointed out that individual households who had better health tended to be richer 5 and 10 years down the road. Those households who had excellent health had a tremendous increase in median wealth (see table 2.1). And Jere Behrman (1996) showed that the returns to investment in health were even greater than the returns to education, overturning the dogma of that time.

Several publications in the 1990s had a critical influence on thinking in the health policy field. The United Nations Development Programme's

Table 2.1 Median Wealth by Self-Reported 1984 Health Status
1996 US$ (thousands)

All households	1984	1989	1994
Excellent	68.3	99.3	127.9
Very good	66.3	81.9	90.9
Good	51.8	59.6	64.9
Poor	39.2	36.0	34.7

Source: Smith 1999.

Human Development Report 1990, conceived and coordinated by Mahbub ul Haq, included health as one of the indicators of human development (UNDP 1990). Haq's writings have been absolutely fundamental to how we understand the social factors that influence health. If Haq had not died, perhaps he would have received a Nobel Prize. Two other seminal publications had Dean Jamison as their lead author: the World Bank's *World Development Report 1993: Investing in Health* and a companion volume, *Disease Control Priorities in Developing Countries.*[2]

These publications gave, for the first time, a clear exposition of why it is necessary for countries to invest in health. They pointed out the channels through which investments in health would produce returns. And they posed the question, What kinds of interventions should one apply in order to improve health in the developing world?

Macroeconomics and Health

Perhaps the major recent contribution to thinking in the health policy field has come from the World Health Organization's Commission on Macroeconomics and Health. I happened to be the co-chair of the commission's Working Group I, which analyzed issues in health, economic growth, and poverty reduction and provided the commission with macroeconomic analysis justifying societal investments in health.

As outlined in the commission's overall report (Commission on Macroeconomics and Health 2001a), health inputs contribute to economic growth through three channels:

- Returns to individual health, through labor market outcomes, a demographic dividend, and increased savings
- The net value of increased income from household investment in human capital
- Societal returns to health, through economic activity such as the tourism industry or agriculture.

Among the relationships that are detailed in the Working Group I report (Commission on Macroeconomics and Health 2001b), three fascinated me. One is the relationship between output per worker and nutritional status, as measured by workers' stature. The data in figure 2.2 are for Denmark, but the relationship is universal: taller adults have higher earnings than shorter adults. And I always ask, Is this because of early nutrition, or for some other reason? Data from the same source show that the relationship goes in the same direction for both Brazil and the United States, but the slope of the curve is steeper in the case of Brazil. This could be interpreted to mean that the impact on height and

---

2 Much of the work for the *World Development Report* was based on *Disease Control Priorities in Developing Countries,* which assessed which diseases posed the biggest obstacles to improvement in population health (Jamison and others 2006; World Bank 1993).

Figure 2.2 Relationship between Output per Worker and Nutritional Status in Denmark

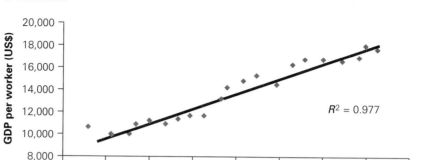

Source: Commission on Macroeconomics and Health 2001b.

Figure 2.3 Growth Rate of Income per Capita, 1965–94

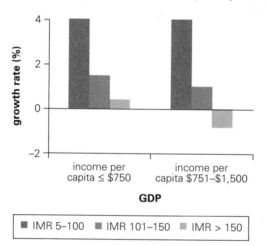

■ IMR 5–100   ■ IMR 101–150   ■ IMR > 150

Source: Commission on Macroeconomics and Health 2001a.

nutritional status was stronger in Brazil because more of the work that produced wealth depended on physical capacity.

The second relationship that fascinates me is the association between income growth per capita and the infant mortality rate. Figure 2.3 illustrates that, regardless of a country's initial income level, income growth is faster where infant mortality rates are low.

The third relationship is illustrated in table 2.2. These data are from a study in Guatemala, in which children were fed supplements early in life and their earnings were observed as adults (Fuentes, Hernández, and Pascual 2001). The researchers found that if children received supplements of up to 32,000 calories in their first three years of life, then those children, grown up to be adults, would earn more than those who received fewer supplemental calories. This is the only study I know of that has looked at children's early nutrition and compared it with their earnings later on. The researchers also

Table 2.2 Early Nutrition and Future Earnings
Q (10 millions)

Calorie supplements	Earnings	Remittances
0–32,000 (206)	3,614	327
32,000 + (237)	7,656	769

Source: Fuentes, Hernández, and Pascual 2001.
Note: Guatemala's currency is the quetzal. Numbers in parentheses are the number of persons receiving the supplement.

found that, among individuals who had migrated, those who had been better fed as children sent back more money as remittances and were less likely to be receiving welfare payments. The findings emphasize that one of the best things you can do is to stimulate early childhood development. The data from those villages and families have been analyzed in more detail recently with the same result (Victora and others 2008; Behrman, this volume). Early childhood nutrition results in more productive adults.

The overall recommendation of the Commission on Macroeconomics and Health was that the world's low- and middle-income countries, in partnership with high-income countries, should scale up the access of the world's poor to essential health services, including through specific interventions.

Current Concerns

My three biggest concerns are the lack of a vulgar metric for health, the failure to use evidence to induce policy change, and the shortage of tools to justify health interventions and expenditures.

Lack of a Vulgar Metric for Health

I am concerned that we lack what I call an appropriate "vulgar metric" for health. In education, there is a vulgar metric—years of schooling—that is easy to use for advocating policy reforms. You can focus a prime minister's attention on years of schooling and tell him, "This is what you can do to change the situation." In health, I worry that too little attention is being paid to developing a comparably useful metric.

Failure to Use Evidence to Induce Policy Change

What concerns me even more is that, although we assemble masses of evidence in our reports, we often make poor use of this evidence to induce policy change. Jeffrey Sachs once said to me, "The problem with macroeconomists is that they don't understand why or how the output of their work can be important." What Sachs did in the commission's report (Commission on Macroeconomics and Health 2001a) was to take as given the macroeconomic arguments that explain the returns to the general economy that justify investing in health and then to say, "Now, *given* that there is macroeconomic evidence of the returns to investment in health, *then* policy makers should take these and these measures."

So how does one translate the information arising from macroeconomic analysis into the kinds of messages that will allow—or even galvanize—heads of government to take action?

I recall an exercise in which Dwight Venner and I were involved, looking at how you get policy makers to pay attention to health issues. In 2001 the 15 heads of Caribbean governments met in Nassau and said, "The health of the region is the wealth of the region."[3] They declared their cognizance of "the critical role of health in the economic development of our people," and they mandated a taskforce or commission, whose job was to "review health and propel health to the center of the development process." I had the honor of chairing that task force, and Dwight Venner was one of our commissioners.

For our report to the heads of government, we had excellent data on the macroeconomic returns to investment in public health, in terms of the effects on tourism and inflows of foreign direct investment (CARICOM Secretariat 2006). I went to every capital and presented our good data to the prime minister and his or her cabinet.

But what galvanized the prime ministers was not so much our macroeconomic evidence on the economic benefits of investment in public health, but the data we showed them on specific diseases. Showing them that the death rates from diabetes in Trinidad and Tobago were almost 10 times greater than those in Canada and the United States got their attention (see figure 2.4). Offering them specific comparative numbers helped them to see that their countries had a major problem.

Figure 2.4 Age-Adjusted Death Rate per 100,000 Population from Diabetes in Caribbean and North American Countries, 2000

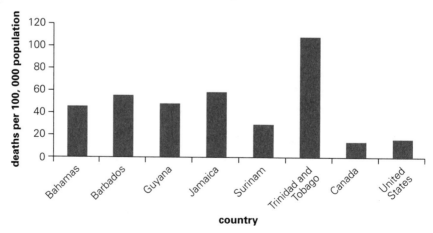

Source: CARICOM Secretariat 2006.

---

3 Nassau declaration on health 2001. http://www.caricom.org/jsp/communications/meetings_statements/nassau_declaration_on_health.jsp?menu=communications.

Table 2.3 Possible Economic Burden from Diabetes and Hypertension in Caribbean Countries
2001 US$ (millions)

Condition	Bahamas	Barbados	Jamaica	Trinidad and Tobago
Diabetes	27.3	37.8	208.8	494.4
Hypertension	46.4	72.7	251.6	259.5
Total	76.7	110.5	460.4	753.9

Source: CARICOM Secretariat 2006.

What engaged them further was the evidence we showed them that the cost of treating two major chronic diseases could consume up to 7 percent of the GDP in their countries (see table 2.3). That information got their attention.

They were so taken by the possible economic impact of these diseases—and by the possibility of reducing this economic burden by preventing them—that 15 of them came together in a Summit on Chronic Noncommunicable Diseases. Perhaps this was the first time in the world that a group of heads of government got together uniquely to discuss health. And they were so convinced of the need that they set up programs to prevent these diseases.

My point is that the heads of Caribbean governments agree that poor health is a problem not only because they understand its impact on economic growth down the road, but also because they *recognize that it constitutes a current economic burden* for their countries and also because they *see that there are levers they can pull* to dramatically reduce the problem.

We as writers of policy reports might agonize over producing the right data and the right analysis—say, on how investments in health relate to the speed of long-term growth—but we need to go a step further. We need to ask ourselves, How can we translate that knowledge into some specific commitment that heads of governments can make. Is there some specific instrument they can use or some lever they can pull?

Tools to Justify Health Interventions and Expenditures

My third concern relates to the shortage of tools to enable the health sector to make the case for (a) appropriate interventions within the sector and (b) spending on health vis-à-vis other sectors. Like convenient metrics, such tools are in short supply.

One of the new ideas that has come forward for measuring the impact of health on wealth is to measure the welfare cost of changes in mortality, rather than using GDP alone—an idea first raised to me by Markus Haacker in relation to HIV/AIDS (Haacker 2004). I still have philosophical difficulty with this concept, but obviously, distinguished economists such as William Nordhaus believe in its validity. Nordhaus (2003) points out that, in the first half of the past century, more than half of the growth in the

United States, if measured in terms of full income, was due to health inputs and that, in the second half, almost as much growth in full income was due to health improvements. These numbers are significant. If you look at decreased mortality from AIDS in developing countries, it is a calculation of full income that gives you a more credible idea of what the impact of the disease will be.

William Petty, who lived from 1623 to 1687, wrote something along similar lines that I have always remembered and often quoted. He computed "above 80 pounds to be the value of each Head of Man, Woman, and child, and of adult persons twice as much; from whence we may learn to compute the loss we have sustained by the plague, by the slaughter of men in war, and by sending them abroad into the service of foreign princes" (Petty 1711).

My last point, also discussed in Jamison and others (2006), is about weighing investment priorities. When a minister of health has, say, a million dollars to spend, economists are very good at telling her which are the most cost-effective health interventions and what, given her million dollars, she should choose to do within the sector. But what do you say when the minister asks, "That is fine, but how do I get the president to invest in improving health systems rather than building a metro? How do I convince the president that one is more productive than the other?"

I believe we have served the health sector poorly by not having politicians understand the relevance of cost-benefit analysis and how it can be applied in their presentations and debates on priorities for the allocation of budgets and the evolution of the national product.

References

Arora, Suchit. 2001. "Health, Human Productivity, and Long-Term Economic Growth." *Journal of Economic History* 61 (September, 3): 699–749.

Bauer, Peter T., and Basil S. Yamey. 1957. *The Economics of Under-developed Countries.* Chicago: University of Chicago Press.

Behrman, Jere R. 1996. *Human Resources in Latin America and the Caribbean.* Washington, DC: Inter-American Development Bank.

Bentham, Jeremy. 1780. *An Introduction to the Principles of Morals and Legislation.* London: T. Payne and Son at the Mews Gate.

CARICOM (Caribbean Community) Secretariat. 2006. *Report of the Caribbean Commission on Health and Development.* Kingston, Jamaica: Ian Randle Publishers for the PAHO (Pan American Health Organization)/WHO (World Health Organization).

Commission on Macroeconomics and Health. 2001a. *Health, Economic Growth, and Poverty Reduction: Report of Working Group I.* Geneva: World Health Organization.

———. 2001b. *Macroeconomics and Health: Investing in Health for Economic Development.* Geneva: World Health Organization.

Conly, Gladys N. 1975. *The Impact of Malaria on Economic Development: A Case Study*. Scientific Publication 297. Washington, DC: Pan American Health Organization, Pan American Sanitary Bureau, Regional Office of the World Health Organization.

Ettling, John. 1981. *The Germ of Laziness: Rockefeller Philanthropy and Public Health in the New South*. Cambridge, MA: Harvard University Press.

Fogel, Robert W. 1986. "Nutrition and the Decline of Mortality." In *Long-Term Factors in American Economic Growth*, ed. Stanley L. Engerman and Robert E. Gallman. Chicago: University of Chicago Press.

Fuentes, J. A., J. Hernández, and M. Pascual. 2001. "The Effects of Early Nutritional Intervention on Human Capital Formation." Report prepared by the Institute of Nutrition of Central America and Panama (INCAP) for Working Group I of the Commission on Macroeconomics and Health, World Health Organization, Geneva.

Giglioli, George. 2006. *Demerara Doctor: An Early Success against Malaria. The Autobiography of a Self-Taught Physician*. London: Smith-Gordon.

Haacker, Martin. 2004. *The Macroeconomics of HIV/AIDS*. Washington, DC: International Monetary Fund.

Jamison, Dean T., Joel Breman, Anthony Measham, George Alleyne, Mariam Claeson, David Evans, Prabhat Jha, Anne Mills, and Philip Musgrove, eds. 2006. *Disease Control Priorities in Developing Countries*. 2d ed. New York: World Bank and Oxford University Press.

Lewis, W. Arthur. 1955. *The Theory of Economic Growth*. Homewood, IL: R. D. Irwin.

Mushkin, Selma J. 1962. "Health as an Investment." *Journal of Political Economy* 70 (5): 129–57.

Nordhaus, William. 2003. "The Health of Nations: The Contribution of Improved Health to Living Standards." In *Measuring the Gains from Medical Research: An Economic Approach*, ed. Kevin M. Murphy and Robert H. Topel, 9–40. Chicago: University of Chicago Press.

Petty, William. 1711. *Essays in Political Arithmetick, or, A Discourse Concerning the Extent and Value of Lands, People, Buildings as the Same Relates to Every Country in General but More Particularly to the Territories of Her Majesty of Great Britain and Her Neighbours of Holland, Zealand, and France*. London: Printed for Henry and George Mortlock.

Ram, Rati, and Theodore W. Schultz. 1979. "Life-Span, Health, Savings, and Productivity." *Economic Development and Cultural Change* 27 (3): 399–421.

Smith, James P. 1999. "Healthy Bodies and Thick Wallets: The Dual Relation between Health and Economic Status." *Journal of Economic Perspectives* 13 (2): 145–66.

UNDP (United Nations Development Programme). 1990. *Human Development Report 1990*. New York: UNDP.

Victora, C. G., L. Adair, C. Fall, P. C. Hallal, R. Martorell, L. Richter, and others. 2008. "Maternal and Child Undernutrition 2: Maternal and Child Undernutrition; Consequences for Adult Health and Human Capital." *Lancet* 371 (January, 9609): 340–57.

Weisbrod, Burton, Ralph Andreano, Robert Baldwin, Erwin Epstein, Allen Kelly, and Thomas Helminiak. 1973. *Disease and Economic Development: The Impact of Parasitic Diseases in St. Lucia.* Madison: University of Wisconsin Press.

World Bank. 1993. *World Development Report 1993: Investing in Health.* Washington, DC: World Bank.

CHAPTER 3
Population Health and Economic Growth

David E. Bloom and David Canning

Improvements in health may be as important as improvements in income when thinking about development and human welfare. Although good health is a goal in its own right—independent of its relationship with income—the link between health and income is important for policy purposes. To the extent that health follows income, income growth should be the priority for developing countries. To the extent that income is a consequence of health, investments in health, even in the poorest developing countries, may be a priority. This argument for health as an investment good is particularly relevant because cheap and easily implementable health policies can improve health dramatically even in the poorest countries.

Empirically, high levels of population health go hand in hand with high levels of national income. This is not unexpected. Higher incomes promote better health through improved nutrition, improved access to safe water and sanitation, and increased ability to purchase more and higher-quality health care. However, health may be not only a consequence but also a cause of high income. This can work through a number of mechanisms (Bloom and Canning 2000). The first is the role of health in labor productivity. Healthy workers lose less time from work due to ill health and are more productive when working. The second is the effect of health on education. Childhood health can have a direct effect on cognitive development and the ability to learn as well as on school attendance. In addition, because adult mortality and morbidity (sickness) can lower the prospective returns to investments in schooling, improving adult health can raise the incentives to invest in education. The third is the effect of health on savings. A longer prospective life span can increase the incentives to save for retirement, generating higher levels of savings and wealth, and a healthy workforce can increase the incentives for business investment. In addition, health care costs can compel families to sell productive assets, forcing them into long-term poverty. The fourth mechanism is the effect of health on the numbers and age structure of the population.

The economic effects of population health can be seen both at the individual and macroeconomic levels. There is no real dispute about the presence of these effects on economic development, but the size of the effects is an important issue. In this chapter we examine the base of evidence that tries to estimate the magnitude of the health impact.

Four difficulties are apparent in assessing existing work in this area. The first is the issue of measurement. "Health" is measured differently in different studies. There is a wide variety of health measures in microeconomic studies. All of these are aimed at measuring some aspect of morbidity at the individual level. Similarly, macroeconomic studies use a variety of indicators, but these focus on measures of the mortality rate, such as life expectancy. It is difficult to compare studies that use such different notions of "health." The second difficulty is causality. Given that income affects health and health affects income, we have to disentangle the two directions of causality. The third issue is one of timing. There is growing evidence of long-term effects of early childhood health on cognitive and physical development, which affect productivity as an adult. This implies that health effects in the macroeconomy may have long time lags, given that the average worker may have been born 40 or more years before, making the macroeconomic relationship difficult to estimate. The fourth issue is the effect of health on the economy, holding all other factors fixed, and the effect on a more general equilibrium framework, where other factors respond to improved health. Some studies measure the partial equilibrium effect, whereas others attempt to capture the induced changes in other factors and the general equilibrium impact.

The issue of population health and economic outcomes is particularly acute in Sub-Saharan Africa. This region has a high burden of tropical infectious disease, such as malaria, tuberculosis, and intestinal worms, and it also suffers from the HIV/AIDS pandemic. We examine the impact of this disease burden on the prospects for economic development in Sub-Saharan Africa.

Determinants of Health

Although we focus on the economic implications of population health, there is clearly two-way causality, as health is partly a consequence of income levels. Preston (1975) demonstrates a positive correlation between

Figure 3.1 Income and Life Expectancy, 2005

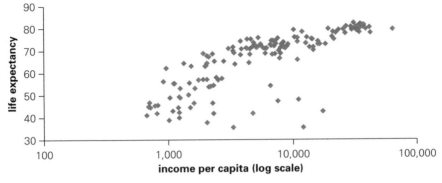

Source: World Bank 2007. Data are for 155 countries in 2005.

Note: Income is in current international dollars, measured at purchasing power parity.

national income levels and life expectancy. Figure 3.1 shows such a "Preston Curve" for recent data. One reason for this link is that higher income levels allow greater access to inputs that improve health, such as food, clean water and sanitation, education, and medical care.

Fogel (2004) emphasizes the role of access to food, while Deaton (2006) puts more weight on public health measures such as clean water and sanitation (see Cutler and Miller 2005). Cutler and McClellan (2001) examine the increasing contribution of medical care to health outcomes. Pritchett and Summers (1996) use the relationship between income level and health to argue for an emphasis on economic growth in poor countries as a method of improving population health. However, the findings of Easterly (1999) weaken this argument. Easterly finds that, although income levels and population health are closely related, the effect of changes in income on population health over reasonable time spans appears to be quite weak. By contrast, relatively inexpensive public health interventions and policies can have remarkable impacts on population health, even in very poor countries. In practice, the major forces behind health improvements have been improvements in health technologies and public health measures that prevent the spread of infectious disease, and not higher income (Cutler, Deaton, and Lleras-Muney 2006).

Overall, Preston's (1975) original view of the determinants of health seems to hold. If we plot the relationship between population health and national income, there is definitely an upward slope, particularly at low income levels. However, plotting the same curve at different points in time (Preston used 1900, 1930, and 1960) yields curves that are higher in later years, indicating an improvement in health over time even if income were to remain fixed. More than 75 percent of the health gains we have observed have come from upward movements of the health-income curve and less than 25 percent have come from movements along the curve as countries get richer. This reinforces the idea that health interventions can improve population health, without the need for prior improvements in income.

Health and Welfare

In this section we examine the role of health as an instrument to generate economic well-being. However, any reasonable view of the contribution of health to human welfare would also include the direct welfare benefits of a long life span and good health. Estimates of the monetary value of life (as measured by the willingness to pay to avoid a small risk of death) are often very large (Viscusi and Aldy 2003). We can use these estimates of the value of life to compare the improvements in welfare that have come about due to improvements in population health and those due to economic growth and higher incomes. Conceptually we can measure the monetary value of health gains by the amount of money people would be willing to pay to forgo these gains (the equivalent variation). For example, we can ask someone living with today's income, health, and life expectancy in the United States what level of income would be required for them to accept living with the average life expectancy and health of Americans in 1900. The income gain they would require is a measure of the value of health and longevity in monetary units and can be very large. Such comparisons suggest that in many countries the value of health gains has been comparable to, or has even surpassed, the value of income gains (Nordhaus 2003). In addition, although income gaps between countries have been very persistent over the last 50 years, there has been large-scale convergence in life expectancy, suggesting that overall levels of world welfare have been converging (Becker, Philipson, and Soares 2005; Bourguignon and Morrisson 2002). The large monetary value of health gains gives a rationale for investing in health quite apart from its instrumental value as an input into productivity.

Health as Human Capital

The idea of health as a form of human capital has a long history (for example, see Mushkin 1962). Grossman (1972) develops a model in which illness prevents work, so the cost of ill health is lost labor time. However, ill health may also have an effect on worker productivity. A major difficulty in measuring the economic effect of health is the two-way causality between wealth and health (Smith 1999). Another difficulty is the lack of consensus on what is meant by health. Different studies use different health measures: self-assessments of health, biomarkers, medical records, limitations on physical functioning, and anthropometric measurements have all been used as health indicators. Each of these approaches may fail to provide a complete picture of an individual's health status, giving rise to a problem of measurement error. In addition, it is necessary to separate the effect of investments in health from the effect of natural or genetic variation in health (Schultz 2005).

One solution to these problems in measuring the effect of health on worker productivity is to establish the causal paths in panel data through the use of timing of health shocks and income or wealth responses (for example, Adams and others 2003). Case, Fertig, and Paxson (2005), controlling for parental influences and education, find that childhood health has a significant impact on adult health and earnings. Yet another approach to establishing causality is to use instrumental variables. For example, Schultz (2002) instruments adult height with childhood health and nutrition to argue that each centimeter gain in height due to improved inputs as a child in Ghana and Brazil leads to a wage increase of between 8 and 10 percent (Strauss and Thomas 1998 provide a survey of studies in this area).

Thomas and Frankenberg (2002) caution against drawing inferences from observational studies and instead advocate an experimental approach. Two randomized experiments using iron supplementation to reduce iron deficiency anemia led to sizable effects on worker productivity in Indonesia (Basta, Soekirman, and Scrimshaw 1979). Quasi-experiments can be used where it is possible to treat changes in health as if such changes were randomly generated. Bleakley (2003) considers the effects of the eradication of hookworm and malaria in the United States in the 1910s and 1920s. These diseases were pandemic in many counties of the American South prior to eradication. Bleakley, controlling for normal wage gains in areas that were not infected, shows that children not exposed to these diseases after eradication had higher incomes as adults than those born before eradication. This body of research on health and human capital generally supports the idea that health affects worker productivity. However, it lacks a good appreciation of which types of health interventions are most important and what rate of return can be achieved by investing in health as a form of human capital. In many developing countries, relatively inexpensive activities designed to prevent the spread of infectious disease (for example, vaccination) can improve population health at low cost, suggesting that even modest income gains from health will generate very high rates of return. By comparison, treating chronic noninfectious disease in developed countries is often costly. There is evidence that susceptibility to chronic disease in later life is determined by health and nutrition as a fetus and in infancy (Barker 1992; Behrman and Rosenzweig 2004), suggesting that early health investments are crucial for adult productivity.

Health, Education, and Cognitive Ability

It is widely agreed that education affects economic outcomes, and health affects education through two mechanisms. The first is the effect of better child health on school attendance, cognitive ability, and learning. Bleakley (2003) finds that deworming of children in the American South had an effect on their educational achievements while in school. Miguel and Kremer (2004) find that deworming of children in Kenya increased school attendance. The second mechanism is the effect of lower mortality and a longer prospective life span on increasing incentives to invest in human capital. This effect increases the benefits of education for the individual

(Kalemli-Ozcan, Ryder, and Weil 2000). In addition, lower infant mortality may encourage parents to invest more resources in fewer children, leading to low fertility but high levels of human capital investment in each child (Kalemli-Ozcan 2002). Evidence for this effect is limited, although Bils and Klenow (2000) do find an effect of life expectancy on investments in education at the national level.

There are several paths from impaired health to the inadequate education of children. Jamison and Leslie (1990) review the links between health conditions and what they see as the three main educational problems in developing countries: children who are not prepared to attend school, the failure of many students to learn in school, and the unequal participation of girls in schooling.

Children's readiness for school may be hindered by cognitive and physical impairments. These problems may begin in utero due to inadequate nutrition and poor health of the mother. The United Nations estimates that roughly 30 million children are born in developing countries annually for whom physical development is impaired as a result of poor nutrition in utero. (United Nations Administrative Committee on Coordination, Subcommittee on Nutrition 2000). For example, cretinism, which can be avoided if iodized salt is provided to the mother, is the most common preventable cause of mental retardation worldwide (Cao and others 1994: 1739). Moreover, malnourished children are less likely to enroll in school, and those who ultimately enroll do so at a later age (UN 2004).

The failure of children in developing countries to learn in school is often attributable to illness. The most important causes of morbidity among school-age children include helminthic infections, micronutrient deficiencies, and chronic protein malnutrition. (Estimates of mortality may be inadequate in assessing the burden of disease among schoolchildren because most illnesses are not fatal.) When not fatal, these conditions impair children's ability to learn by contributing directly to disease, absenteeism, and inattention among children. Micronutrient deficiencies have a variety of adverse health effects. Vitamin A deficiency contributes to measles mortality and diarrheal illness (WHO 2004c) and is the leading cause of preventable pediatric blindness in low-income countries (Sommer and West 1996). Impaired vision is a formidable barrier to receiving an education, particularly in resource-poor settings. Globally, 4.4 million children and 6.2 million women of childbearing age manifest varying degrees of vision impairment from vitamin A deficiency (UN 2004). Iron deficiency is a well-documented cause of impaired cognitive development and lower school achievement and has a high economic cost (Grantham-McGregor and Ani 2001). It is also one of the most prevalent nutrient deficiencies in the world, affecting an estimated 2 billion people (WHO 2004c). Horton and Ross (2003) estimate that income forgone due to iron deficiency ranges from 2 percent of GDP in Honduras to 7.9 percent in Bangladesh. The higher estimates are associated with severe iron deficiency and higher returns to educational attainment in the labor market for a given country.

Biological and cultural forces affect the health of girls and can impede their educational attainment. Attending to remediable medical problems could help to keep girls in school. Menstruation exacerbates iron-deficiency anemia, and, at around the same developmental stage, iodine-deficiency disorders also begin to affect more girls. Pregnancy increases nutrient demands and the risk of morbidity and mortality from a multitude of associated causes. An estimated 15 percent of women develop potentially life-threatening complications associated with pregnancy, such as hemorrhage, infection, unsafe abortion, eclampsia, and obstructed labor (WHO 2004b). Early marriage and childbearing may account for the drop in the number of girls enrolled in secondary and tertiary school. A ubiquitous and disturbing pattern is that, when illness strikes a family, girls often discontinue their studies to assume responsibilities for household chores. (Overviews of the interactions between health and education appear in Bloom 2005, 2006.)

A year of education increases wages by about 10 percent in developing countries (Patrinos and Psacharopoulos 2004). In the United States a standard deviation gain in either mathematics or language test scores corresponds to 8 percent higher wages (Krueger 2003), and there is evidence that in developing countries the effects may be even higher. This suggests that the effects of childhood health on educational outcomes and cognitive development may be even more substantial (Glewwe 1996; Moll 1998). However, wage studies such as these should be interpreted with caution, given how much of production in developing countries is carried out by subsistence farming, where productivity estimates are more difficult to construct (Glewwe 2002).

Health and Saving

Poor health affects both the ability to save and the impetus to save. Sickness can impose large out-of-pocket medical expenses that reduce current and accumulated household savings. This occurs in developed countries (Smith 1999) but is of particular concern in developing countries. In many developing countries the weakness of public and private insurance systems means that out-of-pocket spending by households is the main source of financing for the health system. For example, in India 83 percent of health spending comes from the private sector and 94 percent of private sector spending consists of out-of-pocket expenses (WHO 2007). Health shocks may throw families into poverty if they lack insurance and are forced to sell productive assets, such as land or animals, to pay for medical expenses (Xu and others 2003).

Because poor health tends to be associated with a short life span, increasing population health and expected longevity will have an effect on the planning horizon and will influence life-cycle behavior. With a fixed retirement age, a longer life span elicits greater savings for retirement. Blanchard (1985) considers the theoretical effect of a longer life span in a macroeconomic model. Hurd, McFadden, and Gan (1998) find that expectation of increased longevity leads to greater household wealth in the United States. Bloom, Canning, and Graham (2003) find an effect of life expectancy on national savings, using cross-country data. Lee, Mason, and Miller (2000) argue that rising life expectancy can account for the boom in savings in Taiwan, China, since the 1960s. But the effect of a longer life span need not be increased saving for retirement; people could instead choose to work longer. The behavioral response to longer life spans depends on social security arrangements and retirement incentives (Bloom and others 2007).

In a life-cycle model with a stable age structure and no population or economic growth, the dissaving of the old will exactly match the saving of the young at any level of life expectancy. This suggests that the aggregate effect of a longer life span on savings is temporary and occurs when life expectancy rises. In the long run, the high saving rates of the working-age population will be offset by the dissaving of a large cohort of elderly.

Although we focus on saving, the more important mechanism for accumulating wealth may be investment. In many poor societies, the household is the focus of production and consumption activities. Household savings can take the form of investments in assets that directly affect productivity, such as land, animals, machinery, or seeds. In more advanced economies, savings may be held as investments abroad and do not automatically add to national productive capital. However, in most countries there is a close connection between domestic saving and investment, since international capital markets are not perfect. In addition, a healthy population and workforce may increase productivity and encourage foreign direct investment (Alsan, Bloom, and Canning 2006), while infectious disease can lower productivity and deter investment. These empirical results are supported by historical evidence. The best-known example is the building of the Panama Canal. Yellow fever and communicable diseases claimed the lives of 10,000 to 20,000 workers between 1882 and 1888, forcing Ferdinand de Lesseps and the French to abandon the construction project (Jones 1990).

Health and Demography

The global population explosion of the nineteenth and twentieth centuries was caused not by a rise in fertility but by a fall in mortality. Lower mortality and improved survival rates not only increased population numbers, but also led to significant increases in the number of young people because the largest improvements in mortality were initially in infant mortality. In the long run, reductions in infant mortality lead to a fall in desired fertility, creating a one-time baby boom cohort. As this large cohort ages, the resultant changes in population age structure can have significant economic implications.

Improvements in health and decreases in mortality rates can catalyze a transition from high to low rates of fertility and mortality—the "demographic transition" (Lee 2003). Population growth is the difference between birth and death rates (ignoring migration), and the global population explosion in the twentieth century is attributable to improving health and falling death rates. In developing countries, health advances tend to lower infant and child mortality, leading initially to a surge in the number of children. Reduced infant mortality, larger numbers of surviving children, and rising wages for women can lower desired fertility (see Schultz 1997), leading to smaller cohorts of children in future generations. Better access to family planning can also help couples to match more closely their desired and realized fertility.

This process creates a "baby boom" generation that is larger than both preceding and succeeding cohorts. Subsequent health improvements tend to primarily affect the elderly, reducing old-age mortality and lengthening life spans. In many theoretical models a population explosion reduces income per capita by putting pressure on scarce resources and by diluting the capital-labor ratio. In these models, declines in population spur economic growth in per capita terms. For example, the very high death rates and decline in population due to the Black Death in fourteenth-century Europe appear to have caused a shortage of labor, leading to a rise in wages and the breakdown of the feudal labor system (Herlihy 1997). However, in modern populations there appears to be little connection between overall population growth and economic growth; indeed the twentieth century saw both a population explosion and substantial rises in income levels. Recent evidence from growth models suggests that high population density in coastal areas is conducive to economic growth, implying that scale and specialization effects can outweigh the negative impacts of large populations.

Although it is difficult to find significant effects of overall population growth on economic growth, it is possible to consider the components of population growth separately. High birth and low death rates both generate population growth, but they seem to have quite different effects on economic growth (Bloom and Freeman 1988; Kelley and Schmidt 1995). This may be because, while both forces increase population numbers, they affect the age structure quite differently. The effect of changing age structure due to a baby boom has large effects as the baby boomers enter the workforce and then as they eventually retire. As long as the baby boomers are of working age, economic growth may be spurred by a "demographic dividend" if the baby boom generation can be productively employed. Figure 3.2 shows how the decline in infant mortality rates is leading to a population explosion and high youth dependency rates in Africa. Figure 3.3 shows a similar pattern in East Asia, but in this case falling fertility led to a decline in the number of births after 1970 and current low levels of youth dependency. However, the aging of the large baby boom cohort in East Asia will create high old-age dependency rates in the near future. Bloom, Canning, and Sevilla (2004) find that the demographic dividend

Figure 3.2 Population in Sub-Saharan Africa, by Age, 1960–2040

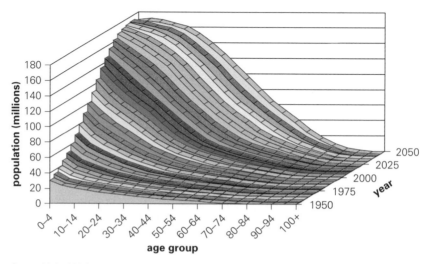

Source: United Nations 2007.

Figure 3.3 Population in East Asia, by Age, 1950–2060

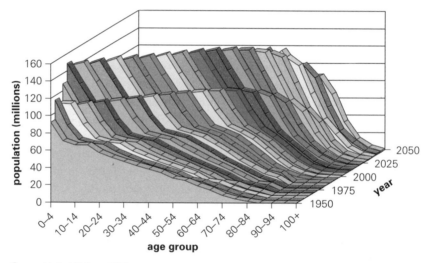

Source: United Nations 2007.

increases the potential labor supply but that its effect on economic growth depends on the policy environment. There is a worry that health improvements and population aging will lead to high dependency rates and a slowdown in economic growth. In addition to longer life spans, however, we are seeing a compression of morbidity; the period of sickness toward the end of life is falling as a proportion of overall life span (Fries 1980, 2003). The idea that old-age dependency starts at 65 is essentially a result of social security retirement arrangements (Gruber and Wise 1998), and healthy aging means that physical dependency now often occurs at much later ages.

Population Health and Economic Growth

Health and Economic Growth

There are two approaches to estimating the effect of health on economic growth. The first is to take estimates of the effect of health from microeconomic studies and use these to calibrate the size of the effects at the aggregate level. The second is to estimate the aggregate relationship directly using macroeconomic data. We begin by considering the calibration approach.

An immediate difficulty is that, in macroeconomic models, population health is usually taken to be life expectancy, or some other mortality measure, as opposed to the morbidity measures used at the individual level. Although the World Health Organization's Global Burden of Disease project now gives estimates of disability rates due to ill health as well as mortality rates, such data are available only for recent years.[1] In addition, even calculating life expectancy requires age-specific mortality rates that are not available for many developing countries, and published figures for life expectancy from the World Bank and United Nations are often constructed from quite incomplete raw data (Bos, Vu, and Stephens 1992). In particular, we often only have reasonable estimates of infant mortality in developing countries, and mortality rates at older ages are imputed using standard life tables. There is a need to improve our measures of population health and to expand them to measures that correspond to morbidity and not just mortality.

Even with a mortality measure such as life expectancy, it is difficult to assess how this can be related to evidence from microeconomic studies on the link between morbidity and productivity. This disjunction can be bridged by assuming a one-to-one relationship between mortality and morbidity rates in a population; however, it is not clear that such a relationship holds, making comparison of the macroeconomic and microeconomic relationships difficult.

The effect of health on individual productivity implies a relationship between population health and aggregate output. Shastry and Weil (2003) calibrate a production function model of aggregate output using microeconomic estimates of the return to health. They assume a stable relationship between average height and adult survival rates so that when adult survival rates improve we can infer a rise in population heights. Using estimates of the effect of height on worker productivity and wages from microeconomic studies, they calibrate what health improvements in the form of lower adult survival rates should mean for aggregate output. They find that cross-country gaps in income levels can be explained in part by differential levels of physical capital, education, and health, with these three factors making roughly equal contributions to differences in income levels. These factors explain a little more than half of the cross-country income gap; the remainder of the gap is ascribed to differences in total factor productivity.

---

1   The World Health Organization data are available at http://www.who.int/healthinfo/bod/en/index.html.

The argument that health is unidimensional so that health indicators can be used interchangeably is useful for analysis, but it is not clear that it is true. In terms of mortality and height indicators, Deaton (2007) makes the point that most of the cross-country variation in height is not related to health and that a population's average height is not a good indicator of its health status. However, changes in population height over time still may reflect changes in health status. Crimmins and Finch (2006) show that the cohorts that underwent substantial improvements in infant mortality in developed countries in the late nineteenth century were the same cohorts that experienced gains in adult height and improvements in adult mortality. However, Akachi and Canning (2007a, 2007b) argue that this relationship appears to hold today in most developing countries, but not in Sub-Saharan Africa. In most developing countries, gains in infant mortality rates and cohorts' eventual adult height are strongly related. In Sub-Saharan Africa, however, cohort average height has stagnated over the last 50 years, while infant mortality has declined rapidly. This indicates that health gains in Sub-Saharan Africa may be more dependent on life-saving medical interventions and less on broad-based improvements in nutrition and the absence of disease that would reduce morbidity.

Table 3.1 shows time trends of height, infant mortality, and nutrition. In terms of infant mortality, we find very similar rates of decline in Sub-Saharan Africa and developing countries in other regions: a decrease of about 2.1 versus 2.4 deaths per 1,000 births each year. However, while the consumption of both protein and calories has been increasing significantly elsewhere, within Sub-Saharan Africa it has remained virtually unchanged over the whole period.

The trends in height are also quite distinct. In Sub-Saharan Africa, heights overall have been decreasing; the cohort born in 1985 is about 0.5 centimeters shorter than the cohort born in 1961. In the rest of the developing world, the height of adult women rose approximately 1.6 centimeters on average during this 24-year period.

Another approach is to estimate directly the effect of population health on economic growth. Estimating the effect of the current level of population

Table 3.1 Regional Time Trends in Adult Height, Infant Mortality, and Nutrition, 1961–85

Region	Adult height	Infant mortality rate	Calories per capita per day	Protein grams per capita per day
Sub-Saharan Africa	−0.021*** (0.003)	−2.120*** (0.052)	0.394 (0.820)	−0.019 (0.025)
Other developing countries	0.066*** (0.003)	−2.359*** (0.037)	16.488*** (0.795)	0.333*** (0.022)

Source: Akachi and Canning 2007a.

Note: These results are based on regressions with country fixed effects and regional time trends. Coefficients give the average annual change of the variable in the region; standard errors are in parentheses. Height trends are estimated with weighted least squares, weighted by the number of individuals used to calculate the cohort average height.

***Significant at 1 percent.

Table 3.2 Annual Growth Rate of Per Capita Income, by Income per Capita and Infant Mortality Rate (1960), 1960–2000

% growth

Initial income, 1960 (constant 2000 US$, purchasing power parity)	Initial infant mortality rate			
	≤50	51–100	101–150	151+
≤$1,000	—	3.9 (1)	2.0 (11)	0.8 (9)
$1,001–$2,000	—	4.8 (3)	1.5 (7)	0.5 (7)
$2,001–$3,500	—	1.6 (6)	1.7 (6)	1.0 (4)
$3,501–$7,000	3.5 (6)	2.1 (9)	0.7 (2)	1.0 (1)
$7,001+	2.5 (17)	0.9 (1)	—	—

Source: Alsan and others 2007.

— Not available.

Note: The number reported is the average growth rate of countries in that income and infant mortality rate interval. The numbers in parentheses represent the number of countries in the interval that are used in constructing the average.

health on current level of income is subject to the problem of reverse causality; income also affects health. One way around this problem is to look at the effect of population health on subsequent economic growth, arguing that timing can determine the direction of causality. This requires the absence of reverse causality through an expectation effect (so that current health is not caused by expected future economic growth).

Growth regressions show that the initial levels of population health are a significant predictor of future economic growth (Bloom, Canning, and Sevilla 2004 provide a survey of this literature). Bhargava and others (2001) argue that the effect of health on economic growth is larger in developing countries than in developed countries. Table 3.2, taken from Alsan and others (2007), gives economic growth rates over the period 1960–2000 for countries grouped by initial income and life expectancy. This table illustrates why studies tend to find health to be a significant predictor of economic growth. At each level of income there is a tendency for the countries with higher initial levels of life expectancy to experience more rapid economic growth.

Although measures of population health are highly predictive of future economic growth, there is a debate about how to interpret the link. The health effect could be interpreted as the macroeconomic counterpart of the worker productivity effect found in individuals. However, Acemoglu, Johnson, and Robinson (2003) argue that differences in health are not large enough to account for much of the cross-country difference in incomes and that the variations in political, economic, and social institutions are more central. They argue that health does not have a direct effect on growth, but serves in growth regressions as a proxy for the pattern of European settlement, which was more successful in countries with a low burden of infectious disease.

One way to address the issue is to see how the effect of health carries with the inclusion of other variables in the growth regression that may account for potential omitted variables. Sala-i-Martin, Doppelhofer, and Miller (2004) test 67 potential variables that might affect economic growth. They start by putting an equal probability of affecting growth on each variable. They then run possible models of a particular size (for example, 5, 7, 9, and 11 explanatory variables) and perform Bayesian updating on the results to find the posterior probability of each variable being included. If the model has only five explanatory variables, then they select the East Asia dummy, primary schooling, price of investment goods, initial income, and fractional tropical area as the most likely explanations of economic growth. However, extending the model to include nine explanatory variables adds life expectancy, malaria prevalence, the fraction of the population that is Confucian, and the population density in coastal areas. This indicates that the predictive power of health for economic growth (as measured by life expectancy and malaria prevalence) is robust to the specification of the growth regression.

Acemoglu and Johnson (2007; also in this volume) raise a second objection to the argument that health affects economic growth. They instrument health using the initial disease burden and worldwide technological progress in disease-specific interventions. They find that instrumented health does not predict the level of income. This result is subject to the criticism of lag times; it may take time for health technologies to be implemented and time for the health improvements in children to work their way into productivity improvements. However, the major innovation in their paper is the argument that health improvements increase longevity and spur population growth and that this population growth puts a strain on other factors, causing income per capita to fall.

As we note in the section on demography, the resultant population growth is usually short-lived. Falling infant mortality usually leads to a fall in fertility, which stabilizes population numbers and generates a demographic dividend through a very low level of youth dependency. However, this effect takes time, and it seems likely that the initial effects of rising child survival (which is where mortality health gains tend to be concentrated in developing countries) on income per capita are negative. Acemoglu and Johnson's work certainly points toward the need for a better understanding of the demographic consequences of health improvements. Given the importance of the effect of a reduction in mortality on fertility behavior for understanding the effects of health improvements, the base of evidence is rather weak. Cleland (2001) argues for a strong effect on fertility based on evidence regarding the timing of the fertility, although he emphasizes that the effect may be delayed. However, at the individual level, the replacement effect of a child's death on the mother's fertility is fairly small. Palloni and Rafalimanana (1999) find that the major effect appears to be community-level expectations of infant mortality, whereas Bongaarts and Watkins (1996) emphasize the role of diffusion of social norms in fertility behavior, making the effects of infant mortality on fertility difficult to estimate from household data.

Even if a causal interpretation of the effect of health on individual productivity and economic growth is accepted, the argument for using health as an input depends on there being low-cost health interventions that can improve population health without first having a high income level. However, the number of such interventions that can be implemented is large (Commission on Macroeconomics and Health 2001).

Disease-Specific Issues

Economists and public health specialists have carried out considerable research on the manner and extent to which specific diseases have economic implications. We discuss below some findings on tropical diseases, malaria, and HIV/AIDS.

Tropical Diseases and Malaria

Sub-Saharan Africa suffers from poor health due to the widespread presence of tropical disease. Many tropical diseases may have a small effect on mortality but a high morbidity burden. Diseases such as malaria, schistosomiasis, and intestinal worms can cause anemia and reduced energy levels and productivity as well as result in significant long-term developmental effects if acquired by children.

Gallup and Sachs (2001) find that countries heavily burdened with malaria experienced significantly lower growth between 1965 and 1990, even after allowing for the effect of life expectancy in each country. New evidence is pointing to large long-term effects on education and productivity outcomes for children who avoid being infected when DDT campaigns are used to eliminate malaria. Bleakley (2006) examines the effect of childhood exposure to malaria in Brazil, Colombia, Mexico, and the United States on income level as an adult. He identifies the effect by looking at the earnings of children born after the DDT intervention in previously malarial areas with those born before the intervention and then compares this with the change in earnings in nonmalarial areas over the same period. He finds very large effects with a removal of childhood malaria, increasing adult earnings by around 50 percent. Cutler and others (2007) undertake a similar study of the DDT eradication program in India in the 1960s and find significant effects on the educational outcomes of children who avoided exposure to malaria due to the program.

There is abundant evidence of the large effects of malaria on adults. Focusing just on working days lost as a result of bouts of illness, Babu and others (2002) note that in malaria-endemic areas adults can expect about two bouts of malarial fever a year, with each bout leading to the loss of

Table 3.3 Prevalence of Preventable Neglected Diseases, by Region

% of the population

Region	Trichuriasis	Ascariasis	Hookworm	Schistosomiasis
Latin America and Caribbean	19	16	10	4
Sub-Saharan Africa	24	25	29	29
Middle East and North Africa	2	7	3	7
South Asia	20	27	16	—
India	7	14	7	—
East Asia and the Pacific	28	36	26	—
China	17	39	16	0.10

Source: De Silva and others 2003.
— Not available.

between five and 10 working days. This amounts to a reduction in labor supply of about 5 percent. Although this effect on working days lost is substantial, the effect of early exposure on children's cognitive development and eventual earnings may be much greater.

Lymphatic filariasis is also transmitted by mosquitoes and has large effects on health and worker productivity (Ramaiah and others 2000). About 120 million people are infected worldwide, mainly in Asia and the Americas. Efforts to attack malaria transmission through targeting the transmission vector are likely to reduce the burden of this disease as well.

Parasitic worm diseases have high rates of prevalence in developing countries (see table 3.3). Iron deficiency anemia, which can result from the parasitic diseases, has insidious effects, lowering energy levels, worker productivity, and wages (Thomas and Frankenberg 2002). Parasitic worm diseases are most common in children, where they affect school attendance, literacy, and physical development (Bleakley 2003; Miguel and Kremer 2004), although the potential for effects on cognitive development are less clear (Dickson and others 2000).

The low costs of interventions that can substantially reduce or eliminate the burden of these parasitic diseases should make such interventions a high priority even in the poorest countries. Annual population- and school-based administration of drugs is safe and effective and costs very little (Molyneux 2004; Molyneux, Hotez, and Fenwick 2005). It promises large benefits, both in terms of reduced morbidity burden and economic gains. These tropical diseases (other than malaria) are now often grouped under the heading of "neglected" diseases. This is because their low mortality burden makes them less of a health priority than high-mortality diseases. In addition, the ill health they cause is not acute and rarely results in patients reporting to medical facilities for treatment. The morbidity associated with these diseases has a very low weight in estimates of the total burden of disease (Murray and Lopez 1996), even though their effects on worker productivity may be large. There is a strong case for focusing on these "neglected" diseases for economic, if not for health, reasons (Canning 2006b).

HIV/AIDS

Approximately 33 million people are infected with HIV (UNAIDS 2008), and AIDS is now the world's leading killer of adults ages 15–59 (WHO 2003). Co-infections of HIV and malaria or tuberculosis can exacerbate an already dire health situation. A high prevalence of some diseases negatively affects economies and is associated with lower economic growth. Although HIV/AIDS has increased mortality rates dramatically, its impact on income per capita is unclear. HIV/AIDS is associated with high mortality, but the period of sickness before death is relatively short. This mutes the worker productivity effects of the disease. Bloom and Mahal (1997) find that HIV/AIDS does not seem to lower the growth rate of income per capita; lower output is matched by lower population numbers due to high death rates. Young (2005) goes further and argues that AIDS mortality significantly reduces fertility and that this, together with the deaths of large numbers of people, will lower population pressure and increase the income per capita of the survivors of the pandemic in South Africa.

Many authors, however, argue that AIDS mortality has significant indirect effects that will reduce economic growth in the long term. Deaths from HIV/AIDS are concentrated among young adult men and women, leading to a higher dependency ratio. Bell, Devarajan, and Gersbach (2004) argue that the creation of a generation of AIDS orphans may lead to lack of care and education for children and to low productivity in the future. This effect may be compounded by fatalism induced by high AIDS mortality and shorter expected life span, which reduce the returns to education. The high level of stigma associated with HIV/AIDS can lower trust in the community, while high mortality and the strains imposed by extreme ill health before death can weaken families, community groups, firms, and government agencies, with long-term consequences for social capital (Haacker 2004).

It is important to remember that income per capita is not a complete measure of welfare. Resources devoted to preventing and treating HIV/AIDS are part of measured income but reduce consumption of other goods, reducing welfare even as measured GDP per capita may remain steady. A more comprehensive welfare measure that included the welfare gain derived from a long life span, as well as annual income, would show a large welfare reduction due to HIV/AIDS (Crafts and Haacker 2004). The main welfare effect of HIV/AIDS is the sickness and death of its victims and the impact of these on the victims' families; the effect on the average income level of the survivors is decidedly secondary.

In terms of policies to combat HIV/AIDS, various prevention options are highly cost-effective and could have a large impact on the course of the epidemic. The high cost of antiretroviral treatment (ART) relative to other interventions that can improve health makes it difficult to justify in very poor countries (Canning 2006a). However, recent evidence suggests that patients on ART are well enough to return to work and that this economic payoff may strengthen the case for treatment (Thirumurthy, Graff Zivin, and Goldstein 2005).

References

Acemoglu, Daron, and Simon Johnson. 2007. "Disease and Development: The Effect of Life Expectancy on Economic Growth." *Journal of Political Economy* 115 (6): 925–85.

Acemoglu, Daron, Simon Johnson, and James Robinson. 2003. "Disease and Development in Historical Perspective." *Journal of the European Economic Association, Papers and Proceedings* 1 (2-3): 397–405.

Adams, Peter, Michael D. Hurd, Daniel L. McFadden, Angela Merrill, and Tiago Ribeiro. 2003. "Healthy, Wealthy, and Wise? Tests for Direct Causal Paths between Health and Socioeconomic Status." *Journal of Econometrics* 112 (1): 3–56.

Akachi, Yoko, and David Canning. 2007a. "Health Capital in Sub-Saharan Africa: Evidence from Adult Heights." Program on the Global Demography of Aging, Harvard University, Cambridge, MA.

———. 2007b. "The Height of Women in Sub-Saharan Africa: The Role of Health, Nutrition, and Income in Childhood." *Annals of Human Biology* 34 (4): 397–410.

Alsan, Marcella, David E. Bloom, and David Canning. 2006. "The Effect of Population Health on Foreign Direct Investment Inflows to Low- and Middle-Income Countries." *World Development* 34 (4): 613–30.

Alsan, Marcella, David E. Bloom, David Canning, and Dean Jamison. 2007. "The Consequences of Population Health for Economic Performance." In *Health, Economic Development, and Household Poverty,* ed. Sara Mills, Lucy Gibson, and Anne Mills, 21–39. Oxford: Routledge.

Babu, B. V., A. N. Nayak, A. S. Acharya, P. K. Jangid, and G. Mallick. 2002. "The Economic Loss Due to Treatment Cost and Work Loss to Individuals with Chronic Lymphatic Filariasis in Rural Communities of Orissa, India." *Acta Tropica* 82 (1): 31–38.

Barker, D. J. P. 1992. *The Fetal and Infant Origins of Adult Disease.* London: BMJ Books.

Basta, S. S., Karyadi Soekirman, and N. S. Scrimshaw. 1979. "Iron Deficiency Anemia and Productivity of Adult Males in Indonesia." *American Journal of Clinical Nutrition* 32 (4): 916–25.

Becker, Gary S., Tomas J. Philipson, and Rodrigo R. Soares. 2005. "The Quantity of Life and the Evolution of World Inequality." *American Economic Review* 95 (1): 277–91.

Behrman, Jere R., and Mark R. Rosenzweig. 2004. "The Returns to Birthweight." *Review of Economics and Statistics* 86 (2): 586–601.

Bell, Clive, Shantayanan Devarajan, and Hans Gersbach. 2004. "Thinking about the Long-Run Economic Costs of AIDS." In *The Macroeconomics of HIV/ AIDS,* ed. Markus Haacker. Washington, DC: International Monetary Fund.

Bhargava, Alok, Dean Jamison, Lawrence Lau, and Christopher Murray. 2001. "Modeling the Effects of Health on Economic Growth." *Journal of Health Economics* 20 (3): 423–40.

Bils, Mark, and Peter J. Klenow. 2000. "Does Schooling Cause Growth?" *American Economic Review* 90 (5): 1160–83.

Blanchard, Olivier J. 1985. "Debt, Deficits, and Finite Horizons." *Journal of Political Economy* 93 (2): 223–47.

Bleakley, Hoyt. 2003. "Disease and Development: Evidence from the American South." *Journal of the European Economic Association* 1 (2-3): 376–86.

———. 2006. "Malaria in the Americas: A Retrospective Analysis of Childhood Exposure." Documentos CEDE 003185, Universidad de los Andes, Centro de Estudios sobre el Desarrollo Económico, Bogotá.

Bloom, David E. 2005. "Education and Public Health: Mutual Challenges Worldwide: Guest Editor's Overview." *Comparative Education Review* 49 (4): 437–51.

———. 2006. "Education, Health, and Development." In *Educating All Children: A Global Agenda,* ed. Joel E. Cohen, David E. Bloom, and Martin Malin, 535–58. Cambridge, MA: American Academy of Arts and Sciences and MIT Press.

Bloom, David E., and David Canning. 2000. "The Health and Wealth of Nations." *Science* 287 (5456): 1207–08.

Bloom, David E., David Canning, and Bryan Graham. 2003. "Longevity and Life-Cycle Savings." *Scandinavian Journal of Economics* 105 (3): 319–38.

Bloom, David E., David Canning, Rick Mansfield, and Michael Moore. 2007. "Demographic Change, Social Security Systems, and Savings." *Journal of Monetary Economics* 54 (1): 92–114.

Bloom, David E., David Canning, and J. P. Sevilla. 2004. "The Effect of Health on Economic Growth: A Production Function Approach." *World Development* 32 (1): 1–13.

Bloom, David E., and Richard B. Freeman. 1988. "Economic Development and the Timing and Components of Population Growth." *Journal of Policy Modeling* 10 (1): 57–82.

Bloom, David E., and Ajay S. Mahal. 1997. "Does the AIDS Epidemic Threaten Economic Growth?" *Journal of Econometrics* 77 (1): 105–24.

Bongaarts, John, and Susan C. Watkins. 1996. "Social Interactions and Contemporary Fertility Transitions." *Population and Development Review* 22 (4): 639–82.

Bos, Eduard, My T. Vu, and Patience W. Stephens. 1992. "Sources of World Bank Estimates of Current Mortality Rates." Policy Research Working Paper 851, World Bank, Washington, DC.

Bourguignon, François B., and Christian Morrisson. 2002. "Inequality among World Citizens: 1820–1992." *American Economic Review* 92 (4): 727–44.

Canning, David. 2006a. "The Economics of HIV/AIDS in Low-Income Countries: The Case for Prevention." *Journal of Economic Perspectives* 20 (3): 121–42.

———. 2006b. "Priority Setting and the 'Neglected' Tropical Diseases." *Transactions of the Royal Society of Tropical Medicine and Hygiene* 100 (6): 499–504.

Cao, Xue-Yi, Xin-Min Jiang, Zhi-Hong Dou, Murdon A. Rakeman, Ming-Li Zhang, Karen O'Donnell, Tai Ma, Kareem Amette, Nancy DeLong, and G. Robert DeLong. 1994. "Timing of Vulnerability of the Brain to Iodine Deficiency in Endemic Cretinism." *New England Journal of Medicine* 331 (26): 1739–44.

Case, Anne, Angela Fertig, and Christina Paxson. 2005. "The Lasting Impact of Childhood Health and Circumstance." *Journal of Health Economics* 24 (2): 365–89.

Cleland, John. 2001. "The Effect of Improved Survival on Fertility: A Reassessment." *Population and Development Review* 27 (1): 60–92.

Commission on Macroeconomics and Health. 2001. *Macroeconomics and Health: Investing in Health for Economic Development.* Geneva: World Health Organization.

Crafts, N. F. R., and Markus Haacker. 2004. "Welfare Implications of HIV/AIDS." In *The Macroeconomics of HIV/AIDS,* ed. Markus Haacker. Washington, DC: International Monetary Fund.

Crimmins, Eileen, and Caleb Finch. 2006. "Infection, Inflammation, Height, and Longevity." *PNAS (Proceedings of the National Academy of Sciences)* 103 (2): 498–503.

Cutler, David M., Angus S. Deaton, and Adriana Lleras-Muney. 2006. "The Determinants of Mortality." *Journal of Economic Perspectives* 20 (3): 71–96.

Cutler, David C., Winnie Fung, Michael Kremer, and Monica Singhal. 2007. "Mosquitoes: The Long-Term Effects of Malaria Eradication in India." NBER Working Paper 13539, National Bureau of Economic Research, Cambridge, MA.

Cutler, David M., and Mark McClellan. 2001. "Productivity Change in Health Care." *American Economic Review* 91 (2): 281–86.

Cutler, David M., and Grant Miller. 2005. "The Role of Public Health Improvements in Health Advances: The Twentieth-Century United States." *Demography* 42 (1): 1–22.

Deaton, Angus. 2006. "The Great Escape: A Review Essay on Fogel's *The Escape from Hunger and Premature Death, 1700–2100.*" *Journal of Economic Literature* 44 (1): 106–14.

———. 2007. "Height, Health, and Development." *PNAS (Proceedings of the National Academy of Sciences)* 104 (33): 13232–37.

De Silva, Nilanthi R., Simon Brooker, Peter J. Hotez, Antonio Montresor, Dirk Engels, and Lorenzo Savoli. 2003. "Soil-Transmitted Helminth Infections: Updating the Global Picture." *Trends in Parasitology* 19 (12): 547–51.

Dickson, Rumona, Shally Awasthi, Paula Williamson, Colin Demellweek, and Paul Garner. 2000. "Effects of Treatment for Intestinal Helminth Infection on Growth and Cognitive Performance in Children: Systematic Review of Randomised Trials." *British Medical Journal* 320 (7251): 1697–1701.

Easterly, William. 1999. "Life during Growth." *Journal of Economic Growth* 4 (3): 239–76.

Fogel, Robert W. 2004. *The Escape from Hunger and Premature Death, 1700–2100: Europe, America, and the Third World.* Cambridge, U.K.: Cambridge University Press.

Fries, J. F. 1980. "Aging, Natural Death, and the Compression of Morbidity." *New England Journal of Medicine* 303 (3): 130–35.

———. 2003. "Measuring and Monitoring Success in Compressing Morbidity." *Annals of Internal Medicine* 139 (5, pt. 2): 455–59.

Gallup, John L. and Jeffrey D. Sachs. 2001. "The Economic Burden of Malaria." *American Journal of Tropical Medicine and Hygiene* 64 (1-2): 85–96.

Glewwe, Paul. 1996. "The Relevance of Standard Estimates of Rates of Return to Schooling for Education Policy: A Critical Assessment." *Journal of Development Economics* 51 (2): 267–90.

————. 2002. "Schools and Skills in Developing Countries: Education Policies and Socioeconomic Outcomes." *Journal of Economic Literature* 40 (2): 436–82.

Grantham-McGregor, Sally, and Cornelius Ani. 2001. "A Review of Studies on the Effect of Iron Deficiency on Cognitive Development in Children." *Journal of Nutrition* 131 (11): S649–S68.

Grossman, Michael. 1972. "On the Concept of Health Capital and the Demand for Health." *Journal of Political Economy* 80 (2): 223–55.

Gruber, Jonathan, and David Wise. 1998. "Social Security and Retirement: An International Comparison." *American Economic Review* 88 (2): 158–63.

Haacker, Makus. 2004. "HIV/AIDS: The Impact on the Social Fabric and the Economy." In *The Macroeconomics of HIV/AIDS*, ed. Markus Haacker. Washington, DC: International Monetary Fund.

Herlihy, David. 1997. *The Black Death and the Transformation of the West.* Cambridge, MA: Harvard University Press.

Horton, Susan, and J. Ross. 2003. "The Economics of Iron Deficiency." *Food Policy* 28 (1): 51–75.

Hurd, Michael, Daniel McFadden, and Li Gan. 1998. "Subjective Survival Curves and Life-Cycle Behavior." In *Inquiries in the Economics of Aging*, ed. David Wise. Chicago: University of Chicago Press.

Jamison, Dean T., and Joanne Leslie. 1990. "Health and Nutrition Considerations in Education Planning: The Cost and Effectiveness of School-Based Interventions." *Food and Nutrition Bulletin* 12 (3): 204–14.

Jones, Tyler. 1990. "The Panama Canal: A Brief History." http://www.ilovelanguages.com/tyler/nonfiction/pan2.html.

Kalemli-Ozcan, Sebnem. 2002. "Does Mortality Decline Promote Economic Growth?" *Journal of Economic Growth* 7 (4): 411–39.

Kalemli-Ozcan, Sebnem, Harl E. Ryder, and David N. Weil. 2000. "Mortality Decline, Human Capital Investment, and Economic Growth." *Journal of Development Economics* 62 (1): 1–23.

Kelley, Allen C., and Robert M. Schmidt. 1995. "Aggregate Population and Economic Growth Correlations: The Role of the Components of Demographic Change." *Demography* 32 (4): 543–55.

Krueger, Alan B. 2003. "Economic Considerations and Class Size." *Economic Journal* 113 (485): F34–63.

Lee, Ronald. 2003. "The Demographic Transition: Three Centuries of Fundamental Change." *Journal of Economic Perspectives* 17 (4): 167–90.

Lee, Ronald, Andrew Mason, and Timothy Miller. 2000. "Life Cycle Saving and the Demographic Transition: The Case of Taiwan." *Population and Development Review* 26 (supplement): 194–219.

Miguel, Edward, and Michael Kremer. 2004. "Worms: Identifying Impacts on Education and Health in the Presence of Treatment Externalities." *Econometrica* 72 (1): 159–217.

Moll, Peter G. 1998. "Primary Schooling, Cognitive Skills, and Wages in South Africa." *Economica* 65 (258): 263–84.

Molyneux, David H. 2004. "'Neglected' Diseases but Unrecognised Successes: Challenges and Opportunities for Infectious Disease Control." *Lancet* 364 (9431): 380–83.

Molyneux, David H., Peter J. Hotez, and Alan Fenwick. 2005. "Rapid-Impact Interventions: How a Policy of Integrated Control for Africa's Neglected Tropical Diseases Could Benefit the Poor." *PLoS Medicine* 2 (11): e336.

Murray, Christopher J. L., and Alan D. Lopez, eds. 1996. *Global Burden of Disease*. Cambridge, MA: Harvard University Press.

Mushkin, Selma J. 1962. "Health as an Investment." *Journal of Political Economy* 70 (5): 129–57.

Nordhaus, William. 2003. "The Health of Nations: The Contribution of Improved Health to Living Standards." In *Measuring the Gains from Medical Research: An Economic Approach*, ed. Kevin H. Murphy and Robert H. Topel. Chicago: University of Chicago Press.

Palloni, Alberto, and Hantamala Rafalimanana. 1999. "The Effect of Infant Mortality on Fertility Revisited: New Evidence from Latin America." *Demography* 36 (1): 41–58.

Patrinos, Harry A., and George Psacharopoulos. 2004. "Returns to Investment in Education: A Further Update." *Education Economics* 12 (2): 111–34.

Preston, Samuel. 1975. "The Changing Relation between Mortality and Level of Economic Development." *Population Studies* 29 (2): 231–48.

Pritchett, Lant, and Lawrence Summers. 1996. "Wealthier Is Healthier." *Journal of Human Resources* 31 (4): 841–68.

Ramaiah, K. D., P. K. Das, E. Michael, and H. Guyatt. 2000. "The Economic Burden of Lymphatic Filariasis in India." *Parasitology Today* 16 (6): 251–53.

Sala-i-Martin, Xavier, Gernot Doppelhofer, and Ronald I. Miller. 2004. "Determinants of Long-Term Growth: A Bayesian Averaging of Classical Estimates (BACE) Approach." *American Economic Review* 94 (4): 813–35.

Schultz, T. Paul. 1997. "The Demand for Children in Low-Income Countries." In *Handbook of Population and Family Economics*. Vol. 1A, ed. Mark R. Rosenzweig and Oded Stark. Amsterdam: North-Holland.

———. 2002. "Wage Gains Associated with Height as a Form of Human Capital." *American Economic Review, Papers and Proceedings* 92 (2): 349–53.

———. 2005. "Productive Benefits of Health: Evidence from Low-Income Countries." In *Health and Economic Growth: Findings and Policy Implications*, ed. Guillem López-Casasnovas, Berta Riveras, and Luis Currais. Cambridge, MA: MIT Press.

Shastry, Gauri K., and David N. Weil. 2003. "How Much of Cross-Country Income Variation Is Explained by Health?" *Journal of the European Economic Association* 1 (2-3): 387–96.

Smith, James P. 1999. "Healthy Bodies and Thick Wallets: The Dual Relation between Health and Economic Status." *Journal of Economic Perspectives* 13 (2): 145–66.

Sommer, Alfred, and Keith West. 1996. *Vitamin A Deficiency: Health, Survival, and Vision*. New York: Oxford University Press.

Strauss, John, and Duncan Thomas. 1998. "Health, Nutrition, and Economic Development." *Journal of Economic Literature* 36 (2): 766–817.

Thirumurthy, Harsha, Joshua Graff Zivin, and Markus P. Goldstein. 2005. "The Economic Impact of AIDS Treatment: Labor Supply in Western Kenya." NBER Working Paper W11871, National Bureau of Economic Research, Cambridge, MA.

Thomas, Duncan, and Elizabeth Frankenberg. 2002. "Health, Nutrition, and Prosperity: A Microeconomic Perspective." *Bulletin of the World Health Organization* 80 (2): 106–13.

United Nations Administrative Committee on Coordination, Subcommittee on Nutrition. 2000. *Fourth Report on the World Nutrition Situation. Nutrition throughout the Life Cycle*. Geneva: Administrative Committee on Coordination, Subcommittee on Nutrition.

UN (United Nations). 2004. *Fifth Report on the World Nutrition Situation: Nutrition for Improved Development Outcomes*. New York: UN. http://www.unsystem.org/scn/Publications/AnnualMeeting/SCN31/ SCN5Report.pdf.

———. 2007. *World Population Prospects: The 2006 Revision*. Washington, DC: UN Population Division, Department of Economic and Social Affairs.

UNAIDS (United Nations Programme on HIV/AIDS). 2008. *Report on the Global HIV/AIDS Epidemic 2008*. Geneva: UNAIDS. http://www.unaids.org/en/KnowledgeCentre/HIVData/GlobalReport/2008/2008_Global_report.asp.

Viscusi, W. Kip, and Joseph E. Aldy. 2003. "The Value of a Statistical Life: A Critical Review of Market Estimates from around the World." *Journal of Risk and Uncertainty* 27 (1): 5–76.

WHO (World Health Organization). 2003. *World Health Report 2003*. Geneva: WHO.

———. 2004a. "Making Pregnancy Safer." Fact Sheet 276, WHO, Geneva.

———. 2004b. "Micronutrient Deficiencies: Iron Deficiency Anaemia." WHO, Geneva. http://www.who.int/nutrition/topics/ida/en/index.html.

———. 2004c. "Micronutrient Deficiencies: Vitamin A Deficiency." WHO, Geneva. http://www.who.int/nutrition/topics/vad/en/.

———. 2007. *World Health Statistics*. Geneva: WHO.

World Bank. 2007. *World Development Indicators 2007*. Washington, DC: World Bank.

Xu, Ke, David Evans, Kei Kawabata, Riadh Zeramdini, Jan Klavus, and Christopher Murray. 2003. "Household Catastrophic Health Expenditure: A Multicountry Analysis." *Lancet* 362 (9378): 111–17.

Young, Alwyn. 2005. "The Gift of the Dying: The Tragedy of AIDS and the Welfare of Future African Generations." *Quarterly Journal of Economics* 120 (2): 243–66.

CHAPTER 4

Disease and Development: The Effect of Life Expectancy on Economic Growth

Daron Acemoglu and Simon Johnson

Improving health around the world today is an important social objective, which has obvious direct payoffs in terms of longer and better lives for millions. There is also a growing consensus that improving health can have equally large indirect payoffs through accelerating economic growth.[1] For example, Gallup and Sachs (2001: 91) argue that wiping out malaria in Sub-Saharan Africa could increase that continent's per capita growth rate by as much as 2.6 percent a year, and a recent report by the World Health

Reprinted with permission from Daron Acemoglu and Simon Johnson, "Disease and Development: The Effect of Life Expectancy on Economic Growth," *Journal of Political Economy* (The University of Chicago Press) 115, no. 6 (2007): 925–85. © 2007 by The University of Chicago. All rights reserved.

The authors thank Leopoldo Fergusson and Ioannis Tokatlidis for excellent research assistance and Josh Angrist, David Autor, Abhijit Banerjee, Tim Besley, Anne Case, Sebnem Kalemli-Ozcan, Torsten Persson, Arvind Subramanian, David Weil, Pierre Yared, and especially Gary Becker, Angus Deaton, Steve Levitt, and an anonymous referee for very useful suggestions. They also thank seminar participants at the Brookings Institution, Brown University, University of Chicago, Harvard University, and Massachusetts Institute of Technology (MIT) development seminar, London School of Economics, University of Maryland, Northwestern University, the National Bureau of Economic Research Summer Institute, Princeton University, the seventh Bureau for Research and Economic Analysis conference on development economics, and the World Bank for comments, and the staff of the National Library of Medicine and MIT's Retrospective Collection for their patient assistance. Acemoglu gratefully acknowledges financial support from the National Science Foundation.

1   See, among others, Alleyne and Cohen (2002); Bloom and Canning (2005); Bloom and Sachs (1998); Gallup and Sachs (2001); Lorentzon, McMillan, and Wacziarg (2005); WHO (2001).

Organization states, "In today's world, poor health has particularly pernicious effects on economic development in Sub-Saharan Africa, South Asia, and pockets of high disease and intense poverty elsewhere" (WHO 2001 : 24) and "Extending the coverage of crucial health services … to the world's poor could save millions of lives each year, reduce poverty, spur economic development, and promote global security" (WHO 2001: i).

The evidence supporting this recent consensus is not yet conclusive, however. Although cross-country regression studies show a strong correlation between measures of health (for example, life expectancy) and the level of both economic development and recent economic growth, these studies have not established a causal effect of health and disease on economic growth. Since countries suffering from short life expectancy and ill health are also disadvantaged in other ways (and often this is the reason for their poor health outcomes), such macro studies may be capturing the negative effects of these other, often omitted, disadvantages. While a range of micro studies demonstrate the importance of health for individual productivity,[2] these studies do not resolve the question of whether health differences are at the root of the large income differences we observe because they do not incorporate *general equilibrium effects*. The most important general equilibrium effect arises due to diminishing returns to effective units of labor, for example, because land or physical capital are supplied inelastically. In the presence of such diminishing returns, micro estimates may exaggerate the aggregate productivity benefits from improved health, particularly when health improvements are accompanied by population increases.

This chapter investigates the effect of general health conditions, proxied by life expectancy at birth, on economic growth. We exploit the large improvements in life expectancy driven by international health interventions, more effective public health measures, and the introduction of new chemicals and drugs starting in the 1940s. This episode, which we refer to as the *international epidemiological transition*, led to an unprecedented improvement in life expectancy in a large number of countries.[3] Figure 4.1 shows this by plotting life expectancy in countries that were initially (circa 1940) poor, middle-income, and rich. It illustrates that, while in the 1930s life expectancy was low in many poor and middle-income countries, this transition brought their levels of life expectancy close to those prevailing in richer parts of the

---

2   See Strauss and Thomas (1998) for an excellent survey of the research through the late 1990s. For some of the more recent research, see Behrman and Rosenzweig (2004); Bleakley (2003, 2007); Miguel and Kremer (2004); Schultz (2002).

3   The term "epidemiological transition" was coined by demographers and refers to the process of falling mortality rates after about 1850, associated with the switch from infectious to degenerative disease as the major cause of death (Omran 1971). Some authors prefer the term "health transition," as this includes the changing nature of ill health more generally (for example, Riley 2001). Our focus is on the rapid decline in mortality (and improvement in health) in poorer countries after 1940, most of which was driven by the fast spread of new technologies and practices around the world (hence the adjective "international"). The seminal works on this episode include Omran (1971), Preston (1975), and Stolnitz (1955).

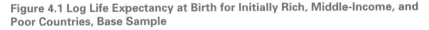

Figure 4.1 Log Life Expectancy at Birth for Initially Rich, Middle-Income, and Poor Countries, Base Sample

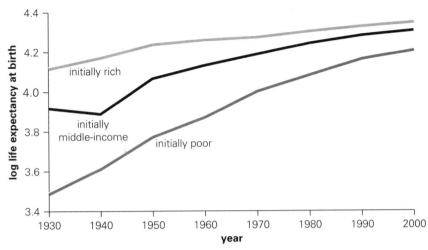

Source: Authors.

world.[4] As a consequence, health conditions in many poor countries today, though still in dire need of improvement, are significantly better than the corresponding health conditions were in the West at the same stage of development.[5]

The international epidemiological transition provides us with an empirical strategy to isolate potentially exogenous changes in health conditions. The effects of the international epidemiological transition on a country's life expectancy were related to the extent to which its population was initially (circa 1940) affected by various specific diseases, for example, tuberculosis, malaria, and pneumonia, and to the timing of the various health interventions.

The early data on mortality by disease are available from standard international sources, although they have not been widely used in the economics literature. These data allow us to create an instrument for changes in life expectancy based on the pre-intervention distribution of mortality from various diseases around the world and the dates of global intervention (for example, the discovery and mass production of penicillin and streptomycin or the discovery and widespread use of the pesticide DDT against mosquito vectors). The only source of variation in this instrument, which we refer to as *predicted mortality*, comes from the interaction of baseline cross-country disease prevalence with global intervention dates for specific diseases.

---

4   This figure is for illustration purposes and should be interpreted with caution, since convergence is not generally invariant to nonlinear transformations. Our empirical strategy does not exploit this convergence pattern; instead, it relies on potentially exogenous changes in life expectancy. In this figure and throughout the chapter, rich countries are those with income per capita in 1940 above the level of Argentina (the richest Latin American country at that time, according to Maddison's data, in our base sample). See table 5A.1 for a list of initially rich, middle-income, and poor countries.

5   For example, life expectancy at birth in India in 1999 was 60 compared to 40 in Britain in 1820, when income per capita was approximately the same level as in India today (Maddison 2001: 30). From Maddison (2001: 264), income per capita in Britain in 1820 was $1,707, while it stood at $1,746 in India in 1998 (all figures in 1990 international dollars).

We document that there were large declines in disease-specific mortality following these global interventions. More important, we show that the predicted mortality instrument has a large and robust effect on changes in life expectancy starting in 1940, but has *no* effect on changes in life expectancy *prior* to this date (that is, before the key interventions).

The instrumented changes in life expectancy have a fairly large effect on population: a 1 percent increase in life expectancy is related to an approximately 1.7–2 percent increase in population over a horizon of 40–60 years. The magnitude of this estimate indicates that the decline in fertility rates was insufficient to compensate for increased life expectancy, a result that we directly confirm by looking at the relationship between life expectancy and total births.

However, we find no statistically significant effect on total GDP (although our two standard error confidence intervals do include economically significant effects). More important, GDP per capita and GDP per working-age population show relative declines in countries experiencing large increases in life expectancy. In fact, our estimates exclude any positive effects of life expectancy on GDP per capita within 40- or 60-year horizons. This is consistent with the overall pattern in figure 4.2, which, in contrast to figure 4.1, shows no convergence in income per capita between initially poor, middle-income, and rich countries. We document that these results are robust to a range of specification checks and to the inclusion of various controls. We also document that our results are not driven by life expectancy at very early ages. The predicted mortality instrument has a large, statistically significant, and robust effect on life expectancy at 20 (and at other ages), and using life expectancy at 20 instead of life expectancy at birth as our measure of general health conditions leads to very similar results.

The most natural interpretation of our results comes from neoclassical growth theory. Increased life expectancy raises population, which initially reduces capital-to-labor and land-to-labor ratios, thus depressing income

Figure 4.2 Log GDP per Capita for Initially Rich, Middle-Income, and Poor Countries, Base Sample

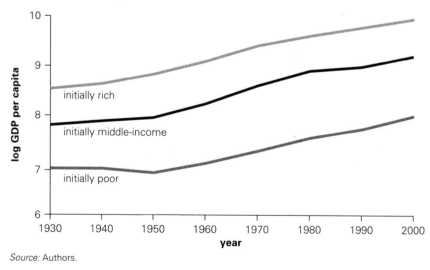

Source: Authors.

The Effect of Life Expectancy on Economic Growth

per capita. This initial decline is later compensated by higher output as more people enter the labor force and as more capital is accumulated. This compensation can be complete and may even exceed the initial level of income per capita if there are significant productivity benefits from longer life expectancy. Yet the compensation may also be incomplete if the benefits from higher life expectancy are limited and if some factors of production—for example, land—are supplied inelastically.

Our findings do *not* imply that improved health has not been a great benefit to less-developed nations during the postwar era. The accounting approach of Becker, Philipson, and Soares (2005), which incorporates information on longevity and health as well as standards of living, suggests that these interventions have considerably improved "overall welfare" in these countries. What these interventions have not done—and in fact *were not* intended to do—is to increase output per capita in these countries.

This chapter is most closely related to two recent contributions: Weil (2007) and Young (2005). Weil calibrates the effects of health using a range of micro estimates and finds that these effects could be quite important in the aggregate.[6] The major difference between Weil's approach and ours is that the conceptual exercise in his paper is concerned with the effects of improved health holding population constant. In contrast, our estimates look at the general equilibrium effects of improved health from the most important health transition of the twentieth century, which takes the form of both improved health and increased life expectancy (and thus population). Young evaluates the effect of the recent HIV/AIDS epidemic in Africa. Using micro estimates and calibration of the neoclassical growth model, he shows that the decline in population resulting from HIV/AIDS may increase income per capita despite significant disruptions and human suffering caused by the disease.[7]

In addition, our work is related to the literature on the demographic transition both in the West and in the rest of the world, including the seminal contribution of McKeown (1976) and the studies by Arriaga and Davis (1969), Caldwell (1986), Deaton (2003, 2004), Fogel (1986, 2004), Kelley (1988), and Preston (1975, 1980). More recent work by Cutler and Miller (2005, 2006) finds that the introduction of clean water accounts for about half of the decline in U.S. mortality in the early twentieth century.

The rest of the chapter is organized as follows. In the next section, we present a simple model to frame the empirical investigation. This is followed by a description of the health interventions and the data on disease mortality rates and life expectancy that we constructed from a variety of primary sources. Then we present the ordinary least squares (OLS) relationships between life expectancy and a range of outcomes, discuss the construction of our instrument, and show the first-stage relationships, robustness checks, falsification exercises, and other supporting evidence. A section presents

---

6   Weil's baseline estimate uses the return to the age of menarche from Knaul's (2000) work on Mexico as a general indicator of "overall return to health." Using Behrman and Rosenzweig's (2004) estimates from returns to differences in birth weight in monozygotic twins, Knaul finds smaller effects.

7   For more pessimistic views on the economic consequences of HIV/AIDS, see Arndt and Lewis (2000); Bell, Devarajan, and Gersbach (2003); Forston (2006); Kalemli-Ozcan (2006).

our main results, followed by a section presenting a number of robustness checks and additional results. A final section summarizes the findings and provides suggestions for future research. An appendix provides further information on data sources and data construction. Two additional appendixes—appendixes B and C from our working paper (Acemoglu and Johnson 2006), which provide further details on data and historical sources—are available on the Web and upon request.

Motivating Theory and Estimating Framework

To frame the empirical analysis, we first derive the medium-run and long-run implications of increased life expectancy in the closed-economy neoclassical (Solow) growth model. Labor and land are supplied inelastically. We proxy all variables related to health in terms of life expectancy at birth. Economy i has the following constant returns to scale aggregate production function:

$$Y_{it} = (A_{it}H_{it})^\alpha K_{it}^\beta L_{it}^{1-\alpha-\beta}, \tag{4.1}$$

where $\alpha + \beta \leq 1$, K_{it} denotes capital, L_{it} denotes the supply of land, and H_{it} is the effective units of labor given by $H_{it} = h_{it}N_{it}$, where N_{it} is total population (and employment), while h_{it} is human capital per person.

Without loss of any generality, we normalize $L_{it} = L_i = 1$ for all i and t. Let us also assume that life expectancy (or more generally health conditions) may increase output (per capita) through a variety of channels, including more rapid accumulation of human capital or direct positive effects on total factor productivity (TFP).[8] To capture these effects in a reduced-form manner, we assume the following isoelastic relationships:

$$A_{it} = \overline{A}_i X_{it}^\gamma \text{ and } h_{it} = \overline{h}_i X_{it}^\eta, \tag{4.2}$$

where X_{it} is life expectancy in country i at time t, and $\overline{A}_i$ and $\overline{h}_i$ designate the baseline differences across countries. Finally, greater life expectancy naturally leads to greater population (both directly and also potentially indirectly by increasing total births as more women live to childbearing age), so we posit the following:

$$N_{it} = \overline{N}_i X_{it}^\lambda. \tag{4.3}$$

Now imagine the effect of a change in life expectancy from some baseline value X_{it0} at t_0 to a new value X_{it_1} at time t_1. First, suppose that, while life expectancy changes (and, as a result, population, productivity, and human capital per worker change), the total capital stock remains fixed at some $\overline{K}_{it_0}$. In this case, substituting equations 4.2 and 4.3 into equation 4.1 and taking logs, we obtain the following log-linear relationship between log life expectancy, $x_{it} \equiv \log X_{it}$, and log income per capita, $y_{it} \equiv \log(Y_{it}/N_{it})$:

$$y_{it} = \beta \log \overline{K}_{it_0} + \alpha \log \overline{A}_i + \alpha \log \overline{h}_i \\ - (1-\alpha)\log \overline{N}_i + [\alpha(\gamma + \eta) - (1-\alpha)\lambda]x_{it}, \tag{4.4}$$

---

8 On the potential effects of life expectancy and health on productivity, see Bloom and Sachs (1998). On their effects on human capital accumulation, see, among others, Kalemli-Ozcan, Ryder, and Weil (2000), Kalemli-Ozcan (2002), or Soares (2005), which point out that, when people live longer, they have greater incentives to invest in human capital.

for $t = t_0, t_1$. This equation shows that the increase in log life expectancy will raise income per capita if the positive effects of health on TFP and human capital, measured by $\alpha(\gamma + \eta)$, exceed the potential negative effects arising from the increase in population because of fixed land and capital supply, $(1 - \alpha)\gamma$.

Although land may be inelastically supplied even in the long run, the supply of capital will adjust as life expectancy, population, and productivity of the factors of production change. Equation 4.4 gives one extreme without such adjustment. The other extreme is the full adjustment of population and the capital stock to the change in life expectancy (which can in practice take longer than 40–60 years; see Ashraf, Lester, and Weil 2007). To model this possibility in the simplest possible way, suppose that country i has a constant saving rate equal to $s_i \in (0, 1)$ and capital depreciates at the rate $\delta \in (0, 1)$ so that the evolution of the capital stock in country i at time t is given by $K_{it+1} = s_i Y_{it} + (1 - \delta)K_{it}$. Suppose also that life expectancy changes from X_{it_0} to a new value X_{it_1} and remains at this level thereafter. After population and the capital stock have adjusted, the steady-state level of capital stock will be $K_i = s_i Y_i / \delta$. Using this value of the capital stock together with equations 4.1, 4.2, and 4.3, we obtain the long-run relationship between log life expectancy and log income per capita:

$$y_{it} = \frac{\alpha}{1-\beta} \log \overline{A}_i + \frac{\alpha}{1-\beta} \log \overline{h}_i + \frac{\beta}{1-\beta} \log s_i - \frac{\beta}{1-\beta} \log \delta$$
$$- \frac{1-\alpha-\beta}{1-\beta} \log \overline{N}_i + \frac{1}{1-\beta}[\alpha(\gamma+\eta) - (1-\alpha-\beta)\lambda]x_{it}, \quad (4.5)$$

again for $t = t_0, t_1$. This equation is similar to equation 4.4, except that it features the saving rate of country i, s_i, instead of its capital stock, and as a result of this adjustment, the effect of life expectancy on income is greater ("more positive"). Intuitively, capital now adjusts to the increase in population and productivity resulting from improvements in life expectancy. In fact, for industrial economies where land plays a small role in production (because only a small fraction of output is produced in agriculture), $1 - \alpha - \beta \simeq 0$ would be a good approximation to reality. In this case, the potential negative effect of population disappears and the impact of log life expectancy on log income per capita is given by $\alpha(\gamma + \eta)/(1 - \beta) \geq 0$. However, for less-developed economies where a significant fraction of production is in the agricultural sector, the effect is still ambiguous and depends on the size of the externalities as measured by γ and η versus the negative effects of population, which are captured by the share of land in GDP, $1 - \alpha - \beta$, as well as the size of the population response, λ.[9]

---

9   See Galor and Weil (2000), Galor (2005), and Hansen and Prescott (2002) for models in which, at different stages of development, the relationship between population and income may change because of a change in the composition of output or technology. In these models, during an early Malthusian phase, land plays an important role as a factor of production, and there are strong diminishing returns to capital. Later in the development process, the role of land diminishes, allowing per capita income growth. Hansen and Prescott (2002), for example, assume a Cobb-Douglas production function during the Malthusian phase with a share of land equal to 0.3.

Our estimating equation follows directly from equations 4.4 and 4.5. In particular, adding an error term and potential covariates, these equations yield equation 4.6:

$$y_{it} = \pi x_{it} + \zeta_i + \mu_t + Z'_{it}\beta + \varepsilon_{it}, \qquad (4.6)$$

where y is log income per capita; x is log life expectancy (at birth);[10] ζ_i denotes a full set of fixed effects that are functions of the parameters $\bar{A}_i$, $\bar{h}_i$, $\bar{N}_i$, and $\bar{K}_i$ (or s_i) in equations 4.4 and 4.5; μ_t incorporates time-varying factors common across all countries; and Z_{it} denotes a vector of other controls. The coefficient π is the parameter of interest, equal to $[\alpha(\gamma + \eta) - (1 - \alpha)\lambda]$ when equation 4.4 applies or to $[\alpha(\gamma + \eta) - (1 - \alpha - \beta)\lambda]/(1 - \beta)$ when equation 4.5 applies. Including a full set of country fixed effects, ζ_i is important, since the country characteristics, $\bar{A}_i$, $\bar{h}_i$, $\bar{N}_i$, $\bar{K}_{it_0}$, and s_i, will be naturally correlated with life expectancy (or health) and thus with the error term ε_{it}. In addition, many other country-specific factors will simultaneously affect health and economic outcomes. Fixed effects at least remove the time-invariant components of these factors.

Motivated by equations 4.4 and 4.5, and since we do not expect the yearly or decadal changes in life expectancy to have their full effect on income per capita or on other economic variables, we estimate equation 4.6 in *long differences*—that is, in a panel including only two dates, t_0 and t_1 (in practice either 1940 and 1980 or 1940 and 2000). These long-difference regressions also make interpretation easier because they directly measure the effect of change in life expectancy between two dates on the change in economic variables between the same two dates. Since in the long-difference specification we only have two dates, equation 4.6 is also (algebraically) equivalent to estimating the first-differenced specification:

$$\Delta y_i = \pi \Delta x_i + \Delta \mu + \Delta Z'_i \beta + \Delta \varepsilon_i, \qquad (4.6)$$

where $\Delta y_t \equiv y_{it_1} - y_{it_0}$, and Δx_i, $\Delta \mu$, $\Delta Z'_i$, and $\Delta \varepsilon_i$ are defined similarly.

Throughout, in addition to log income per capita, we look at a number of other outcome variables. These include log population, log births, and the age composition of the population, which will be informative to show the impact of the increase in life expectancy on population, fertility behavior, and also changes in age composition (which are important for interpreting the results related to GDP). They also include total GDP and GDP per working-age population. The last variable is particularly important, since GDP per capita might be affected by changes in the dependency ratio, defined as the ratio of nonactive population to total population (however, over 40- or 60-year horizons, there is little change in dependency ratios).

Finally, despite the presence of fixed effects controlling for fixed country characteristics such as $\bar{A}_i$, $\bar{h}_i$, $\bar{N}_i$, $\bar{K}_{it_0}$, and s_i, OLS estimates of equation 4.6 will not yield the causal effects of life expectancy (or health) on economic outcomes, because of the presence of potentially time-varying factors simultaneously affecting health and economic outcomes. For example,

---

10 In view of equations 4.4 and 4.5 and the regression models used in the existing literature, we use log life expectancy on the right-hand side throughout. All of the results reported in this chapter are very similar if we use the level of life expectancy instead (results available upon request).

countries that increased their relative growth rates between 1940 and 1980 also may have invested more in health during this period, increasing life expectancy. More generally, societies that are able to solve their economic problems are also more likely to solve their disease control problems. These considerations imply that the (population) covariance term $\text{Cov}(x_{it}, \varepsilon_{it})$ in equation 4.6 is not equal to 0, because, even conditional on fixed effects, health is endogenous to economics. For this reason, our main focus is on the instrumental variables (IV) estimates using the cross-country variation induced by the international epidemiological transition described in the introduction to this chapter. We next provide more details on this episode, on the data used in our study, and on our IV strategy.

Background and Data

Despite early improvements in public health in Western Europe, the United States, and a few other places from the mid-nineteenth century until 1940, there were limited improvements in health conditions in most of the Americas, Africa, and Asia and even in Southern and Eastern Europe.[11] In part, this was because there were few effective drugs against the major diseases in these areas, so most of the measures were relatively expensive public works (for example, to drain swamps). Colonial authorities showed little enthusiasm for such expenditures.

The situation changed dramatically from around 1940 mainly because of three factors (see, for example, Davis 1956; Preston 1975; Stolnitz 1955). First, there was a wave of global innovations in drugs and chemicals. Many of these products offered cures effective against major killers in developing countries. The most important was the discovery and subsequent mass production of penicillin, which provided an effective treatment against a range of bacterial infections (Easterlin 1999; National Academy of Sciences 1970). Penicillin, which was only used in small quantities even in the most developed countries through the mid-1940s (Conybeare 1948: 66), became widely available by the early 1950s (see, for example, Valentine and Shooter 1954).[12] Further antibiotic development quickly followed, most notably

---

11 During the 1920s and 1930s, there were measures to reduce mortality from smallpox and cholera in Indonesia, smallpox and plague in the Philippines, malaria in India, malaria and respiratory and diarrheal diseases in British Guyana (see, for example, Mandle 1970; Preston 1980). Gwatkin (1980: 616) states, "But such increases [in life expectancy] were modest compared with those that came later, for soon after World War II annual gains in life expectancy averaging over a year were recorded for periods of up to a decade in such diverse places as Taiwan [China], Malaysia, Sri Lanka, Mauritius, Jamaica, and Mexico." On public health improvements in Western Europe and the United States, see, for example, Cutler, Deaton, and Lleras-Murray (2006).

12 Fleming isolated penicillin in the 1930s but could not produce it in any significant quantity; Florey and Chain made the breakthroughs essential for the use of penicillin as a drug and they shared the Nobel Prize with Fleming in 1945 (see, for example, Chain 1980). The first large-scale use of penicillin was in 1943, by Allied armies in North Africa. Andrew Moyer's patent in 1948 is often regarded as a major step in its mass production. The invention of penicillin led to a wave of discovery of other antibiotics, including streptomycin, chloromycetin, aureomycin, and terramycin (National Academy 1970: 147). Waksman discovered streptomycin in 1944 and was awarded the Nobel Prize in 1952 (see Keers 1978).

---

with the discovery of streptomycin, which was effective against tuberculosis. Between 1940 and 1950, the major bacterial killers became treatable and, in most cases, curable. Diseases that could now be treated, for most people without serious side effects, included pneumonia, dysentery, cholera, and venereal diseases. Antibiotics also reduced deaths indirectly caused by (and attributed to) viruses, such as influenza, which often kill by weakening the immune system and allowing secondary bacterial infections to develop.

Also important during the same period was the development of new vaccines, for example, against yellow fever.[13] The major chemical innovation of this era was the discovery of DDT, which allowed a breakthrough in attempts to control malaria, one of the major killers of children in less-developed regions of the world.[14] Aggressive use of inexpensive DDT led to the rapid eradication of malaria in Taiwan (China), much of the Caribbean, the Balkans, parts of northern Africa, northern Australia, and large parts of the South Pacific and all but eradicated malaria in Sri Lanka and India (see, for example, Davis 1956).

The second pillar of the improvements in public health was the establishment of the World Health Organization (WHO), which greatly facilitated the spread of medical and public health technology to poorer countries. From the 1950s, the WHO, together with other United Nations–related bodies, most significantly, the United Nations Children's Fund (UNICEF), was the driving force behind the public health (for example, antimalaria campaigns) and immunization drives (for example, against smallpox).[15]

---

13 The yellow fever vaccine was invented by Max Theiler in 1930 and became widely available in the 1940s. Theiler was awarded a Nobel Prize in 1951. More vaccine inventions followed in the 1950s and 1960s (for example, against smallpox and measles), but antibiotics already provided usually effective treatment against those diseases.

14 DDT was first synthesized in 1874, but its insecticide properties were discovered much later—in 1939, by Paul H. Müller. Müller received a patent for the insecticide in 1940 and was awarded a Nobel Prize in 1948 (Alilio, Bygbjerg, and Breman 2004: 270). Desowitz (1991: 62–63), for example, describes the impact of DDT as follows: "There was nothing quite like [DDT] before and has been nothing quite like it since. Here was a chemical that could be sprayed on the walls of a house, and for up to six months later any insect that alighted or rested on that wall would die. It was virtually without toxicity to humans. And, for the icing on the chemical cake, it was dirt-cheap to manufacture."

15 It is notable that Brazil and China, both poor countries at the time, took the initiative in pushing for the formation of the World Health Organization (WHO 1998). A central goal of the organization was to diffuse medical practices and technology to poorer countries. Between the world wars, the League of Nations was responsible for international disease interventions and worked with other European organizations, for example, against typhus in Eastern Europe (see also Office International d'Hygiene Publique 1933). However, in contrast with the WHO, the League of Nations showed less interest in and had few resources for combating diseases in less-developed countries, limiting itself to monitoring epidemics that might spread to the West.

On UNICEF, Lee and others (1996) report, "[Founded in 1946] . . . Unicef was given the task of utilising its resources 'for child health purposes generally.' When the WHO came on to the scene two years later it was accepted that coordination on health matters was needed. This led to the creation of the WHO/Unicef joint committee on health policy, with the WHO, importantly, designated as the lead health organisation." The U.S. military also played a significant role in developing treatments for diseases like cholera and in spreading the use of DDT and penicillin (Bhattacharya 1994).

The third factor was a change in international values. As Preston (1975: 243) emphasizes, after the 1930s: "Universal values assured that health breakthroughs in any country would spread rapidly to all others where the means for implementation existed."

These three factors combined caused a dramatic improvement in life expectancy in much of the world, especially in the lesser developed parts of the globe, starting in the 1940s. Most new drugs, chemicals, and public health knowledge were available in almost all countries by 1950. As a result, by the late 1940s and early 1950s, there were significant improvements in health conditions and life expectancy in Central America, South Asia, and parts of Eastern and Southern Europe compared to richer countries.

Coding Diseases

We collected comparable data on 15 of the most important infectious diseases across a wide range of countries and constructed cross-country mortality rates for these diseases before the 1940s. These 15 diseases are tuberculosis, malaria, pneumonia, influenza, cholera, typhoid, smallpox, whooping cough, measles, diphtheria, scarlet fever, yellow fever, plague, typhus fever, and dysentery or diarrhea-related diseases (see appendix B in our working paper for more details). In all cases, the primary data source is national health statistics, as collected and republished by the League of Nations (until 1940) and the WHO and the United Nations (after 1945). We tried several different ways of constructing these data, all of which produced similar results.

In addition, we confirmed these quantitative assessments of geographic disease incidence with data and qualitative evidence in Lancaster (1990, especially ch. 48), the maps and discussion of Cliff, Haggett, and Smallman-Raynor (2004), and the maps of disease incidence published by the American Geographical Society (1951a, 1951b, 1951c, 1951d) immediately after World War II. The appendix to this chapter, as well as appendix C in the working paper, provides details on sources and construction. Information on the etiology and epidemiology of each disease is obtained from the comprehensive recent surveys in Kiple (1993) and other sources (see appendix B in the working paper). We also checked that our data are comparable with those reported in Preston and Nelson (1974).

The other building block for our approach is the date of *global intervention* for each specific disease, that is, dates of significant events that potentially reduced mortality around the world from the disease in question. These events are described below (and in appendix B), and the relevant dates were obtained from WHO epidemiological reports as well as Easterlin (1999), Hoff and Smith (2000), Kiple (1993), National Academy of Sciences (1970), and Preston (1975).

Among the 15 diseases (in fact, among all diseases), tuberculosis was the largest single cause of death around the world in 1940. It is primarily caused by *Mycobacterium tuberculosis*, which is transmitted through the air. Vaccination was available from the 1920s, but the breakthrough cure was the 1944 invention of streptomycin.[16] Use of this drug spread quickly and has remained important. Following this discussion of the invention and introduction of penicillin and streptomycin, we code the intervention against tuberculosis in the 1940s.

The other major cause of death was pneumonia, which results from a variety of infectious agents and toxins, including various bacterial and viral pathogens. Frequently, it appears as a secondary bacterial infection that causes death. The primary causes are often tuberculosis, influenza, and more recently AIDS. Antibiotics—for example, penicillin—proved highly effective against bacterial pneumonia in the 1940s (although by now resistant strains have developed).[17] Also, beginning in the 1940s, there were partially effective vaccines against pneumonia. In our baseline instrument, the intervention against pneumonia takes place in the 1940s.

The third major disease at this time was malaria, which is caused by four types of parasites, transmitted by the bite of an infected female *Anopheles* mosquito. Control of mosquito vectors had been under way since the late nineteenth century, but became much more effective with the discovery that DDT was an effective insecticide (see Expert Committee on Malaria 1947: 26–28). The use of DDT became widespread in the late 1940s (particularly following a successful demonstration in Greece) and was intensified following the 1955–57 WHO decision to campaign systematically to eradicate malaria (see Bradley 1992; WHO 2004).[18] In our baseline instrument, the intervention against malaria is taken to be the extensive use of DDT during the 1940s (chloroquine was also invented during the 1940s and quickly replaced mepacrine as the antimalarial drug of choice, until chloroquine-resistant parasites developed).[19]

Life Expectancy, Population, and GDP Data

Other key variables for our investigation include life expectancy at birth, life expectancy at different ages, and total births, which are all obtained

16 Previously, tuberculosis could be treated by surgery, but even in the United Kingdom resources for this were limited and not available to many patients (Conybeare 1948: 61). One discussant of Conybeare (1948) made the point, based on data from the United Kingdom's statistical reviews, that, comparing 1939 with 1931–35, "in the general population tuberculosis had not recently been a decreasing risk at all." This was on the eve of the dramatic impact of streptomycin (Keers 1978).

17 Sulphonamides were also used against pneumonia, but were soon superceded by penicillin (Conybeare 1948: 65; National Academy of Sciences 1970: 144–46). In any case, these drugs were not widely available, even in the United Kingdom, until the very end of the 1930s (Conybeare 1948).

18 While it is generally accepted that DDT played a major role in the dramatic declines in malaria prevalence, there is some controversy in the demography literature about whether broader public health interventions of the 1940s were also essential (see, for example, Langford 1996). Following the WHO campaign, it became apparent that some mosquitos could develop resistance to insecticides. However, the view from the WHO was that, if used properly, spraying with DDT remained effective. E. J. Pampana (1954), chief of the Malaria Section of the WHO, called for a change in strategy, but this strategy still centered around insecticide spraying.

19 Alternatively, one might take the major intervention against malaria to be the WHO campaign and thus code the date of global intervention as the 1950s. Acemoglu and Johnson (2006) show that all the results reported here are robust to this alternate coding.

from historical United Nations (UN) data (various issues of the *Demographic Yearbook*) and League of Nations reports.[20] Since we need population and GDP data before World War II, we use the data from Maddison (2003). Postwar demographic data are from UN data sources. We also construct life expectancy at different ages for a subset of our base sample using these same UN sources. Results using life expectancy at age 20 are reported below.

Our full sample contains 75 countries from Western Europe, Oceania, the Americas, and Asia, although when we restrict the sample to countries that have the relevant data for predicted mortality, life expectancy, and second-stage variables in 1940 and 1980 (or 2000), and when we exclude Eastern Europe and Russia, our base sample consists of 47 countries.[21] Eastern Europe and Russia are excluded from the base sample due to concerns about the quality of their GDP data.[22] Because of lack of reliable data on life expectancy in 1940, Africa is not in our base sample, although below we briefly discuss the robustness of our main results to including data from Africa.

We focus on 1940 and 1980 as our base sample. Post-1980 is excluded from our base sample because the emergence of AIDS appears to have led to a divergence in life expectancy between some poor countries and the richer nations.[23] In order to approximate the longer-run effects of health on economic outcomes, we also look at the changes between 1940 and 2000. In addition, we look at pre-1940 changes in our falsification exercises.

Table 4.1 provides basic descriptive statistics on the key variables (see also the raw data in table 5A.1). The first column is for the whole world, while the second column refers to our base sample. A comparison of these two columns indicates that, despite the absence of Africa from our base sample, averages of life expectancy, population, GDP, and GDP per capita are broadly similar between the whole world and our sample. The next three columns show numbers separately for the three groups of countries used in figures 4.1 and 4.2—initially rich, middle-income, and poor countries (measured in terms of GDP per capita in 1940). These columns show

---

20 These data are often based on rough estimates. For example, life expectancy is calculated by combining data on age-specific death rates at a point in time, but often approximations are made using standard life tables (Lancaster 1990: ch. 3; Kiple 1993: IV.4). Preston (1975) previously used some of the prewar data for the 1930s; see appendix C in the working paper.

21 The 47 countries in our base sample are listed in table 5A.1. In addition, we have data from 1950 onward (but not for 1940) on Algeria, Bolivia, Arab Republic of Egypt, Islamic Republic of Iran, Iraq, Lebanon, Morocco, Singapore, South Africa, Tunisia, Turkey, and Vietnam. These countries are included in our panel regressions, for example, in panel B of table 4.5 and table 4.6, but not in the long-difference regressions of tables 4.2 and 4.3, panel A of table 4.5, and tables 4.7–4.10. For two-square least squares (2SLS) results including these countries, see Acemoglu and Johnson (2006).

22 The only communist country in our sample is China. Excluding China or including Eastern European countries has no effect on any of our results (see Acemoglu and Johnson 2006).

23 In addition, malaria reappeared in the 1970s and 1980s because of reduced international efforts, the international ban on the use of DDT, and the emergence of insecticide-resistant mosquitoes and drug-resistant strains of malaria. Tuberculosis has also returned as a secondary infection associated with AIDS.

Table 4.1 Descriptive Statistics

Indicator	Whole world (1)	Base sample (2)	Initially rich countries (3)	Initially middle-income countries (4)	Initially poor countries (5)	Above median change in predicted mortality, 1940–80 (6)	Below median change in predicted mortality, 1940–80 (7)
Life expectancy at birth in 1900	30.90 (8.83)	37.59 (10.31)	49.36 (3.67)	36.92 (8.13)	28.77 (5.42)	31.50 (5.71)	43.95 (10.26)
Life expectancy at birth in 1940	46.70 (11.59)	49.30 (12.67)	65.13 (1.86)	50.93 (9.37)	40.63 (8.39)	39.66 (7.99)	59.35 (7.90)
Life expectancy at birth in 1980	61.13 (11.02)	67.60 (7.41)	74.30 (1.13)	69.66 (4.57)	61.92 (7.18)	62.91 (7.28)	72.49 (3.24)
Life expectancy at age 20 in 1940		63.61 (6.20)	70.41 (1.08)	64.51 (3.91)	56.96 (4.36)	59.32 (5.34)	67.70 (3.73)
Life expectancy at age 20 in 1980		73.08 (2.89)	75.73 (0.87)	73.59 (2.42)	70.27 (2.05)	71.40 (2.77)	74.69 (1.95)
Predicted mortality in 1940		0.47 (0.27)	0.17 (0.05)	0.48 (0.21)	0.53 (0.32)	0.70 (0.18)	0.23 (0.08)
Log population in 1940	8.94 (1.54)	9.10 (1.53)	9.34 (1.34)	8.82 (1.40)	9.14 (1.79)	8.99 (1.59)	9.22 (1.49)
Log population in 1980	8.88 (1.62)	9.81 (1.47)	9.76 (1.29)	9.44 (1.25)	10.00 (1.75)	9.93 (1.48)	9.68 (1.48)
Log GDP in 1940	9.78 (1.67)	9.94 (1.58)	11.08 (1.39)	9.75 (1.49)	9.19 (1.71)	9.39 (1.51)	10.51 (1.49)
Log GDP in 1980	9.99 (1.98)	11.59 (1.48)	12.47 (1.33)	11.41 (1.35)	10.88 (1.52)	11.09 (1.43)	11.98 (1.43)
Log GDP per capita in 1940	7.64 (0.69)	7.73 (0.72)	8.64 (0.15)	7.84 (0.33)	6.95 (0.32)	7.30 (0.51)	8.19 (0.63)
Log GDP per capita in 1980	7.98 (1.07)	8.62 (0.95)	9.61 (0.13)	8.88 (0.44)	7.79 (0.73)	8.06 (0.82)	9.20 (0.70)
Log GDP per working-age population in 1940	8.19 (0.63)	8.27 (0.63)	9.03 (0.14)	8.36 (0.30)	7.51 (0.30)	7.86 (0.50)	8.71 (0.45)
Log GDP per working-age population in 1980	9.13 (0.80)	9.18 (0.85)	10.04 (0.11)	9.40 (0.39)	8.36 (0.71)	8.65 (0.79)	9.75 (0.46)

Source: Authors' calculations.

Note: The table reports the mean values of variables in the samples described in the column heading, with their standard deviations in parentheses. The base sample is 47 countries. Initially rich countries had log GDP per capita over 8.4 in 1940; middle-income countries had log GDP per capita between 7.37 and 8.4; and low-income countries had log GDP per capita below 7.37 in 1940. Predicted mortality is measured per 100 per year. The last two columns report descriptive statistics for subsamples in which the change in predicted mortality between 1940 and 1980 was above or below the median value in the base sample (−0.409). See the text and the appendix for details and definitions.

the same patterns as figures 4.1 and 4.2: there is a large convergence in life expectancy among the three groups of countries between 1940 and 1980, but no convergence in GDP per capita. These columns also give information on predicted mortality, which is our instrument for life expectancy. Columns 6 and 7 of this table are discussed below.

OLS Estimates

Tables 4.2 and 4.3 report OLS regressions of equation 4.6 for the main variables of interest listed above. These results are useful both to show the (conditional) correlations in the data and for comparison to the IV estimates reported below. All regressions in these tables and throughout the chapter (except some first-stage estimates) are for the *long-difference specification* as described above, with data for 1940 and 1980 or for 1940 and 2000.

Table 4.2 focuses on population-related outcomes. Panel A is for log population, panel B is for log births (we do not have the data necessary to compute fertility rates), and panel C is for the age composition of the population measured by the percentage of the population under the age of 20. The first column includes all countries for which we have the relevant data. The remaining columns focus on our base sample, consisting of countries for which we can construct predicted mortality rates.

Several features are notable in table 4.2. First, the "whole world" sample gives very similar results to our base sample for 1960–2000. Second, the results in our base sample for 1960–2000 are also similar to the results for 1940–80. For example, in panel A the effect of log life expectancy on log population in column 1 is 1.6 (s.e.= 0.30), while in our base sample over the same time period, the same coefficient is estimated as 1.75 (s.e.= 0.40). In column 3, when we focus on our main sample period, 1940–80, the estimate is 1.62 (s.e.= 0.19). The magnitudes of these estimates are reasonable. They suggest that a 1 percent increase in life expectancy is associated with a 1.6–1.75 percent increase in population. If births are held constant, a 1 percent increase in life expectancy would be associated with a 1 percent increase in population (since each individual would live for 1 percent longer). Naturally, an increase in life expectancy is also associated with an increase in births, since more women survive to childbearing age, so we should expect a somewhat larger effect than 1 percent. The results in panel B, which show a significant increase in total number of births associated with the increase in life expectancy, confirm this interpretation. In particular, a 1 percent increase in life expectancy is associated with a 2–2.7 percent increase in total births.

Column 4 reports estimates for the sample of initially low- and middle-income countries (as defined in table 5A.1). This subsample is useful for verifying that our results are not driven by a comparison of initially rich to initially low- and middle-income countries. The association between life expectancy and population (and life expectancy and births) is slightly stronger in this sample than in the base sample.

Table 4.2 Life Expectancy, Population, Births, and Percent of Population Under 20: OLS Estimates

Indicator	Whole world	Base sample		Low- and middle-income countries only	Base sample	Low- and middle-income countries only
	(1)	(2)	(3)	(4)	(5)	(6)
Panel A: Dependent variable is log population						
Time period	Just 1960 and 2000	Just 1960 and 2000	Just 1940 and 1980	Just 1940 and 1980	Just 1940 and 2000	Just 1940 and 2000
Log life expectancy	1.60 (0.30)	1.75 (0.40)	1.62 (0.19)	1.86 (0.26)	2.01 (0.22)	2.25 (0.32)
Number of countries	120	59	47	36	47	36
Panel B: Dependent variable is log number of births						
Time period	Just 1960 and 1990	Just 1960 and 1990	Just 1940 and 1980	Just 1940 and 1980	Just 1940 and 1990	Just 1940 and 1990
Log life expectancy	2.09 (0.37)	2.01 (0.40)	2.35 (0.27)	2.57 (0.40)	2.19 (0.27)	2.66 (0.42)
Number of countries	115	47	45	34	45	34
Panel C: Dependent variable is % of population under age 20						
Time period	Just 1960 and 2000	Just 1960 and 2000	Just 1940 and 1980	Just 1940 and 1980	Just 1940 and 2000	Just 1940 and 2000
Log life expectancy	0.045 (0.087)	0.045 (0.087)	0.094 (0.029)	0.124 (0.042)	0.053 (0.038)	0.132 (0.058)
Number of countries	40	40	40	29	40	29

Source: Authors' calculations.

Note: OLS regressions with a full set of year and country fixed effects. Robust standard errors are reported in parentheses. Long-difference specifications have two observations per country, one for the initial date and one for the final date. In all regressions the independent variable is the log of life expectancy at birth. "Whole world" is the set of countries for which we have data on the variables in the regression shown. The base sample is the set of countries for which we can estimate 2SLS regressions. The assignment of countries to the low-, middle-, and high-income categories is based on income per capita levels for 1940. See the text and the appendix for definitions and details.

Table 4.3 Life Expectancy, GDP, GDP per Capita, and GDP per Working-Age Population: OLS Estimates

Variable	Whole world	Base sample		Low- and middle-income countries only	Base sample	Low- and middle-income countries only
	(1)	(2)	(3)	(4)	(5)	(6)
Panel A: Dependent variable is log GDP panel						
Time period	Just 1960 and 2000	Just 1960 and 2000	Just 1940 and 1980	Just 1940 and 1980	Just 1940 and 2000	Just 1940 and 2000
Log life expectancy	1.17 (0.56)	1.55 (0.35)	0.78 (0.33)	0.65 (0.42)	0.85 (0.28)	0.43 (0.38)
Number of countries	120	59	47	36	47	36
B: Dependent variable is log GDP per capita						
Time period	Just 1960 and 2000	Just 1960 and 2000	Just 1940 and 1980	Just 1940 and 1980	Just 1940 and 2000	Just 1940 and 2000
Log life expectancy	−0.42 (0.58)	−0.19 (0.54)	−0.81 (0.26)	−1.17 (0.38)	−1.14 (0.27)	−1.79 (0.41)
Number of countries	120	59	47	36	47	36
Panel C: Dependent variable is log GDP per working-age population						
Time period	Just 1960 and 2000	Just 1960 and 2000	Just 1940 and 1980	Just 1940 and 1980	Just 1940 and 2000	Just 1940 and 2000
Log life expectancy	−1.01 (0.60)	−1.03 (0.60)	−0.78 (0.26)	−1.10 (0.38)	−1.26 (0.24)	−1.78 (0.38)
Number of countries	51	47	46	35	46	35

Source: Authors' calculations.

Note: OLS regressions with a full set of year and country fixed effects. Robust standard errors are reported in parentheses. Long-difference specifications with two observations per country, one for the initial date and one for the final date. In all regressions the independent variable is the log of life expectancy at birth. "Whole world" is the set of countries for which we have data on the variables in the regression shown. The base sample is the set of countries for which we can estimate 2SLS regressions. The assignment of countries to the low-, middle-, and high-income categories is based on income per capita levels for 1940. See the text and the appendix for definitions and details.

Columns 5 and 6 look at 1940 and 2000 rather than 1940 and 1980 as in our baseline specification. The longer window is useful to gauge whether longer-run effects are different from those that can be detected in a 40-year period. In panel A, there is a slightly stronger association between life expectancy and population from 1940 to 2000 than from 1940 to 1980 (for example, the base sample estimate now increases to 2.01, with a standard error of 0.22).

Panel B shows the estimates for the log number of births. The various specifications show a robust and statistically significant 2–2.6 percent increase in total births in response to a 1 percent increase in life expectancy.

Finally, panel C shows that in our base sample, increases in life expectancy are associated with an increase in the percentage of the population that is under the age of 20, although the magnitude of the effect is not large. For example, the estimate in column 3 (0.094) indicates that a 10 percent increase in life expectancy is associated with a 1 percentage point increase in the fraction of the population that is under the age of 20. This implies that the relationship between life expectancy and working-age population is very similar to that between life expectancy and total population.

Table 4.3 presents results that parallel those in table 4.2, but now the dependent variables are log GDP, log GDP per capita, and log GDP per working-age population.[24] The structure of the table is identical to that of table 4.2. Panel A shows a positive relationship between log life expectancy and log GDP. For example, the results in columns 1 and 2 indicate that a 1 percent increase in life expectancy is associated with a 1.2–1.5 percent increase in GDP. Notably, the effect of life expectancy on GDP is much smaller when we focus on our base sample for 1940–80 (column 3). This is exactly what one would expect if a larger fraction of changes in life expectancy were driven by exogenous factors in this sample than in the samples for columns 1 and 2.[25]

While panel A shows a positive relationship between life expectancy and total income, panels B and C show that this increase in total GDP is insufficient to compensate for the increase in total population and working-age population. As a result, there is a negative (sometimes significant) relationship between GDP per capita and GDP per working-age population and life expectancy. There is no evidence of a positive effect of life expectancy on GDP per capita in table 4.3. Nevertheless, since these estimates are not necessarily causal, the true effects of life expectancy on income per capita

---

24 We define working-age population as population between the ages of 15 and 60. Estimates of the age distribution of the population and hence of the working-age population for this time period are often rough.

25 In particular, OLS estimates of the effect of log life expectancy on log GDP (or log GDP per capita or log GDP per working-age population) typically will be biased upward because of reverse causality and common shocks to income and health. If much of the change in life expectancy in our base sample between 1940 and 1980 comes from exogenous variation due to the international epidemiological transition, then this upward bias will be reduced. The reduction of the coefficient on log life expectancy from 1.55 to 0.78 between columns 2 and 3 in table 4.3 likely reflects this change in the composition of the source of variation in life expectancy between these two samples.

might be larger or smaller than those shown in table 4.3. The rest of the chapter investigates this question.

Predicted Mortality and First Stages

Because of reverse causality and omitted-variable problems, OLS estimates of equation 4.6 are unlikely to uncover the causal effect of life expectancy on economic variables. We now outline a source of exogenous variation in life expectancy that may help us to estimate these causal effects.

The Predicted Mortality Instrument

Prior to the international epidemiological transition, there was considerable variation in the prevalence of diseases across the world. For example, during the 1940s, while malaria was endemic in parts of South Asia and Central America, it was relatively rare in much of Western Europe and in the Southern Cone of Latin America. We therefore expect variation in the effects of global interventions on life expectancy in different countries depending on the baseline distribution of diseases. For example, DDT should reduce malarial infections and mortality and increase life expectancy in Central America and South Asia relative to Western Europe or the Southern Cone of Latin America.

Motivated by this reasoning, our instrument, *predicted mortality,* is constructed as follows:

$$M_{it}^I = \sum_{d \in D} [(1 - I_{dt})M_{di40} + I_{dt}M_{dFt}], \tag{4.7}$$

where M_{dit} denotes mortality in country i from disease d at time t, I_{dt} is a dummy for intervention for disease d at time t (it is equal to 1 for all dates after the intervention), and D denotes the set of the 15 diseases listed above. It is measured as the number of deaths per 100 individuals per year. M_{di40} refers to the pre-intervention mortality from disease d in the same units, while M_{dFt} is the mortality rate from disease d at the *health frontier* of the world at time t. In our baseline instrument, we take M_{dFt} to be equal to zero.[26] Predicted mortality, M_{it}^I, thus uses a country's initial mortality rate from the 15 diseases until there is a global intervention, and after the global intervention, the mortality rate from the disease in question declines to the frontier mortality rate.

We then use our measure of predicted mortality, M_{it}^I, as an instrument for life expectancy in the estimation of equation 4.6. In particular, we posit the following first-stage relationship between log life expectancy and predicted mortality:

$$x_{it} = \psi M_{it}^I + \tilde{\zeta}_i + \tilde{\mu}_t + Z_{it}'\tilde{\beta} + u_{it}. \tag{4.8}$$

---

26 We also calculated an alternative measure of predicted mortality using the average mortality rate from disease d at time t among the richest countries, but since these rates are close to zero, this alternative measure is very similar to our baseline predicted mortality series and yields identical results.

The key exclusion restriction for our IV strategy is $\text{Cov}\left(M_{it}^I, \varepsilon_{it}\right) = 0$, where $\varepsilon_{it} = 0$ is the error term in the second-stage equation (equation 4.6).

Equation 4.7 makes it clear that the only source of variation in predicted mortality comes from the interaction of the baseline distribution of diseases with global interventions (in particular, M_{di40} applies until the time of the relevant global intervention). Whether a country has successfully eradicated a disease or has been quick to adopt international technologies has *no* effect on M_{it}^I; the dummy I_{dt} turns on for all countries at the same time. This makes our exclusion restriction, $\text{Cov}\left(M_{it}^I, \varepsilon_{it}\right) = 0$, plausible. Since variations in M_{it}^I are unrelated to any actions or economic events in the country, there is no obvious reason for it to be correlated with economic or population shocks in the country in question.

The only potential threat to the exclusion restriction would be that the baseline mortality rates, M_{di40}, are correlated with future changes in population or income. To show that this is unlikely to be the case, we show the robustness of our IV results to the inclusion of differential trends that are parameterized as functions of various baseline characteristics (see equations 4.11 and 4.13). In addition, we report a range of falsification exercises illustrating that the variable M_{it}^I has *no* predictive power for life expectancy or other economic variables *before* the international epidemiological transition.

Alternative Instruments

We also constructed a number of alternative instruments to investigate the robustness of our results. The first is the *global mortality instrument*:

$$M_{it}^I = \sum_{d \in D} \frac{M_{dt}}{M_{d40}} M_{di40}, \qquad (4.9)$$

where M_{di40} denotes mortality in country i from disease d in 1940, $M_{dt} (M_{d40})$ is global mortality from disease d in year t (1940), calculated as the unweighted average across countries in our sample. The advantage of this instrument is that it does not use any information on global intervention dates, instead relying on aggregate changes in worldwide disease-specific mortality rates.[27] The estimates using the global mortality instrument therefore show that none of our results depends on the coding of intervention dates.

We also constructed alternative instruments using different (reasonable) timings of interventions, especially whenever there was any potential doubt about the exact dates. In addition, we experimented with an instrument constructed using only the three big killers: malaria, tuberculosis, and pneumonia. The results with these alternative instruments are very similar to the baseline estimates and are not reported to save space (see Acemoglu and Johnson 2006).

---

27 Constructing this instrument requires us to track all diseases through changes in the classification of death over time. As explained further in the appendix, this is not possible for dysentery and diarrhea-related diseases or yellow fever, which are therefore excluded from the global mortality instrument.

The Effect of Life Expectancy on Economic Growth

Zeroth-Stage Estimates

Our approach is predicated on the notion that global interventions reduce mortality from various diseases. Therefore, before documenting the first-stage relationship between our predicted mortality measure and log life expectancy, we show the effect of various global interventions on mortality from specific diseases. In this exercise, in addition to the available data on the infectious diseases listed above, we also use deaths from cancers and malignant tumors as a control disease, since these were not affected by the global interventions.[28]

Table 4.4 reports the estimates from the following "zeroth-stage regression":

$$M_{idt} = \theta I_{dt} + \mu_t + \pi_d + \delta_i + \nu_{it}. \tag{4.10}$$

The dependent variable is mortality in country i from disease d at time t, and the regression includes a full set of time, disease, and country dummies. The coefficient of interest, θ, measures whether there is a decline in mortality from a specific disease associated with an intervention.

Table 4.4 reports estimates of equation 4.10. In all cases, as expected, the estimate of θ is negative and significant. For example, in column 1, θ is estimated to be -24.15 (s.e. $= 5.67$), which indicates an average reduction of 24 deaths per 100,000 population due to the interventions. In column 2, when we add lagged intervention, the coefficient on the intervention dummy is largely unchanged (-24.47), while the lagged intervention itself is also significant, likely reflecting the gradual diffusion of global interventions within our sample (recall that the intervention date corresponds to the time of the major global breakthrough).

More challenging is the specification in column 3, which includes contemporaneous and lead interventions. This specification investigates whether it is the interventions or preexisting trends that are responsible for the declines in mortality. Reassuringly, the estimate of the negative coefficient on contemporaneous intervention, θ, is unaffected, while the lead intervention has an insignificant coefficient, with the opposite (positive) sign of about a third of the magnitude of the effect of contemporaneous intervention. These results therefore show that mortality from specific diseases around the world fell sharply following the global health interventions, but not before.

Columns 4–7 investigate whether one of the main diseases is responsible for the results in columns 1–3, by excluding tuberculosis, pneumonia, malaria, and influenza one at a time. Without tuberculosis or pneumonia, which were the major diseases of this era, the coefficient estimates are somewhat smaller, but still highly significant (-17.72 and -18.59, with

---

28 The zeroth-stage regressions are estimated on an unbalanced panel going back to 1930. The 1930 data enable us to look for potential lead effects. For the reasons noted in footnote 27, we do not have sufficient data to include yellow fever and dysentery and diarrhea-related diseases in this table (see the appendix for details).

Table 4.4 The Effect of Interventions on Disease Mortality: Zeroth Stage

Variable	Base sample (1)	Base sample (2)	Base sample (3)	Without tuberculosis (4)	Without pneumonia (5)	Without malaria (6)	Without influenza (7)
Intervention	−24.15 (5.67)	−24.47 (5.19)	−22.78 (6.11)	−17.72 (5.14)	−18.59 (5.25)	−26.41 (5.58)	−25.16 (5.78)
Lagged intervention		−18.81 (4.25)					
Lead intervention			7.27 (4.14)				
R^2	0.47	0.48	0.47	0.49	0.49	0.49	0.48
Number of observations	1,723	1,723	1,723	1,577	1,613	1,610	1,578

Source: Authors' calculations.

Note: OLS regressions with a full set of disease, year, and country fixed effects. Robust standard errors, adjusted for clustering by country-disease pair, are in parentheses. Unbalanced panels have data for 1930, 1940, 1950, and 1960. Dependent variable is deaths per 100,000 from disease i in country j at year t. The base sample is 13 infectious diseases plus cancer and malignant tumors for which data are available (this excludes dysentery or diarrhea and yellow fever). Independent variables are dummy for intervention (for example, intervention for tuberculosis equals 1 for 1950 and 1960, 0 otherwise), dummy for lead intervention (for example, intervention for tuberculosis equals 1 for 1940, 1950, and 1960), and dummy for lagged intervention (for example, intervention for tuberculosis equals 1 for 1960).

Figure 4.3 Change in Log Life Expectancy and Change in Predicted Mortality, 1940–80, Base Sample

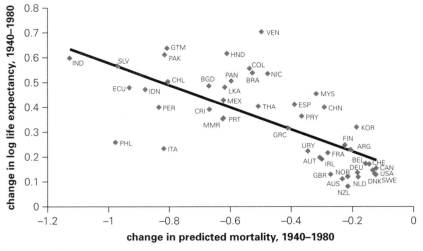

Source: Authors.

standard errors of 5.14 and 5.25, respectively).[29] Without malaria or influenza, the coefficient estimates are very similar to the baseline.

First-Stage Estimates

We next turn to the first-stage relationship between life expectancy and predicted mortality. While the zeroth-stage regression in equation 4.10 is at the disease-country-time level, the structural relationships of interest, captured in equation 4.6, and thus our first-stage relationships, are at the country-time level.

Figure 4.3 shows the first-stage relationship visually. The horizontal axis depicts the change in predicted mortality between 1940 and 1980, while the vertical axis shows the change in log life expectancy during the same time period. A strong negative relationship is clearly visible in figure 4.3. Predicted mortality declined by a large amount in India, the Philippines, Indonesia, and parts of Central America, while remaining largely unchanged in parts of Western Europe, Argentina, Uruguay, Republic of Korea, Australia, and New Zealand. Life expectancy, in turn, increased by a large amount in the first group of countries, and much less in the second group. The pattern shown in figure 4.3 can also be seen in table 4.1, columns 6 and 7. These columns show the descriptive statistics for countries with above and

---

29 Tuberculosis and pneumonia were much more important than the other diseases as major causes of death at this time and also accounted for a very large fraction of the decline in mortality during this episode. For example, in our base sample the (unweighted) cross-country average of deaths per 100,000 due to tuberculosis was 177.24 in 1940 and declined to 26.90 in 1960 (a decline of more than 150 deaths per 100,000). The same numbers for pneumonia were 208.14 in 1940 and 62.07 in 1960 (a decline of 146 deaths per 100,000). Both the death rates in 1940 and the declines were much smaller for other diseases. For example, the decline between 1940 and 1960 was just under 20 deaths per 100,000 for malaria, just over 6 deaths per 100,000 for typhoid, approximately 4 deaths per 100,000 for influenza, smallpox and cholera, and much smaller for the remaining diseases.

Figure 4.4 Change in Log Life Expectancy and Change in Predicted Mortality, 1940–80, Low- and Middle-Income Countries

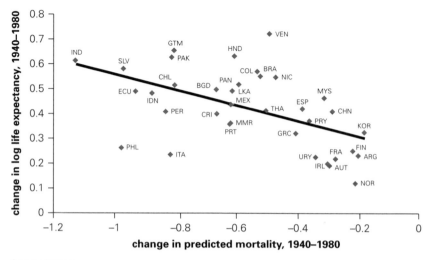

Source: Authors.

below median changes in predicted mortality between 1940 and 1980. The second and the third rows show that there is a much larger increase in life expectancy at birth (over 22 years) for countries with above median changes in predicted mortality versus those with below median changes (a change of 13 years).

Figure 4.4 depicts the same relationship without the richest countries. It shows that the first-stage relationship is not driven by the comparison of initially rich countries to initially low- and middle-income countries.[30]

Table 4.5 shows the first-stage relationship in regression form by estimating equation 4.8. Panel A reports long-difference specifications, which are similar to the OLS regressions reported in tables 4.2 and 4.3. For completeness and comparison, panel B reports panel regressions, with each observation corresponding to a decade. These regressions always include country and year dummies, and we report standard errors that are fully robust against serial correlation at the country level (for example, Wooldridge 2002: 275).

The first column includes all countries for which we have life expectancy and predicted mortality data. It shows an estimate of Ψ equal to -0.39

---

30 Predicted mortality has a similar effect on life expectancy at different ages (see table 4.10 for life expectancy at 20). It also has an impact on infant mortality, although this relationship is somewhat less robust. In particular, change in predicted mortality between 1940 and 1980 reduces infant mortality between 1940 and 1980, but this effect becomes statistically significant only when we look at infant mortality between 1940 and 2000. Moreover, if we look at log infant mortality rather than the level of infant mortality, the sign of the relationship is reversed. This is largely because some countries with relatively large increases in life expectancy had relatively small falls in infant mortality and also because many rich economies experienced large *proportional* declines in infant mortality (though much smaller changes in life expectancy); see, for example, Lancaster (1990: ch. 32). This pattern is not entirely surprising in view of the fact that the main killers of this era—tuberculosis, pneumonia, and malaria—mainly affected adults and children above the age of one.

Table 4.5 Predicted Mortality and Life Expectancy: First-Stage Estimates

Variable	All countries (1)	Base sample (2)	Base sample (3)	Baseline predicted mortality — Low- and middle-income countries only (4)	Base sample, interaction with institutions (5)	Base sample, interaction with initial (1930) log GDP per capita (6)	Base sample, interaction with continent dummies (7)	Using global mortality rate — Base sample (8)	Using global mortality rate — Low- and middle-income countries only (9)
Panel A: Long differences									
Time period	Just 1940 and 1980	Just 1940 and 1980	Just 1940 and 2000	Just 1940 and 1980	Just 1940 and 1980	Just 1940 and 1980	Just 1940 and 1980	Just 1940 and 1980	Just 1940 and 1980
Predicted mortality	−0.39 (0.07)	−0.45 (0.06)	−0.56 (0.07)	−0.31 (0.08)	−0.35 (0.07)	−0.25 (0.09)	−0.30 (0.07)	−0.46 (0.10)	−0.31 (0.13)
R^2	0.93	0.95	0.95	0.95	0.96	0.96	0.96	0.95	0.95
Number of observations	150	94	94	72	94	94	94	94	72
Number of countries	75	47	47	36	47	47	47	47	36
Panel B: Panel regressions									
Time period	1940–80	1940–80	1940–2000	1940–80	1940–80	1940–80	1940–80	1940–80	1940–80
Predicted mortality	−0.29 (0.06)	−0.33 (0.06)	−0.41 (0.06)	−0.23 (0.07)	−0.27 (0.06)	−0.24 (0.09)	−0.25 (0.06)	−0.41 (0.07)	−0.26 (0.09)
R^2	0.93	0.93	0.91	0.93	0.94	0.95	0.96	0.93	0.93
Number of observations	405	283	401	228	271	243	283	263	208
Number of countries	84	59	59	48	56	49	59	59	48

Source: Authors' calculations.

Note: OLS regressions with a full set of year and country fixed effects. Robust standard errors, adjusted for clustering, are in parentheses. Panel A consists of long-difference specifications with two observations per country, one for initial date and one for final date. Panel B consists of unbalanced panel regressions with one observation per country and per decade. The dependent variable is the log of life expectancy at birth. "All countries" are those for which we have disease data; base sample countries are those not missing data on second-stage outcome variables. Columns 1 to 7 use baseline predicted mortality as the independent variable, while columns 8 and 9 use the predicted global mortality. See the text and the appendix for the construction of the predicted mortality instrument, definitions, and data sources. Countries are assigned to the low- and middle-income categories on the basis of 1940 income per capita. Regressions in columns 5 to 7 also include year dummies interacted with institutions measured as constraints on the executive in 1950, 1960, and 1970 from Polity IV (column 5); the log of GDP per capita in 1930 (column 6); and a full set of continent dummies, specifically Africa, Asia, the Americas, and Europe, with Oceania as the omitted category (column 7).

with a standard error of 0.07, which is significant at less than 1 percent. Column 2 is for our base sample and is the first stage corresponding to our main 2SLS (two-stage least squares) regressions in tables 4.8 and 4.9. The estimate of Ψ is now –0.45 (s.e. = 0.06), which is again significant at less than 1 percent.[31] This estimate implies that an improvement in predicted mortality of 0.47 (per 100 or 470 per 100,000, which is the mean improvement between 1940 and 1980 in our base sample) leads approximately to a 21 percent increase in life expectancy (mean life expectancy in our sample in 1940 was 49.30, so this is an increase of about 10.5 years, while the actual mean improvement in life expectancy between 1940 and 1980 was 17 years). This implies that changes in predicted mortality account for almost two-thirds of the increase in life expectancy between 1940 and 1980. Perhaps more important, 10.5 years is approximately equal to the decline in the gap between initially rich versus initially poor and middle-income countries, so that the closing of the health gap during this time period appears to be accounted for almost entirely by the variation driven by the international epidemiological transition.

Column 3 repeats the same regression for 1940 and 2000. Now the estimate of Ψ is slightly larger, -0.56 (s.e. = 0.07). Column 4 looks at only low- and middle-income countries. The estimate of Ψ is slightly smaller and less precise than in column 2, but it is still significant at less than 1 percent (-0.31, with a standard error of 0.08).

Panel B repeats the same regressions using a panel with decadal observations. The results are still highly significant but slightly smaller, which is reasonable since these regressions exploit shorter-run responses to changes in predicted mortality.

As noted, a major concern regarding the validity of our instrument is its potential correlation with baseline country characteristics. Whether this explains the first-stage relationship is investigated in columns 6–8. These columns report regressions of the following form:

$$x_{it} = \psi M_{it}^I + \tilde{\zeta}_i + \tilde{\mu}_t + \sum_{t=1940}^{1980} \mathbf{c}_t' \boldsymbol{\omega}_i + u_{it}, \tag{4.11}$$

where c_i denotes "time-invariant" characteristics of country i, in particular, either a measure of average quality of institutions (computed as the average of the constraints on the executive from the Polity IV data set over 1950–70) in column 5, the 1930 value of GDP per capita in column 6, or a vector of continent dummies in column 7. Since equation 4.11 includes a full set of time interactions with c_i, differential trends related to these characteristics are taken out. In long-difference regressions reported in panel A, this specification is equivalent to including an interaction between the 1980 (or the 2000) dummy and the baseline characteristics.

The results in both panels of table 4.5 show that controlling for these characteristics has little effect on our results. For example, the coefficient

---

31 Since the t statistics in the basic first-stage relationships are above 5, there is no issue of weak instruments, and in the 2SLS regressions below we use the standard Wald confidence intervals (see, for example, Stock, Wright, and Yogo 2002).

estimate in column 5, panel A, is -0.35 (s.e. $= 0.07$), which is slightly smaller than the baseline in column 2, but still significant at less than 1 percent. The coefficient estimates in columns 6 and 7 are -0.25 and -0.30, respectively, and are both statistically significant at less than 1 percent. The results in panel B are similar.

Finally, columns 8 and 9 report results using the global mortality instrument defined in equation 4.9. Once again, the results are similar. For example, the estimate of Ψ for the base sample in column 8 of panel A is -0.46 (s.e. $= 0.10$), while the estimate for low- and middle-income countries is -0.31 (s.e. $= 0.13$), both of which are very close to the results in columns 2 and 4.

Overall, the results in table 4.5 show a large and robust effect of the predicted mortality instrument on life expectancy. We next investigate the robustness of these results further.

Mean Reversion, Lags, and Leads

The specifications in table 4.5 do not allow for mean reversion in life expectancy and also assume that it is contemporaneous predicted mortality that affects life expectancy. In more general specifications we may find that it is the lags or leads of predicted mortality that affect life expectancy. In particular, if it is the leads of (future changes in) predicted mortality that affect life expectancy, this would shed doubt on our interpretation of the first-stage relationship. Table 4.6 investigates these issues using the specifications with decadal observations from panel B of table 4.5. Column 1 repeats our baseline specification (from column 2 of panel B in table 4.5). Column 2 reports OLS estimates from the following model:

$$x_{it} = v x_{it-1} + \Psi M_{it}^l + \delta_i' + \mu_t' + u_{it}, \qquad (4.12)$$

which allows lagged log life expectancy to affect current log life expectancy. There is indeed evidence for mean reversion; the coefficient v in the second row is estimated to be 0.44 (s.e. $= 0.09$). Nevertheless, the negative relationship between predicted mortality and life expectancy remains. The parameter of interest, Ψ, is now estimated at -0.18 (s.e. $= 0.08$) and implies a long-run impact similar to that in our baseline specification—the long-run impact in this case is $-0.18/(1 - 0.44) \approx -0.32$.

Because we have a relatively short panel, OLS estimation of equation 4.12 leads to inconsistent estimates. To deal with this problem, in column 3 we follow the method of Anderson and Hsiao (1982). This involves first-differencing equation 4.12, so that $\Delta x_{it-1} = v \Delta x_{it-1} + \Psi \Delta M_{it}^l + \Delta \mu_t' + \Delta u_{it}$, where the fixed country effects are removed by differencing. Although this equation cannot be estimated consistently by OLS either, in the absence of serial correlation in the original residual, u_{it}, there will be no second-order serial correlation in Δu_{it}, so x_{it-2} will be uncorrelated with Δu_{it} and can be used as instrument for Δx_{it-1} to obtain consistent estimates. Similarly M_{it-1}^l is used as an instrument for ΔM_{it}^l. This procedure leads to very similar results to the OLS estimates. The estimate of Ψ is -0.27 (s.e. $= 0.14$).

Although the instrumental variable estimator of Anderson and Hsiao (1982) leads to consistent estimates, it is not efficient since, under the

Table 4.6. First-Stage Estimates: Mean Reversion and Robustness

Variable	OLS		Lagged LE instrumented by second lag of LE	GMM (Arellano-Bond)	OLS				
	(1)	(2)	(3)	(4)	(5)	(6)	(7)	(8)	(9)
Predicted mortality	−0.33	−0.18	−0.27	−0.19	−0.20	−0.33	−0.20	−0.31	−0.14
	(0.06)	(0.08)	(0.14)	(0.06)	(0.06)	(0.08)	(0.07)	(0.06)	(0.08)
Lagged log life expectancy		0.44	0.32	0.71					0.45
		(0.09)	(0.39)	(0.06)					(0.09)
Lagged predicted mortality					−0.17		−0.17		
					(0.03)		(0.03)		
Lead predicted mortality						0.19	0.14		
						(1.04)	(1.04)		
Lagged log GDP per capita								−0.06	−0.07
								(0.04)	(0.02)
P-value of test for second-order autocorrelation				0.83					
Hansen J test (p-value)				0.014					
R^2	0.93	0.95	0.95		0.94	0.93	0.95	0.93	0.95
Number of observations	283	267	231	248	283	283	283	273	257
Number of countries	59	59	57	59	59	59	59	59	59

Source: Authors' calculations.

Note: OLS (columns 1–2 and 5–9) and 2SLS (columns 3–4) regressions with a full set of year and country fixed effects. Robust standard errors, adjusted for clustering by country, are in parentheses. All columns are unbalanced panels with one observation per decade, per country, using base sample countries. The dependent variable is the log of life expectancy at birth. Panel regressions are for 1940–80. Lagged values are 10 years earlier, and lead predicted mortality is 10 years ahead. Assignment of countries to low-, middle-, and high-income categories is based on 1940 income per capita. In column 3, the second lag of log life expectancy is used as an instrument for lagged log life expectancy. In column 4, GMM (Arellano-Bond) uses all available lags of log life expectancy as instruments.

assumption of no further serial correlation in u_{it}, not only x_{it-2}, but all earlier lags of x_{it} in the sample are also uncorrelated with Δu_{it} and can be used as additional instruments. Arellano and Bond (1991) develop a generalized method-of-moments (GMM) estimator using all of these moment conditions. When all of these moment conditions are valid, this GMM estimator is more efficient than the estimator of Anderson and Hsiao (1982). GMM estimation, which we use in column 4, leads to similar but more precisely estimated coefficients. The estimate of Ψ in the full sample is now -0.19 (s.e.$= 0.06$). Tests for second-order autocorrelation in the residuals, reported at the bottom of the column, show that there is no evidence of additional serial correlation. However, the Hansen J-test shows that the overidentification restrictions are rejected, presumably because different lags of life expectancy lead to different estimates of the mean reversion coefficient. This rejection is not a major concern for our empirical strategy since the exact magnitude of the mean reversion coefficient, v, is not of direct interest to us (because the models in equations 4.8 and 4.12 are the first stages in our 2SLS regressions, all we need is for M^I_{it-1} not to have a direct effect on the second-stage outcomes).

Columns 5–7 investigate the effect of lagged and lead mortality. In column 5, contemporaneous and lagged mortality are included together. Both of these are significant, since in many countries global health interventions were implemented gradually over time.

The more important challenge for our approach is the inclusion of lead predicted mortality. Because global interventions did not start before 1940, lead mortality should have no effect on life expectancy. Column 6 investigates this by including contemporaneous and lead mortality together. In this case, the estimate of the effect of contemporaneous predicted mortality is -0.33 (s.e. $= 0.06$), while lead mortality is not significant and has the wrong sign. Column 7 includes contemporaneous, lag, and lead predicted mortality together, and in this case both contemporaneous and lag mortality are statistically significant, while lead mortality remains highly insignificant. These results suggest that, consistent with our hypothesis, it was indeed the global interventions of the 1940s onward that led to the increase in life expectancy in countries previously affected by these diseases, rather than some preexisting trends in life expectancy. The issue of preexisting trends is investigated more directly in the next subsection and in table 4.7.

Finally, columns 8 and 9 show that controlling for the effect of income per capita has little impact on the relationship between predicted mortality and life expectancy.

Preexisting Trends and Falsification

Table 4.6 shows that life expectancy responds to contemporaneous changes in predicted mortality and does not respond to future changes. This suggests that our first stage is unlikely to be driven by preexisting trends. Nevertheless, the exercise in table 4.6 uses only data from 1940 onward. An alternative falsification exercise is to look at changes in life expectancy

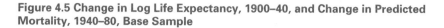

Figure 4.5 Change in Log Life Expectancy, 1900–40, and Change in Predicted Mortality, 1940–80, Base Sample

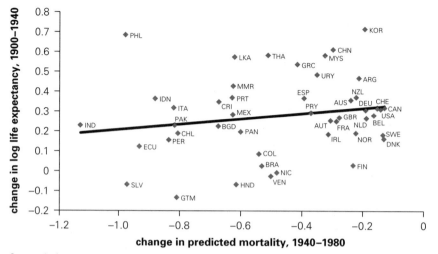

Source: Authors.

Figure 4.6 Change in Log Life Expectancy, 1930–40, and Change in Predicted Mortality, 1940–80, Base Sample

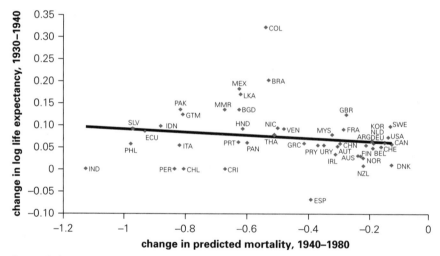

Source: Authors.

during the pre-intervention period, 1900–40, and see whether they correlate with future (post-1940) changes in predicted mortality. This is done in figures 4.5 and 4.6 and in table 4.7.

Figure 4.5 shows the change in log life expectancy 1900–40 against the change in predicted mortality 1940–80 (see also columns 6 and 7 in table 4.1). There is no evidence of a negative relationship similar to those in figures 4.3 and 4.4. In fact, there is a slight positive slope (although column 1 of table 4.7 shows that this relationship is not significant). Figure 4.6 further substantiates the lack of preexisting trends. It shows changes in log life expectancy just before the international epidemiological transition, between 1930 and 1940, against the predicted mortality instrument.

Table 4.7 Falsification Exercise and Reduced Forms

Variable	Base sample (1)	Low- and middle-income countries (2)	Base sample (3)	Low- and middle-income countries (4)	Base sample (5)	Low- and middle-income countries (6)	Base sample (7)	Low- and middle-income countries (8)
Panel A: Falsification exercise								
Dependent variable	Change in life expectancy from 1900 to 1940		Change in log population from 1900 to 1940		Change in log GDP from 1900 to 1940		Change in log GDP per capita from 1900 to 1940	
Change in predicted mortality from 1940 to 1980	0.13 (0.11)	0.21 (0.16)	−0.17 (0.15)	−0.13 (0.24)	0.009 (0.24)	0.05 (0.36)	0.02 (0.17)	0.04 (0.23)
R^2	0.04	0.06	0.03	0.01	0.0001	0.0008	0.0005	0.0008
Number of countries	47	36	45	34	31	20	31	20
Panel B: Reduced forms								
Dependent variable	Change in life expectancy from 1940 to 1980		Change in log population from 1940 to 1980		Change in log GDP from 1940 to 1980		Change in log GDP per capita from 1940 to 1980	
Change in predicted mortality from 1940 to 1980	−0.44 (0.06)	−0.30 (0.08)	−0.74 (0.15)	−0.62 (0.21)	−0.14 (0.22)	0.11 (0.28)	0.58 (0.15)	0.71 (0.20)
R^2	0.5	0.27	0.29	0.17	0.008	0.004	0.18	0.18
Number of countries	47	36	47	36	47	36	47	36

Source: Authors' calculations.

Note: OLS regressions. Robust standard errors are in parentheses. Both panels regress change in the variable indicated from initial to final date on change in predicted mortality from 1940 to 1980. Predicted mortality is measured in deaths per 100 population. Panel A uses the subset of the base sample for which data on all outcome variables are available.

Once again, there is no evidence of a significant negative relationship. These figures therefore suggest that our measure of predicted mortality explains changes in life expectancy *after* 1940 but *not before* 1940.

Panel A of table 4.7 confirms these results using regression analysis and also shows that there is no preexisting trend when we look at the sample of low- and middle-income countries. Table 4.7 also looks for potential preexisting trends in our outcome measures (to save space, we focus on population, GDP, and GDP per capita). Columns 3 and 4 (panel A) show that there is no differential preexisting trend in log population between 1900 and 1940 either for the entire sample or for the sample excluding the initially richest countries. Columns 5–8 show similar results for log GDP and log GDP per capita.

These results therefore indicate that there were no preexisting trends related to changes in predicted mortality either in life expectancy or in our key outcome variables.[32] This gives us greater confidence in using predicted mortality as an instrument to investigate the effect of life expectancy on a range of economic outcomes.

Main Results

We now present our main results, which are the 2SLS estimates of the effect of log life expectancy on six outcome variables: log population, log total births, the fraction of the population under the age of 20, log GDP, log GDP per capita, and log GDP per working-age population. For each outcome, we report long-difference regressions for 1940 and 1980 (see Acemoglu and Johnson 2006 for similar results using decadal observations, as in panel B of table 4.5 and table 4.6). We also report regressions for 1940 and 2000, which may better approximate "longer-run" changes.

Population

Figure 4.7 shows a strong negative reduced-form relationship between change in log population 1940–80 and change in predicted mortality over the same period. This pattern can also be seen in reduced-form regressions in panel B of table 4.7, both for the entire sample and for low- and middle-income countries. It implies that countries with a larger decline in predicted mortality experienced a larger increase in log population, that is, more population growth. Given the negative relationship between predicted mortality and life expectancy in figure 4.4, this translates into a positive effect of life expectancy on population. This is confirmed in panel A of table 4.8, which reports 2SLS regressions of log population on log life expectancy.

In column 1 we look at long differences between 1940 and 1980. The coefficient estimate is 1.67 (s.e. = 0.50), which is statistically significant at 1 percent. This estimate is very similar to the OLS estimate in column 3,

---

32 For a more qualitative confirmation that there were no preexisting trends before 1940, see Carr-Saunders (1936). In this comprehensive review of population trends, there is no hint of the remarkable increases in life expectancy and population that were to occur shortly.

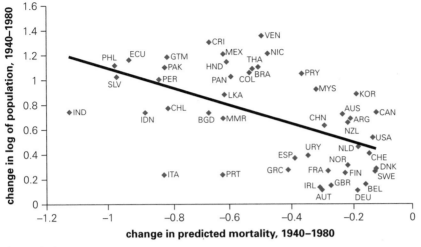

Source: Authors.

panel A, of table 4.2. This coefficient increases to 1.96 when we look at the longer horizon, 1940–2000. This suggests that in countries that benefited from the international epidemiological transition, population continued to increase in the 1980s, most likely because the increase in population until the 1980s led to an increase in total number of births (which is confirmed in panel B).

The coefficient estimates are also larger for low- and middle-income countries. For 1940–80, the coefficient is now 2.04 (s.e. = 1.01), and for 1940–2000, it is 2.18 (s.e. = 0.93). Both of these coefficients are significant at 5 percent.

Columns 5 and 6 estimate specifications that include controls for preexisting trends. In particular, similar to equation 4.11, the second-stage equation in these columns takes the following form:

$$y_{it} = \pi x_{it} + \zeta_i + \mu_t + \sum_{t=1940}^{1980} \mathbf{c}'_i \boldsymbol{\omega}_t + \varepsilon_{it}, \tag{4.13}$$

where $\mathbf{c}_i$ includes average institutions (measured as in the section on predicted mortality and first stages and table 4.5) or initial (1930) log population. Remarkably, in both cases this has little effect on the estimate of π. In column 5, this estimate is 1.63, in column 6, the estimate of π is 1.68, and in both cases the estimate is statistically significant at less than 1 percent.[33] Finally, column 7 shows that using the global mortality instrument leads to very similar results (a coefficient of 1.70, with a standard error of 0.48).

Overall, we conclude that life expectancy has a large, relatively precise, and robust effect on population. The elasticity of population in response

---

33 In column 6, the interaction with initial population is also significant. In addition, results including the interaction with initial log GDP per capita or continent dummies are also very similar and are not reported to economize on space.

Table 4.8 The Effect of Life Expectancy on Population, Total Births, and Population under Age 20: 2SLS Estimates

Variable	Baseline predicted mortality instrument						Global mortality instrument, base sample
	Base sample		Low- and middle-income countries only		Base sample, interaction with institutions	Base sample, interaction with initial (1930) value of dependent variable	
	(1)	(2)	(3)	(4)	(5)	(6)	(7)
Panel A: Dependent variable is log population							
Time period	Just 1940 and 1980	Just 1940 and 2000	Just 1940 and 1980	Just 1940 and 2000	Just 1940 and 1980	Just 1940 and 1980	Just 1940 and 1980
Log life expectancy	1.67	1.96	2.04	2.18	1.63	1.68	1.70
	(0.50)	(0.53)	(1.01)	(0.93)	(0.73)	(0.44)	(0.48)
Post year dummy * institutions or initial log population					−0.006	−0.055	
					(0.05)	(0.03)	
Number of countries	47	47	36	36	47	47	47
Panel B: Dependent variable is log total births							
Time period	Just 1940 and 1980	Just 1940 and 1990	Just 1940 and 1980	Just 1940 and 1990	Just 1940 and 1980	Just 1940 and 1980	Just 1940 and 1980
Log life expectancy	2.53	2.15	2.92	2.67	2.40	2.53	2.52
	(0.70)	(0.64)	(1.36)	(1.20)	(1.09)	(0.70)	(0.72)
Post year dummy * institutions or initial log of total births					−0.018	−0.056	
					(0.09)	(0.05)	
Number of countries	45	45	34	34	45	44	45
Panel C: Dependent variable is fraction of population under age 20							
Time period	Just 1940 and 1980	Just 1940 and 2000	Just 1940 and 1980	Just 1940 and 2000	Just 1940 and 1980	Just 1940 and 1980	Just 1940 and 1980
Log life expectancy	0.12	0.05	0.18	0.16	0.15	0.26	0.12
	(0.06)	(0.08)	(0.14)	(0.17)	(0.08)	(0.31)	(0.057)
Post year dummy * institutions or initial fraction of young population					0.005	−0.30	
					(0.01)	(0.52)	
Number of countries	40	40	29	29	40	40	40

Source: Authors' calculations.

Note: 2SLS regressions with a full set of year and country fixed effects. Robust standard errors are in parentheses. All regressions in all panels are long-difference specifications, with two observations per country, one for the initial date and one for the final date. Dependent variables are, in panel A, the log of population, in panel B, the log of total births, and in panel C, the fraction of total population that is 20 years old or younger. In all panels, the independent variable is the log of life expectancy at birth, which is instrumented by the baseline predicted mortality in columns 1 to 6 and by the predicted global mortality in column 7. First stages are reported in table 4.5. In column 5, regressions include interactions of year dummies with institutions, measured by the average of constraints on the executive in 1950, 1960, and 1970 from Polity IV. In column 6, regressions include interactions of year dummies with the initial (1930) log of population in panel A, the initial (1930) log of total births in panel B, and the initial (1940) percent of population ages 20 or younger in panel C.

to life expectancy at birth is estimated consistently to lie between 1.65 and 2.15, which is similar to the OLS estimates.

Births and Age Composition

Panel B of table 4.8 presents 2SLS estimates for the effect of log life expectancy on log total births. The structure is identical to that of panel A, except that, because we lack data for 2000, the longer-term specification uses 1940 and 1990. Consistent with the magnitude of the response of population to life expectancy, these results show relatively large effects of life expectancy on total births. The coefficient estimates vary between 2.15 and 2.9 and are typically significant at less than 1 percent (except in column 3, where the estimate is significant at 5 percent). The estimates are also remarkably robust across different samples and are robust to controlling for preexisting trends and to the use of the alternative instrument.

There is some evidence that the effect on total number of births is declining (the estimates for 1940–90 are smaller than those for 1940–80). In Acemoglu and Johnson (2006), we use decadal observations to show that this is a consistent pattern. Therefore, the fertility response to the decline in mortality appears to be slightly delayed. This is consistent with the results in Bleakley and Lange (2006) and Kelley (1988).

Panel C shows that the increase in life expectancy is associated with an increase in the fraction of the population under the age of 20 between 1940 and 1980. However, this effect goes away when we look at 1940–2000, or even in the 1940–80 sample when we look at different specifications. Our interpretation of these results is that there is a slight effect on the age composition immediately following the international epidemiological transition, both because antibiotics, DDT, and public health measures saved the lives of children and because those surviving to childbearing age contributed to the increase in births. However, this effect largely abates by 2000. We have also verified that the results are essentially identical with the dependency ratio (the ratio of inactive to total population) and that the effect of life expectancy at birth on working-age population is very similar to its effect on total population (results available upon request). This is also consistent with the patterns reported in panel C.

GDP, GDP per Capita, and GDP per Working-Age Population

Figure 4.8 shows the reduced-form relationship between change in log (total) GDP and change in predicted mortality during 1940–80. As also shown in panel B of table 4.7 (both for the base sample and for low- and middle-income countries), there is a slight (but not statistically significant) downward slope, which indicates that countries with larger declines in predicted mortality experienced somewhat higher GDP growth between 1940 and 1980.

Panel A of table 4.9 presents the corresponding 2SLS estimates. In column 1, the estimate of the key parameter is 0.32 (s.e. = 0.84), while the estimate using 1940 and 2000 in column 2 is 0.42 (s.e. = 0.52). Both of these

Figure 4.8 Change in Log of Total GDP and Change in Predicted Mortality, 1940–80, Base Sample

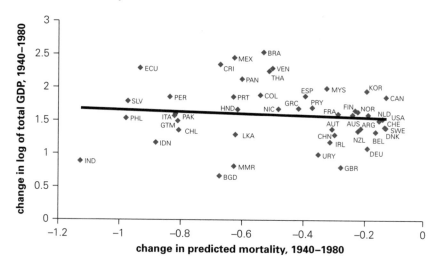

Source: Authors.

estimates suggest that there is a slight positive effect on GDP, although it is imprecisely estimated and thus not statistically significant. In both cases, the standard errors are large enough that economically significant positive effects on total GDP cannot be ruled out. For example, the two standard error bands always include a response of GDP to life expectancy with an elasticity that could be as high as 1.5. It is also interesting that the estimate for 1940–2000 is somewhat larger than that for 1940–80, which may correspond to a delayed response of GDP to the increase in population and health conditions. This is consistent with the neoclassical growth model.[34]

The remaining columns show that the effect of life expectancy on GDP is somewhat smaller or even negative when we focus on low- and middle-income countries or when we include baseline interactions. We interpret these estimates as suggesting that the increase in life expectancy and the associated increase in population had a relatively small effect on total GDP, perhaps with a somewhat larger effect over 60 years than in the first few decades after the decline in mortality. Although the relatively large standard errors make it impossible for us to pin down the exact magnitude or the timing of the impact of life expectancy on GDP, we view the lack of a somewhat larger positive effect on total GDP as a potential puzzle.

The response of total GDP reveals that the effect of the increase in life expectancy on GDP per capita is negative. Panel B of table 4.9 confirms this pattern by presenting the 2SLS estimates of the effect of log life expectancy on GDP per capita. There is a significant negative effect of life expectancy on GDP per capita in columns 1 and 2. For example, in column 1, the

---

34 In Acemoglu and Johnson (2006), we report additional findings consistent with a somewhat delayed response of GDP to life expectancy. The recent paper by Ashraf, Lester, and Weil (2007) shows that, even when health has positive effects on long-run income per capita, population dynamics will lead to considerable delays before any increase in income per capita is observed.

The Effect of Life Expectancy on Economic Growth

Table 4.9 The Effect of Life Expectancy on GDP, GDP per Capita, and GDP per Working-Age Population: 2SLS Estimates

| Variable | Baseline predicted mortality instrument | | | | Base sample, interaction with institutions | Base sample, interaction with initial (1930) value of dependent variable | Global mortality instrument, base sample |
| | Base sample | | Low- and middle-income countries only | | | | |
	(1)	(2)	(3)	(4)	(5)	(6)	(7)
Panel A: Dependent variable is log GDP							
Time period	Just 1940 and 1980	Just 1940 and 2000	Just 1940 and 1980	Just 1940 and 2000	Just 1940 and 1980	Just 1940 and 1980	Just 1940 and 1980
Log life expectancy	0.32 (0.84)	0.42 (0.52)	−0.39 (1.44)	−0.58 (1.09)	−0.11 (0.99)	−0.069 (0.73)	0.46 (0.73)
Post year dummy * institutions or initial log GDP					−0.063 (0.055)	−0.109 (0.059)	
Number of countries	47	47	36	36	47	47	47
Panel B: Dependent variable is log per capita GDP							
Time period	Just 1940 and 1980	Just 1940 and 1990	Just 1940 and 1980	Just 1940 and 1990	Just 1940 and 1980	Just 1940 and 1980	Just 1940 and 1980
Log life expectancy	−1.32 (0.56)	−1.51 (0.57)	−2.35 (1.13)	−2.70 (1.40)	−1.64 (0.77)	−1.59 (1.22)	−1.21 (0.52)
Post year dummy * institutions or initial log GDP per capita					−0.49 (0.060)	−0.073 (0.278)	
Number of countries	47	47	36	36	47	47	47
Panel C: Dependent variable is log GDP per working-age population							
Time period	Just 1940 and 1980	Just 1940 and 2000	Just 1940 and 1980	Just 1940 and 2000	Just 1940 and 1980	Just 1940 and 1980	Just 1940 and 1980
Log life expectancy	−1.35 (0.63)	−1.62 (0.54)	−2.43 (1.30)	−2.63 (1.31)	−1.82 (0.88)	−1.87 (1.39)	−1.23 (0.57)
Post year dummy * institutions or initial log GDP per working-age population					−0.068 (0.065)	−0.758 (0.369)	
Number of countries	46	46	35	35	46	46	46

Source: Authors' calculations.

Note: 2SLS regressions with a full set of year and country fixed effects. Robust standard errors are in parentheses. All regressions in all panels are long-difference specifications, with two observations per country, one for the initial date and one for the final date. Dependent variables are, in panel A, the log of GDP, in panel B, the log of GDP per capita, and in panel C, the log of GDP per working-age population. In all panels, the independent variable is the log of life expectancy at birth, which is instrumented by the baseline predicted mortality in columns 1 to 6 and by the predicted global mortality in column 7. First stages are reported in table 4.5. In column 5, regressions include interactions of year dummies with institutions, measured by the average of constraints on the executive in 1950, 1960, and 1970 from Polity IV. In column 6, regressions include interactions of year dummies with the initial (1930) log of GDP in panel A, the initial (1930) log of GDP per capita in panel B, and the initial (1930) log of GDP per working-age population in panel C.

estimate of π in equation 4.6 is -1.32 (s.e. = 0.56). The estimates are somewhat more negative when we focus on low- and middle-income countries in columns 3 and 4.

Columns 5, 6, and 7 show that the estimates are very similar when we include the interaction between the post-year dummy and average institutions or the initial value of GDP per capita or when we use the global mortality instrument.

One concern with these results is that, to the extent that the increase in population is largely at young ages, GDP per capita may be low precisely because the denominator has increased, while the working-age population has not. The results in panel C of table 4.8, which show only limited changes in age composition, suggest that this is unlikely to be the case. Panel C of table 4.9 investigates this issue directly by estimating models with log of GDP per working-age population on the left-hand side. The results are very similar to those in panel B and indicate that the effect of life expectancy on GDP per working-age population is also negative.

Overall, the 2SLS estimates show no evidence that the large increase in life expectancy in many parts of the world starting in the 1940s led to a significant increase in GDP per capita. Instead, the increase in life expectancy was associated with a significant increase in population and a considerably smaller increase in total GDP.[35]

We can also evaluate these estimates in terms of the neoclassical growth model. First, suppose that the results for 1940–80 correspond to the impact of life expectancy on income per capita with the capital stock held constant. From equation 4.4, the coefficient of interest in this case is $\pi = [\alpha(\gamma + \eta) - (1 - \alpha)\lambda]$. Recall that λ is the response of population to changes in life expectancy, so according to the estimates for the base sample in panel A, table 4.8, we have $\lambda \approx 1.7$. The coefficient α corresponds to the share of labor. Since the countries that benefited most from longer life expectancy include many low-income countries where land is an important factor of production, we take the share of land as one-third, that is, $1 - \alpha - \beta \approx 1/3$ (see footnote 9) and thus set $\alpha \approx 1/3$ and $\beta \approx 1/3$. This would imply that our estimate of $\pi = [\alpha(\gamma + \eta) - (1 - \alpha)\lambda] \approx -1.3$ is consistent with $\gamma + \eta$ being close to zero or even slightly negative. If, in contrast, we were to take λ to be around 2 as suggested by the high-end estimates from low- and middle-income countries in table 4.8, $\lambda + \eta$ would be small but positive. Similar and somewhat less positive results follow if we take the estimates for 1940–2000 to correspond to the long-run effects in equation 4.5. Recall that in this case $\pi = [\alpha(\gamma + \eta) - (1 - \alpha - \beta)\lambda]/(1 - \beta)$. From column 2 in panel A of table 4.8, $\lambda \approx 2$, and from panel B of table 4.9, $\pi \approx -1.5$. Again taking $\alpha \approx 1/3$ and $\beta \approx 1/3$,

---

35 The comparison of these results to the OLS estimates in table 4.3 (together with the pattern discussed in footnote 25) also suggests that the zero OLS relationship between life expectancy and GDP per capita is likely to be a combination of a short-run negative effect of life expectancy on GDP per capita and a positive effect of income on life expectancy. See also Pritchett and Summers (1996) for estimates of the impact of income per capita on life expectancy.

the estimate for π can be rationalized by having negative values for $\gamma + \eta$. These computations suggest that the results reported here could be reconciled with the simple neoclassical growth model, but only if the share of land in GDP is about one-third and the positive effects of health on TFP and education are limited. Since a share of land in GDP of about one-third is quite large,[36] other factors, beyond those captured by the neoclassical growth model, may be important for understanding the effects of life expectancy on income per capita.

Further Results

We verified that our results are not affected by the fact that we are combining data on causes of death (individual diseases) from two sources. In particular, using only the 32 countries for which we have disease data from one source—Federal Security Agency (1947)—has little effect on our first-stage, reduced-form, or 2SLS results. We also checked the robustness of our results to dropping all data for which we had to use information on life expectancy from neighboring countries. The first-stage, reduced-form, or 2SLS estimates in this smaller sample of 39 countries are again very similar to the baseline results.

In addition, in Acemoglu and Johnson (2006) we show that the results reported in tables 4.8 and 4.9 are robust to a variety of additional specifications. First, in panel specifications with decadal observations, we can include data from Sub-Saharan African countries.[37] The inclusion of African data produces very similar estimates to the baseline results. We also show there that the results are robust to excluding countries that were demographically most affected by World War II.[38] We also estimate regressions dropping countries that were involved in developing the new "miracle" drugs and chemicals of the 1940s and 1950s: the United Kingdom, the United States, Germany, and Switzerland. The exclusion of these countries again has no effect on the baseline results. Finally, we estimate specifications that control for mean reversion in the second stage, again with little effect on the main results.

---

36 For example, Hansen and Prescott (2002) suggest a value of 0.3 for $1 - \alpha - \beta$, 0.1 for β, and 0.6 for α in preindustrial societies.

37 There is no life expectancy data for Sub-Saharan Africa before 1950, and post-1950 data may be less reliable for this region than for the rest of the world. Nevertheless, in general terms, we know that health in Africa improved, at least for a while, after World War II. For example, Cutler, Deaton, and Lleras-Muney (2006: 17) write, "Life expectancy [in Africa] rose by more than 13 years from the early 1950s to the late 1980s, before declining in the face of HIV/AIDS." Estimates in Gwatkin (1980: fig. 2) also suggest that increases in life expectancy were at least as dramatic in Africa as in other developing countries, but only until average life expectancy for these societies reached 40; at that point the rate of increase slowed sharply. This could point to a failure to sustain health improvements or some other factor and needs further investigation.

38 The countries most affected by World War II in our base sample are Austria, China, Finland, Germany, and Italy (see Urlanis 2003). Excluding these countries has little effect on the first- or second-stage estimates (see Acemoglu and Johnson 2006).

A potential concern, already discussed, is whether the international epidemiological transition mainly affected life expectancy at birth, with little effect on adult mortality. This is *not* the case. In particular, tuberculosis and pneumonia, two of the main killers in our sample, affected the entire age distribution. As a result, our predicted mortality instrument has a strong effect on life expectancy at various ages. In table 4.10 we focus on life expectancy at 20 (defined as total life expectancy conditional on having reached the age of 20) and present results using this variable as the proxy for health rather than life expectancy at birth. Panels A–D report results for the outcome variables of tables 4.8 and 4.9. Panel E shows the corresponding first stages and documents the impact of predicted mortality on life expectancy at 20.

Panel E shows a strong relationship between life expectancy at 20 and predicted mortality. For example, in the base sample for 1940–80, which now includes 45 countries, the coefficient estimate of predicted mortality in a regression of log life expectancy at 20 is −0.17 (s.e. = 0.039). This first-stage relationship is also shown in figure 4.9. The first stage is similar in the other columns, which focus on low- and middle-income countries, on longer-term changes (1940–2000), and on results using the global mortality instrument. As noted in footnote 30, the effects of predicted mortality on life expectancy at 5, 10, 15, and 30 are also similar, although the impact on infant mortality is somewhat weaker.

The 2SLS results in panels A–D are also similar to those in tables 4.8 and 4.9. There is a positive effect on population and births, a positive and insignificant effect on total GDP, and a negative effect on GDP per capita. Results for GDP per working-age population are once again similar to those for GDP per capita.

Concluding Remarks

A recent consensus in academic and policy circles holds that differences in disease environments and health conditions lie at the root of large income differences across countries today and argues that improving health not only will improve lives but also will by itself spur rapid economic growth.

This chapter investigated these claims by estimating the effect of life expectancy on economic growth. The innovation in our approach is to exploit the international epidemiological transition, which led to potentially exogenous differential changes in mortality from a number of major diseases across the world. As a result of new chemicals, drugs, and international health campaigns, mortality from tuberculosis, pneumonia, malaria, and various other diseases declined sharply in many parts of the world, while countries that were largely unaffected by these diseases did not experience similar improvements in health and mortality. Exploiting these differential changes in predicted mortality as an instrument for life expectancy, we estimated the effect of life expectancy on a range of economic variables, most importantly population and GDP.

Table 4.10 The Effect of Life Expectancy at Age 20 on Population, Total Births, GDP, and GDP per Capita: 2SLS and First-Stage Estimates

| Variable | Baseline predicted mortality instrument | | | | Global mortality instrument, base sample |
| | Base sample | Low- and middle-income countries only | Base sample | Low- and middle-income countries only | |
	(1)	(2)	(3)	(4)	(5)
Panel A: Dependent variable is log population					
Time period	Just 1940 and 1980	Just 1940 and 1980	Just 1940 and 2000	Just 1940 and 2000	Just 1940 and 1980
Log life expectancy at 20	4.54 (2.11)	5.04 (3.64)	6.54 (2.45)	7.16 (4.22)	4.75 (2.02)
Number of countries	45	34	46	35	45
Panel B: Dependent variable is log total births					
Time period	Just 1940 and 1980	Just 1940 and 1980	Just 1940 and 1990	Just 1940 and 1990	Just 1940 and 1980
Log life expectancy at 20	6.60 (2.64)	6.98 (4.40)	7.33 (3.78)	9.21 (7.10)	6.73 (2.67)
Number of countries	43	32	40	29	43
Panel C: Dependent variable is log GDP					
Time period	Just 1940 and 1980	Just 1940 and 1980	Just 1940 and 2000	Just 1940 and 2000	Just 1940 and 1980
Log life expectancy at 20	1.17 (2.55)	−0.39 (3.45)	1.53 (1.84)	−1.71 (3.51)	1.64 (2.30)
Number of countries	45	34	46	35	45
Panel D: Dependent variable is log per capita GDP					
Time period	Just 1940 and 1980	Just 1940 and 1980	Just 1940 and 2000	Just 1940 and 2000	Just 1940 and 1980
Log life expectancy at 20	−3.27 (1.45)	−5.24 (2.95)	−4.91 (2.36)	−8.68 (5.75)	−3.05 (1.47)
Number of countries	45	34	46	35	45
Panel E: First stages of IV estimations, dependent variable is log life expectancy at 20					
Time period	Just 1940 and 1980	Just 1940 and 1980	Just 1940 and 2000	Just 1940 and 2000	Just 1940 and 1980
Predicted mortality	−0.17 (0.039)	−0.13 (0.049)	−0.17 (0.032)	−0.14 (0.041)	−0.17 (0.06)
R^2	0.93	0.92	0.96	0.96	0.92
Number of countries	45	34	46	35	45

Source: Authors' calculations.

Note: In panels A–D, 2SLS regressions with a full set of year and country fixed effects; in panel E, corresponding first stages. Robust standard errors are in parentheses. All regressions are long-difference specifications, with two observations per country, one for the initial date and one for the final date. Dependent variables are as follows: in panel A, the log of population; in panel B, the log of total births; in panel C, the log of GDP; in panel D, the log of GDP per capita; and in panel E, the log of life expectancy at age 20. The log of life expectancy at 20 is also the independent variable for panels A through D. It is instrumented by baseline predicted mortality in columns 1–4 and by global predicted mortality in column 5.

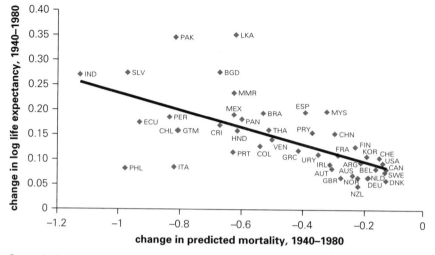

Source: Authors.

Our results indicate that the increase in life expectancy led to a significant increase in population; birth rates did not decline sufficiently to compensate for the increase in life expectancy. We find a small positive effect of life expectancy on total GDP over the first 40 years, and this effect grows somewhat over the next 20 years, but not enough to compensate for the increase in population. Overall, the increases in life expectancy (and the associated increases in population) appear to have reduced income per capita. There is no evidence that the increase in life expectancy led to faster growth of income per capita or output per worker. This evidence sheds doubt on the view that health has a first-order impact on economic growth.

Considerable caution is necessary in interpreting our results for at least two reasons. The most important limitation is that, because our approach exploits the international epidemiological transition around the 1940s, the results may not be directly applicable to today's world; the international epidemiological transition was a unique event, and similar changes in life expectancy today may not lead to an increase in population and the impact on GDP per capita may be more positive. Second, the diseases that take many lives in the poorer parts of the world today are not the same ones as those 60 years ago; most notably HIV/AIDS is a major killer today, but not in 1940. Many of the diseases we focus on have serious impacts on children (with the notable exception of tuberculosis), while HIV/AIDS affects individuals at the peak of their labor productivity and could have a larger negative impact on growth. Further study of the effects of the HIV/AIDS epidemic on economic outcomes as well as more detailed analysis of different measures of health on human capital investments and economic outcomes are major areas for future research.

Appendix. Data Sources and Construction

Data on population, GDP, and GDP per capita are from Maddison (2003), specifically the downloadable data available to purchasers of his book. Working-age population is defined as population between the ages of 15 and 60 and is obtained from the online United Nations (UN) demographic database from 1950 (http://esa.un.org/unpp). Population structure for 1940 is from the UN *Demographic Yearbook 1948* (United Nations 1949: 108–58, table 4). We use data for 1940 or the closest available year or range of years.

Life expectancy in 1940 and earlier are from various UN *Demographic Yearbooks*. Key yearbooks are the original 1948 edition and subsequent issues for 1949–50, 1951, and particularly the retrospective section of the *Demographic Yearbook 1967* (United Nations various years). We use the most recently revised UN data available to calculate the unweighted averages of male and female life expectancy for 1940 (we also check these data against United Nations 2000, but the coverage of this generally begins no earlier than 1948). When there are no data for 1940, but such data exist for neighboring years—for example, 1938 and 1942—we use linear interpolation to obtain an estimate for 1940. In a few cases, we use information from neighboring countries when they have similar crude death rates (from the UN *Demographic Yearbooks*). Appendix C in our working paper provides further details and gives the specifics for each country.

Life expectancy from 1950 onward was downloaded from the online UN demographic database; these data are in five-year intervals, so we use 1950–55 for 1950 and 1960–65 for 1960, and so forth. Life expectancy in 1900, used in the falsification tests, is from Maddison (2001: 30, table 1-5a). These estimates for life expectancy in 1900 for Europe, Latin America, and Asia are consistent with the numbers in Arriaga and Davis (1969), Bengtsson and others (2004), and Riley (2001).

To classify the cause of death, we use the abridged list of the 1938 revision of the International Classification of Disease. This list is comprehensive and has 44 categories. We omit any diseases that are not infectious or could be degenerative, such as "diseases of the heart" (Abridged List no. 24), and residual categories, such as "other infectious or parasitic diseases" (Abridged List no. 14). Syphilis (Abridged List no. 9) and puerperal fever or infection (Abridged List no. 35), which results from an infection after childbirth, are also omitted because their prevalence depends on sexual and fertility behaviors, which fall outside our focus here. Finally, we further omit diseases that were never major causes of death, even though they may have had serious effects on health (for example, acute poliomyelitis). In all, there are 15 infectious diseases for which we can obtain comparable cross-country data on deaths per 100,000 in 1940 (or 1939 or a close year). Of these 15, three are reviewed in more detail in the main text and 12 are covered in appendix B of our working paper. We have checked that the data we use in or around 1940 are not significantly affected by the impact of World War II;

this is generally possible, as in most cases some combination of United Nations sources yields numbers for at least two early years. For European countries affected by the war, we prefer data from 1937 or 1938, where available. Also, in our robustness checks, we drop all data from countries where Urlanis (2003) deems that war had a major demographic impact.

The classification of death rates by cause changed in 1948, and some of our data for 1950 and after are available only according to the abbreviated list of the 1948 revision of the International Classification of Disease. For example, the UN *Demographic Yearbook* (1954) reports cause of death in and around 1950 for some countries using the 1938 classification and for others using the 1948 classification. The terminology of the abridged list for the 1938 classification and the abbreviated list for the 1948 classification is as used in the *Demographic Yearbook*. Most of our 15 diseases can be tracked through this reclassification, but dysentery or diarrhea-related diseases cannot. Consequently, we have information for this category only for 1940, which is what we need to construct the predicted mortality instrument, but not sufficient for the zeroth-stage regressions in table 4.4 or for the global mortality instrument. In addition, there are not enough data to track yellow fever over time, so this disease is not included in table 4.4 or in the global mortality instrument.

For our data on cause of death in 1940, we start with the *Summary of International Vital Statistics, 1937–1944*, published by the Federal Security Agency (1947) of the U.S. government immediately after World War II. This source provides comparable comprehensive data on cause of death around 1940, as well as longer time series on the more important diseases (that is, death rates by country), primarily from League of Nations sources; however, it does not use all the available data (Federal Security Agency 1947: 2). For this reason, we fill gaps for 1940 using the original sources, which are national health statistics collected, cleaned, and republished between the wars by the League of Nations Health Organization (see Federal Security Agency 1947: 1–3); we also use information from the League of Nations and its direct postwar successors for earlier and later data, as discussed in appendix C of our working paper. A key issue is the area covered by the registration of deaths in various countries. Apart from the very richest countries in 1940, there was seldom universal registration of death, with a death certificate signed by a doctor. Consequently, some of the data are for major cities, while others are for all towns or for the entire population. Unfortunately, our sources do not always document clearly the precise coverage of the underlying data (for lower-income countries, the data almost certainly overweigh towns relative to rural areas, and diseases related to urban overcrowding are likely to be overrepresented). Nevertheless, our results are robust to using only the more reliable data.

The League of Nations established comparable international health statistics for a large number of countries, but to our knowledge never published a comprehensive retrospective of the data. Their first relevant publication was issue 7 of the *Annual Epidemiological Report*, which appeared in October

1923. But only from 1929 (covering the year 1927) did this publication include death rates from specific causes (League of Nations Health Organization 1929). Early issues of this publication are also referred to as Statistics of Notifiable Diseases. The first six issues focused on Eastern Europe, particularly typhus and malaria epidemics in Russia. For a comprehensive list of publications by the League of Nations on health, see Aufricht (1951: 176–77 in particular). For an explanation of the structure and purpose of the League of Nations Health Organization, see League of Nations Health Organization (1931). For more on the early development of internationally comparable health statistics, see Stocks (1950).

We use the death rates by disease for 1930 from the League of Nations Health Organization (1933). For 1940 we supplement the information discussed above with WHO (1951), which provides data for 1939–46, based on the League of Nations' work. For cholera, yellow fever, plague, and typhus, we have comparable data for 1940 but not 1930. For malaria in 1930, we use data from the League of Nations' Malaria Commission (League of Nations Health Organization 1932). We also checked our data against information on location of malaria in the 1940s from American Geographical Society (1951a). Data on deaths by disease for 1950 and 1960 are from the UN *Demographic Yearbook* for 1954, 1962, and 1966. Data for 1970 are from the UN *Demographic Yearbook* for 1974 and data for 1980 are from the UN *Demographic Yearbook* for 1985.

We further confirmed that our data do not miss major epidemics by reviewing every available interwar issue of the League of Nations' Weekly Epidemiological Record (WER). For example, for the distribution of cholera in 1938, see WER, March 3, 1938. For the distribution of smallpox in 1930, see WER, August 21, 1930; for 1938, see WER, March 3, 1938; for the early 1940s, see WER, January 3, 1946. For the prewar distribution of diphtheria, with a focus on Europe, see WER, December 21, 1939. For the distribution of plague in 1938, see WER, March 3, 1938. For more detail on the pre-1940 distribution of typhus, see WER, September 14, 1939. For the endemic yellow fever zone in 1951, see the supplement to the WER, September 25, 1952. We also confirm that our numbers are consistent with contemporary qualitative assessments, in particular in the annual reports of the League of Nations and World Health Organization. Further details on these checks and data sources are provided in our working paper.

Predicted mortality in 1940 is calculated by adding deaths per 100,000 from the 15 component diseases (for ease of exposition, we then convert this number to deaths per 100 of population). Preston (1980) points out that data on precise cause of death should be handled with care; for example, it is notoriously difficult to determine how many deaths are due directly and indirectly to malaria. While this is an important warning in general, our analysis is about changes in total predicted mortality from infectious disease, and because most of the global interventions were clustered in the late 1940s and early 1950s, this issue is less of a concern here.

Table 4A.1 Key Data for Base Sample

Country	Initial income	Year	Predicted mortality	Life expectancy	Population	GDP	GDP per capita
Argentina	Middle	1940	0.205	55.50	14,169	58,963	4,161
		1980	0.000	69.59	28,370	232,802	8,206
Australia	Rich	1940	0.232	66.80	7,042	43,422	6,166
		1980	0.000	74.44	14,616	210,642	14,412
Austria	Middle	1940	0.299	60.20	6,705	26,547	3,959
		1980	0.000	72.65	7,549	103,874	13,759
Bangladesh	Poor	1940	0.668	29.90	41,966	25,044	597
		1980	0.000	48.47	88,077	48,239	548
Belgium	Rich	1940	0.156	61.80	8,346	38,072	4,562
		1980	0.000	73.25	9,847	142,458	14,467
Brazil	Poor	1940	0.525	36.70	41,114	51,381	1,250
		1980	0.000	62.67	122,958	639,093	5,198
Canada	Rich	1940	0.121	64.20	11,688	62,744	5,368
		1980	0.000	74.72	24,593	397,814	16,176
Chile	Middle	1940	0.803	42.00	5,093	16,596	3,259
		1980	0.000	69.30	11,094	63,654	5,738
China	Poor	1940	0.291	43.90	518,770	291,603	562
		1980	0.000	65.31	981,235	1,046,781	1,067
Colombia	Middle	1940	0.535	37.90	9,174	17,386	1,895
		1980	0.000	65.91	26,583	113,375	4,265
Costa Rica	Middle	1940	0.667	49.30	620	1,093	1,763
		1980	0.000	72.70	2,299	11,290	4,911
Denmark	Rich	1940	0.121	65.50	3,832	19,606	5,116
		1980	0.000	74.29	5,123	78,010	15,227
Ecuador	Poor	1940	0.930	39.30	2,466	3,344	1,546
		1980	0.000	63.26	7,920	32,706	4,129
El Salvador	Poor	1940	0.970	32.50	1,630	1,811	1,111
		1980	0.000	57.10	4,566	10,748	2,354
Finland	Middle	1940	0.223	57.30	3,698	11,909	3,220
		1980	0.000	73.19	4,780	61,890	12,949
France	Middle	1940	0.279	60.00	41,000	165,729	4,042
		1980	0.000	74.25	53,870	813,763	15,106
Germany	Rich	1940	0.183	63.50	69,835	377,284	5,403
		1980	0.000	72.63	78,298	1,105,099	14,114
Greece	Middle	1940	0.409	54.40	7,280	16,183	2,223
		1980	0.000	74.36	9,643	86,505	8,971
Guatemala	Middle	1940	0.806	30.40	2,200	6,033	2,742
		1980	0.000	57.35	7,235	26,632	3,681
Honduras	Poor	1940	0.610	32.50	1,150	1,334	1,160
		1980	0.000	60.01	3,635	7,014	1,930

Country	Initial income	Year	Predicted mortality	Life expectancy	Population	GDP	GDP per capita
India	Poor	1940	1.126	30.00	321,565	265,455	686
		1980	0.000	54.39	679,000	637,202	938
Indonesia	Poor	1940	0.878	34.30	70,175	86,682	1,235
		1980	0.000	54.81	147,490	275,805	1,870
Ireland	Middle	1940	0.306	59.80	2,958	9,028	3,052
		1980	0.000	72.67	3,401	29,047	8,541
Italy	Middle	1940	0.816	58.70	44,341	155,424	3,505
		1980	0.000	73.92	56,451	742,299	13,149
Korea, Rep. of	Poor	1940	0.186	48.70	15,627	22,536	1,442
		1980	0.000	66.84	38,124	156,846	4,114
Malaysia	Poor	1940	0.317	42.60	5,434	6,945	1,278
		1980	0.000	66.87	13,764	50,333	3,657
Mexico	Middle	1940	0.621	43.60	20,393	37,767	1,852
		1980	0.000	66.76	68,686	431,983	6,289
Myanmar	Poor	1940	0.621	36.60	16,594	12,274	740
		1980	0.000	52.10	33,283	27,381	823
Netherlands	Rich	1940	0.180	67.40	8,879	42,898	4,831
		1980	0.000	75.72	14,144	207,979	14,705
New Zealand	Rich	1940	0.214	67.70	1,636	10,308	6,300
		1980	0.000	73.20	3,170	39,141	12,347
Nicaragua	Poor	1940	0.476	34.50	830	1,139	1,372
		1980	0.000	58.72	2,804	6,043	2,155
Norway	Middle	1940	0.214	67.30	2,973	12,152	4,088
		1980	0.000	75.74	4,086	61,811	15,129
Pakistan	Poor	1940	0.813	30.00	28,169	20,137	715
		1980	0.000	55.12	85,219	98,907	1,161
Panama	Middle	1940	0.595	42.40	697	1,199	1,721
		1980	0.000	70.12	1,956	9,961	5,091
Paraguay	Middle	1940	0.364	46.60	1,111	1,947	1,752
		1980	0.000	66.83	3,193	10,549	3,304
Peru	Middle	1940	0.832	40.60	6,298	11,483	1,823
		1980	0.000	60.38	17,295	72,723	4,205
Philippines	Poor	1940	0.976	47.30	16,585	26,326	1,587
		1980	0.000	61.09	50,940	121,012	2,376
Portugal	Middle	1940	0.623	50.30	7,675	12,396	1,615
		1980	0.000	71.39	9,778	78,655	8,044
Spain	Middle	1940	0.387	50.20	25,757	53,585	2,080
		1980	0.000	75.53	37,488	344,987	9,203
Sri Lanka	Poor	1940	0.617	42.30	6,134	7,673	1,251
		1980	0.000	68.20	14,900	27,550	1,849

Country	Initial income	Year	Predicted mortality	Life expectancy	Population	GDP	GDP per capita
Sweden	Rich	1940	0.125	66.70	6,356	30,873	4,857
		1980	0.000	75.86	8,310	124,130	14,937
Switzerland	Rich	1940	0.144	64.10	4,226	27,032	6,397
		1980	0.000	75.85	6,385	119,909	18,779
Thailand	Poor	1940	0.506	42.60	15,513	12,820	826
		1980	0.000	63.60	47,026	120,116	2,554
United Kingdom	Rich	1940	0.270	65.00	48,226	330,638	6,856
		1980	0.000	73.78	56,314	728,224	12,931
United States	Rich	1940	0.132	63.80	132,637	929,737	7,010
		1980	0.000	73.66	227,726	4,230,558	18,577
Uruguay	Middle	1940	0.344	56.50	1,965	7,193	3,661
		1980	0.000	70.43	2,920	19,205	6,577
Venezuela, R. B. de	Middle	1940	0.496	33.90	3,784	15,307	4,045
		1980	0.000	68.34	14,768	149,735	10,139

Source: Authors' calculations.

Note: Life expectancy is at birth, population is in thousands, and GDP is in millions (1990 international Geary-Khamis dollars). Predicted mortality is as defined in the text; units are per 100 per year.

References

Acemoglu, Daron, and Simon Johnson. 2006. "Disease and Development: The Effect of Life Expectancy on Economic Growth." Working Paper 12269 (June), National Bureau of Economic Research, Cambridge, MA. http://www.nber.org/papers/w12269.

Alilio, Martin S., Ib C. Bygbjerg, and Joel G. Breman. 2004. "Are Multilateral Malaria Research and Controls Programs the Most Successful? Lessons from the Past 100 Years in Africa." *American Journal of Tropical Medicine and Hygiene* 71 (supplement 2, August): 268–78.

Alleyne, George A. O., and Daniel Cohen. 2002. "The Report of Working Group I of the Commission on Macroeconomics and Health." WHO, Commission on Macroeconomics and Health, Geneva (April).

American Geographical Society. 1951a. *Distribution of Cholera, 1816–1950.* New York: American Geographical Society.

———. 1951b. *World Distribution of Malaria Vectors.* New York: American Geographical Society.

———. 1951c. *World Distribution of Plague.* New York: American Geographical Society.

———. 1951d. *World Distribution of Rickettial Diseases: Louse-Borne and Flea-Borne Typhus.* New York: American Geographical Society.

Anderson, Theodore W., and Cheng Hsiao. 1982. "Formulation and Estimation of Dynamic Models Using Panel Data." *Journal of Econometrics* 18 (January): 47–82.

Arellano, Manuel, and Stephen R. Bond. 1991. "Some Specification Tests for Panel Data: Monte Carlo Evidence and an Application to Employment Equations." *Review of Economic Studies* 58 (April): 277–98.

Arndt, Channing, and Jeffrey D. Lewis. 2000. "The Macro Implications of HIV/AIDS in South Africa: A Preliminary Assessment." *South African Journal of Economics* 68 (December): 380–92.

Arriaga, Eduardo E., and Kingsley Davis. 1969. "The Pattern of Mortality Change in Latin America." *Demography* 6 (August): 223–42.

Ashraf, Quamrul, Ashley Lester, and David Weil. 2007. "When Does Improving Health Raise GDP?" Unpublished manuscript, Brown University, Providence, RI (May).

Aufricht, Hans. 1951. *Guide to League of Nations Publications: A Bibliographical Survey of the Work of the League, 1920–1947.* New York: Columbia University Press.

Becker, Gary S., Tomas J. Philipson, and Rodrigo R. Soares. 2005. "The Quantity and Quality of Life and the Evolution of World Inequality." *American Economic Review* 95 (March): 277–91.

Behrman, Jere R., and Mark R. Rosenzweig. 2004. "The Returns to Birthweight." *Review of Economics and Statistics* 86 (May): 586–601.

Bell, Clive, Shantanyanan Devarajan, and Hans Gersbach. 2003. "The Long-Run Economic Costs of AIDS: Theory and an Application to South Africa." Working Paper (June), World Bank, Washington, DC.

Bengtsson, Tommy, Cameron Campbell, James Z. Lee, and others. 2004. *Life under Pressure: Mortality and Living Standards in Europe and Asia, 1700–1900.* Cambridge, MA: MIT Press.

Bhattarcharya, S. K. 1994. "History of Development of Oral Rehydration Therapy." *Indian Journal of Public Health* 38 (April-June): 39–43.

Bleakley, Hoyt. 2003. "Disease and Development: Evidence from the American South." *Journal of European Economic Association* 1 (April-May): 376–86.

———. 2007. "Disease and Development: Evidence from Hookworm Eradication in the American South." *Quarterly Journal of Economics* 122 (February): 73–117.

Bleakley, Hoyt, and Fabian Lange. 2006. "Chronic Disease Burden and the Interaction of Education, Fertility, and Growth." Unpublished manuscript, University of California, San Diego.

Bloom, David E., and David Canning. 2005. "Health and Economic Growth: Reconciling the Micro and Macro Evidence." Working Paper (February), Stanford University, Freeman Spogli Institute for International Economics, Palo Alto, CA.

Bloom, David E., and Jeffrey D. Sachs. 1998. "Geography, Demography, and Economic Growth in Africa." *Brookings Papers on Economic Activity* 2: 207–95.

Bradley, D. J. 1992. "Malaria: Old Infections, Changing Epidemiology." *Health Transition Review* 2 (supplement): 137–52.

Caldwell, J. C. 1986. "Routes to Low Mortality in Poor Countries." *Population and Development Review* 12 (June): 171–220.

Carr-Saunders, A. M. 1936. *World Population: Past Growth and Present Trends.* Oxford: Clarendon Press.

Chain, Sir Ernst. 1980. "A Short History of the Penicillin Discovery from Fleming's Early Observations in 1929 to the Present Time." In *The History of Antibiotics*, ed. John Parascandola. Madison, WI: American Institute of the History of Pharmacy.

Cliff, Andrew, Peter Haggett, and Matthew Smallman-Raynor. 2004. *World Atlas of Epidemic Diseases*. Oxford: Arnold Publishers/Oxford University Press.

Conybeare, John. 1948. "The Effects on Mortality of Recent Advances in Treatment." *Journal of the Institute of Actuaries* 74: 57–81.

Cutler, David, Angus Deaton, and Adriana Lleras-Muney. 2006. "The Determinants of Mortality." *Journal of Economic Perspectives* 20 (Summer): 97–120.

Cutler, David, and Grant Miller. 2005. "The Role of Public Health Improvements in Health Advances: The 20th Century United States." *Demography* 42 (February): 1–22.

———. 2006. "Water, Water Everywhere: Municipal Finance and Water Supply in American Cities." In *Corruption and Reform: Lessons from America's Economic History*, ed. Edward L. Glaeser and Claudia Goldin. Chicago: University of Chicago Press.

Davis, Kingsley. 1956. "The Amazing Decline of Mortality in Underdeveloped Areas." *American Economic Review* 46 (May): 305–18.

Deaton, Angus. 2003. "Health, Inequality, and Economic Development." *Journal of Economic Literature* 41 (March): 113–58.

———. 2004. "Health in an Age of Globalization." In *Brookings Trade Forum*, ed. Susan Collins and Carol Graham. Washington, DC: Brookings Institution Press.

Desowitz, Robert S. 1991. *The Malaria Capers: More Tales of Parasites and People; Research and Reality*. New York: W. W. Norton.

Easterlin, Richard. 1999. "How Beneficent Is the Market? A Look at the Modern History of Mortality." *European Review of Economic History* 3 (December): 257–94.

Expert Committee on Malaria. 1947. "Extract from the Report on the First Session." *Bulletin of the World Health Organization* 1 (1): 21–28.

Federal Security Agency. 1947. *Summary of International Vital Statistics, 1937–1944*. Washington, DC: U.S. Public Health Service, National Office of Vital Statistics.

Fogel, Robert William. 1986. "Nutrition and the Decline in Mortality since 1700: Some Preliminary Findings." In *Long-term Factors in American Economic Growth*, ed. Stanley L. Engerman and Robert E. Gallman, 439–55. Chicago: University of Chicago Press.

———. 2004. *The Escape from Hunger and Premature Death, 1700–2100*. New York: Cambridge University Press.

Forston, Jane. 2006. "Mortality Risks in Human Capital Investment: The Impact of HIV/AIDS in Sub-Saharan Africa." Unpublished manuscript, Princeton University, Princeton, NJ.

Gallup, John Luke, and Jeffrey D. Sachs. 2001. "The Economic Burden of Malaria." *American Journal of Tropical Medicine and Hygiene* 64 (1 supplement, January): 85–96.

Galor, Oded. 2005. "From Stagnation to Growth: Unified Growth Theory." In *Handbook of Economic Growth*, ed. Philippe Aghion and Steven Durlauf, 171–294. Amsterdam: Elsevier, North-Holland.

Galor, Oded, and David Weil. 2000. "Population, Technology, and Growth: From Malthusian Stagnation to the Demographic Transition and Beyond." *American Economic Review* 90 (September): 806–28.

Gwatkin, Davidson R. 1980. "Indications of Change in Developing Country Mortality Trends: The End of an Era?" *Population and Development Review* 6 (December): 615–44.

Hansen, Gary D., and Edward C. Prescott. 2002. "Malthus to Solow." *American Economic Review* 92 (September): 1205–17.

Hoff, Brent, and Carter Smith III. 2000. *Mapping Epidemics: A Historical Atlas of Disease*. New York: Franklin Watts.

Kalemli-Ozcan, Sebnem. 2002. "Does the Mortality Decline Promote Economic Growth?" *Journal of Economic Growth* 7 (December): 411–39.

———. 2006. "AIDS, Reversal of the Demographic Transition, and Economic Development: Evidence from Africa." Unpublished manuscript, University of Houston.

Kalemli-Ozcan, Sebnem, Harl E. Ryder, and David Weil. 2000. "Mortality Decline, Human Capital Investment, and Economic Growth." *Journal of Development Economics* 62 (June): 1–23.

Keers, R. Y. 1978. *Pulmonary Tuberculosis: A Journey Down the Centuries*. London: Bailliere Tindall.

Kelley, Allen C. 1988. "Economic Consequences of Population Change in the Third World." *Journal of Economic Literature* 26 (December): 1685–728.

Kiple, Kenneth F. 1993. *The Cambridge World History of Human Disease*. Cambridge, U.K.: Cambridge University Press.

Knaul, Felicia Marie. 2000. "Health, Nutrition, and Wages: Age at Menarche and Earnings in Mexico." In *Wealth from Health: Linking Social Investments to Earnings in Latin America*, ed. William D. Savedoff and T. Paul Schultz. Washington, DC: Inter-American Development Bank.

Kuznets, Simon. 1960. "Quantitative Aspects of the Economic Growth of Nations. V. Capital Formation Proportions: International Comparisons for Recent Years." *Economic Development and Cultural Change* 8 (pt. 2, July): 1–96.

Lancaster, Henry O. 1990. *Expectations of Life: A Study in the Demography, Statistics, and History of World Mortality*. New York: Springer-Verlag.

Langford, C. M. 1996. "Reasons for the Decline in Mortality in Sri Lanka Immediately after the Second World War: A Re-examination of the Evidence." *Health Transition Review* 6 (April): 3–23.

League of Nations Health Organization. 1929. *Statistics of Notifiable Diseases for the Year 1927*. Geneva: League of Nations Health Organization, Information Section.

———. 1931. *History of International Health Organization Documents*. Geneva: League of Nations Health Organization, Information Section. http://whqlibdoc.who.int/hist/chronicles/health_org_1931.pdf.

————. 1932. *Enquiry into the Quinine Requirements of Malarial Countries and the World Prevalence of Malaria.* C.H./Malaria/185, Publications III, Health (December). Geneva: League of Nations Health Organization, Information Section.

————. 1933. *Statistics for Notifiable Diseases for the Year 1931.* Annual Report 16. Geneva: League of Nations, Health Organization.

Lee, Kelley, Sue Collinson, Gill Walt, and Lucy Gilson. 1996. "Who Should Be Doing What in International Health: A Confusion of Mandates in the United Nations?" *British Medical Journal* 312 (February): 302–07.

Lorentzon, Peter, John McMillan, and Romain Wacziarg. 2005. "Death and Development." Working Paper 11620 (September), National Bureau of Economic Research, Cambridge, MA.

Maddison, Angus. 2001. *The World Economy: A Millennial Perspective.* Paris: OECD, Development Centre Studies.

————. 2003. *The World Economy: Historical Statistics.* Paris: OECD, Development Centre Studies.

Mandle, Jay R. 1970. "The Decline in Mortality in British Guiana, 1911–1960." *Demography* 7 (August): 301–15.

McKeown, Thomas. 1976. *The Modern Rise of Population.* New York: Academic Press.

Miguel, Edward, and Michael Kremer. 2004. "Worms: Identifying Impacts on Education and Health in the Presence of Treatment Externalities." *Econometrica* 72 (January): 159–217.

National Academy of Sciences. 1970. *The Life Sciences.* Washington, DC: Committee on Research in Life Sciences, Committee on Science and Public Policy.

Office International d'Hygiene Publique. 1933. *Vingt-cinq ans d'activite de l'Office International d'Hygiene Publique.* Paris.

Omran, Abdel R. 1971. "The Epidemiologic Transition." *Milbank Memorial Fund Quarterly* 49 (December): 509–38.

Pampana, E. J. 1954. "Changing Strategy in Malaria Control." *Bulletin of the World Health Organization* 11 (4-5): 513–20.

Preston, Samuel H. 1975. "The Changing Relation between Mortality and Level of Economic Development." *Population Studies* 29 (July): 231–48.

————. 1980. "Causes and Consequences of Mortality Declines in Less Developed Countries during the Twentieth Century." In *Population and Economic Change in Developing Countries*, ed. Richard A. Easterlin. Chicago: University of Chicago Press.

Preston, Samuel H., and Verne E. Nelson. 1974. "Structure and Change in Causes of Death: An International Summary." *Population Studies* 28 (March): 19–51.

Pritchett, Lant, and Lawrence H. Summers. 1996. "Wealthier Is Healthier." *Journal of Human Resources* 31 (Autumn): 841–68.

Riley, James C. 2001. *Rising Life Expectancy: A Global History.* Cambridge, U.K.: Cambridge University Press.

Schultz, T. Paul. 2002. "Wage Gains Associated with Height as a Form of Health Human Capital." *American Economic Review* 92 (May): 349–53.

Soares, Rodrigo R. 2005. "Mortality Reductions, Educational Attainment, and Fertility Choice." *American Economic Review* 95 (July): 780–95.

Stock, James H., Jonathan H. Wright, and Motohiro Yogo. 2002. "A Survey of Weak Instruments and Weak Identification in Generalized Method of Moments." *Journal of Economics and Statistics* 20 (October): 518–29.

Stocks, Percy. 1950. "Contributions of Statistics to World Health." *Bulletin of World Health Organization* 2 (4): 731–41.

Stolnitz, George J. 1955. "A Century of International Mortality Trends: I." *Population Studies* 9 (July): 24–55.

Strauss, John, and Duncan Thomas. 1998. "Health, Nutrition, and Economic Development." *Journal of Economics Literature* 36 (June): 766–817.

United Nations. 2000. *Demographic Yearbook: Historical Supplement 1948–1997.* CD-ROM, New York and Geneva: United Nations.

———. Various years (1949–85). *Demographic Yearbook.* Lake Success, New York.

Urlanis, B. 2003. *Wars and Population.* Honolulu: University Press of the Pacific, reprint of 1971 ed.

Valentine, F. C. O., and R. A. Shooter. 1954. *Findlay's Recent Advances in Chemotherapy.* Vol. 3: *Antibiotics.* New York: Blakiston Company.

Weil, David N. 2007. "Accounting for the Effect of Health on Growth." *Quarterly Journal of Economics* 122 (August): 1265–306.

Wooldridge, Jeffery M. 2002. *Econometric Analysis of Cross Section and Panel Data.* Cambridge, MA: MIT Press.

WHO (World Health Organization). 1951. *Annual Epidemiological and Vital Statistics, 1939–46.* Geneva: WHO.

———. 1998. *Milestones on the Way towards the World Health Organization.* Geneva: WHO. http://www.who.int/archives/who50/en/milestones.htm.

———. 2001. *Macroeconomics and Health: Investing in Health for Economic Development.* Geneva: WHO. http://www3.who.int/whosis/cmh.

———. 2004. *Fifty Years of the World Health Organization in the Western Pacific Region.* Report to the Regional Committee for the Western Pacific. Geneva: WHO.

Young, Alwyn. 2005. "The Gift of the Dying: The Tragedy of AIDS and the Welfare of Future African Generations." *Quarterly Journal of Economics* 120 (May): 423–66.

CHAPTER 5
Disease and Development: Evidence from Hookworm Eradication in the American South

Hoyt Bleakley

The importance of the burden of tropical disease in impeding economic development has received considerable attention in recent years. The establishment and maintenance of an environment free of infectious disease is an important public good. The very nature of the transmission mechanism of such diseases implies a manifest externality. This might serve as a rationale for collective action to reduce the incidence of infectious disease. However, little is known about the long-term benefits of such actions, and therefore there is nothing to compare with the short-term costs.

Reprinted with permission from Hoyt Bleakley, "Disease and Development: Evidence from Hookworm Eradication in the American South," *The Quarterly Journal of Economics* (The MIT Press) 122, no. 1 (February 2007): 73–117. © 2007 by the President and Fellows of Harvard College and the Massachusetts Institute of Technology.

This is a revised version of the first chapter of the author's doctoral dissertation (Bleakley 2002b), which was partially summarized in Bleakley (2003). The author thanks Daron Acemoglu, Joshua Angrist, David Autor, Gary Becker, Eli Berman, Patrick Buckley, Garland Brinkley, Dora Costa, Mark Duggan, Michael Greenstone, Jonathan Guryan, Christian Hansen, Gordon Hanson, Lakshmi Iyer, Simon Johnson, Lawrence Katz, Fabian Lange, Mark Lewis, Robin McKnight, Derek Neal, John Strauss, Robert Triest, Burton Weisbrod, Jonathan Zinman, several anonymous referees, and seminar participants at Boston University, the University of Chicago, Harvard University, Illinois State University, the Massachusetts Institute of Technology, Northwestern University, Princeton University, the University of California, Berkeley, University of California, San Diego, the University of Southern California, and Yale University for useful comments, and Michael Pisa, Tareq Rashidi, and Elizabeth Stone for excellent research assistance.

Unfortunately, simple correlations of public health and economic outcomes are unlikely to measure the causal effect because public health is endogenous. Indeed, it is likely a normal good: rich areas, purchase more of it. To measure the contribution of a disease-free environment, we need to analyze plausibly exogenous improvements in public health. Targeted public health interventions are a possible source of such variation.

This chapter focuses on one specific intervention targeted toward hookworm disease in the American South. The hookworm eradication campaign (circa 1910–15) began soon after (a) the discovery that a variety of health problems among Southerners could be attributed to the disease and (b) the donation by John D. Rockefeller of a substantial sum to the campaign. The Rockefeller Sanitary Commission (RSC) surveyed infection rates in the affected areas and found that an average of 40 percent of school-age children in the American South suffered from hookworm infection. The RSC then sponsored treatment dispensaries that traveled these areas, providing deworming medications and educating local physicians and the public about prevention. Follow-up studies indicate that the campaign brought about a substantial immediate reduction in hookworm disease and, furthermore, that the seeds were sown for preventing its return.

The introduction of this treatment (broadly defined) combines with the cross-area differences in pretreatment infection rates to form the basis of my identification strategy. As the RSC surveys demonstrated, different areas of the country had distinct incidences of the hookworm disease. Areas with high infection rates had more to gain from the newly available treatments, whereas areas with little hookworm disease did not. This heterogeneity allows for a treatment-control strategy.

Moreover, the eradication campaign began—and was ultimately successful—because of critical innovations to knowledge. I argue that such innovations were neither related to nor in anticipation of the future growth prospects of the affected areas and therefore should not be thought of as endogenous in this context. For example, the discovery of the transmission mechanism for hookworm was made by a European doctor whose initial experimental evidence consisted of accidentally infecting himself while diagnosing a patient. At that time, hookworm infection in the American South was not even recognized as a problem.

Hookworm disease, while rarely fatal, has potentially severe chronic symptoms. The hookworm is a parasite that lodges itself in the victim's digestive system and burrows into the intestinal wall, tapping into the host's bloodstream. Listlessness, anemia, and stunting of growth are common symptoms among infected children. Because schoolwork is an energy-intensive activity for children, it is plausible that hookworm disease would depress the returns to human capital investment.

After hookworm eradication, school enrollment, regular school attendance, and literacy increased markedly in counties that had previously suffered from high rates of hookworm infection. This is true in absolute terms as well as relative to comparison counties that had lower levels of hookworm infection. I find this result using either a two-period double difference or a multiperiod setup that allows for differential trends across areas. Furthermore, the conclusion is robust to controlling for a variety of alternative hypotheses, including crop-specific shocks, demographic shifts, the near-simultaneous reduction in malaria, parental socioeconomic status, and certain policy changes. Estimates using indirect least squares imply that a child infected with hookworm had a 20 percent lower probability of school enrollment, although it is impossible to rule out the possibility that the intervention had effects through channels besides measured hookworm infection. Replicating this design using state-of-birth-level variation in hookworm infection yields similar estimates for these variables, although the results for enrollment are imprecise.

Next, I present analogous results for adults as a specification check. A priori we would expect that adults would be substantially less affected by the hookworm eradication campaign because adults were substantially less likely to have hookworm (RSC 1911; Smillie and Augustine 1925). Moreover, human capital investments not made in childhood due to hookworm would be water under the bridge once the disease environment improved. However, if the results for children were due to changes in income or migration patterns, we would see changes in adult outcomes as well. Instead, I find evidence that there was little contemporaneous impact on adults, measured along several important dimensions: literacy, labor force participation, and occupation.

I also follow up on the cohorts that potentially benefited from hookworm eradication during childhood. Here I contrast individuals based on (a) the pre-eradication hookworm burden in their state of birth and (b) their year of birth relative to the RSC. Cohorts more exposed to the eradication efforts went on to earn substantially higher incomes as adults. This pattern is seen using data on wage and salary incomes from the 1940 census. Again using indirect least squares (and subject to the same caution as above), I estimate that being infected with hookworm throughout childhood led to a reduction in adult wages of approximately 40 percent. I also consider occupational proxies of income, which are defined over a broad range of census years, and show that the shift in the hookworm-income relationship coincided with childhood exposure to the eradication campaign, rather than with some preexisting trend or autoregressive process. No statistically significant long-term effect of hookworm is found on the years of schooling (in accordance with the imprecise result for enrollment using state variation), but both literacy and returns to schooling increased with exposure to hookworm eradication.

The rest of this chapter is organized as follows. The first section describes the symptoms and history of the disease, in particular how the circumstances of the discovery of the hookworm problem in the South and the subsequent antihookworm campaign lend themselves to a strategy for identifying the effect of hookworm. The second section describes the data employed, the third and fourth present the contemporaneous results using sequential cross sections, and the fifth section presents the long-term follow-up. The last section summarizes the findings and suggests areas of future study.

Hookworm and the Rockefeller Sanitary Commission

Hookworm is an intestinal parasite that lodges itself in the human intestine and absorbs nutrients from the victim's bloodstream. The symptoms of hookworm infection (*uncinaria*) are lethargy and anemia. In rare cases, the anemia can become so severe as to cause death. The life cycle of the hookworm is dependent on unsanitary conditions. The nematodes lay their eggs in the intestine, but the larvae are passed out of the digestive system in feces. Hookworm is therefore transmitted through skin contact with infected fecal matter. The larvae then burrow their way in through the skin. The lifespan of a hookworm is much shorter than that of a human, and so continuous reinfection is required to generate any sustained worm load.

There are two angles for managing hookworm: treatment and prevention. The treatment consists of simply taking a deworming medicine. Preventative measures include limiting skin contact with polluted soil (through the use of shoes, for example) and dealing with excrement in ways that minimize soil pollution in the first place (for example, the use of sanitary latrines).

The Eradication Campaign

The Rockefeller Sanitary Commission for the Eradication of Hookworm Disease was formed in 1910 with the donation of $1 million by John D. Rockefeller. Some years before, an American doctor (Charles W. Stiles) had recognized hookworm symptoms in Southerners. Through intermediaries, Dr. Stiles had convinced Rockefeller that taking on hookworm was a good foray into large-scale charity. The commission began by conducting surveys of hookworm infection rates among children across the region. It surveyed more than 600 counties in the South and found hookworm infection to be over 40 percent among children.

Soon after, the treatment campaign began. First, the RSC sent teams of health care workers to counties to administer and dispense deworming treatments free of charge. RSC dispensaries visited a large and mostly contiguous fraction of the South, and the campaign treated more than 400,000 individuals with deworming medication.[1] Second, the RSC sought to educate doctors, teachers, and the general public on how to recognize the symptoms of hookworm disease so that fewer cases would go untreated. Another part of this publicity campaign included education about the importance of hygiene, especially with regard to the use of sanitary privies. In this period, oftentimes even public buildings such as schools and churches did not have such hygienic facilities. Follow-up surveys conducted afterward showed a substantial decline in hookworm infection (RSC 1915). Although the stated goal of eradication was not achieved, the hookworm infection rate of the region dropped by more than half, and fewer extreme cases of the disease went unnoticed and untreated.

---

1   Thymol, taken orally, was the recommended treatment of the time.

Because the deworming treatments are short-term solutions, eradication requires (a) sustained monitoring (and treatment as needed) and (b) a reduction in the probability of reinfection. Follow-up efforts by private and government actors likely played a key role in consolidating the gains from the RSC campaign and continuing the progress toward complete eradication.[2] State governments ramped up their funding of antihookworm campaigns as the RSC was winding down. Local and state governments eventually took over some of its activities. The successor to the RSC, the Rockefeller Foundation's International Health Board (IHB), continued to be involved at a lower level of funding. The IHB sponsored a handful of demonstration projects of the "intensive method," which combined the deworming treatments and publicity campaigns of the RSC with technical assistance in building latrines at homes and public buildings. The state boards of health largely adopted this method and applied it to a degree throughout their jurisdictions. Harder to measure, but of considerable importance, the hookworm problem entered into the public consciousness.

Testimonials Following the Campaign

Anecdotal evidence suggests that the RSC had an impact on human capital. Periodically, educators would write the commission thanking it for its efforts and describing the improvements following hookworm treatment. The following letter is from the school board of Varnado, Louisiana (RSC 1912):

> As a result of your treatment for hookworm in our school, we find that children who were ranking fifth and sixth in their classes now rank second and third. Their lessons are not so hard for them: they pay better attention in class and they have more energy.... In short, we have here in our school-rooms today about 120 bright, rosy-faced children, whereas had you not been sent here to treat them we would have had that many pale-faced, stupid children.

Farmer (1970) relates the following testimonials from the same period:

> Teachers, school officials, and editors continued to be amazed at the difference in children after treatment for hookworm disease. A. J. Caldwell, Principal of Hammond High School in Louisiana, wrote that there was a decided improvement in the students in his school. One girl, who was in the fifth grade and did not attend school regularly because she was so pale and weak, started regaining her color and strength after treatment and finished the school term at the top of her class. C. C. Wright, Superintendent of Schools in Wilkes County, North Carolina, was an ardent supporter of the eradication program after examination of the pupils in his district revealed over 50 percent infection. Treatment cured

---

2   An interesting episode for comparison comes from Puerto Rico. Around the same time as the RSC, a commission from the U.S. Army sponsored treatment and education campaigns throughout that Caribbean island. Large gains against hookworm were realized immediately after the campaign. Unfortunately, the colonial government provided very little follow-up support, and these gains had almost completely disappeared a decade later. Moreover, recent work in Kenya by Kremer and Miguel (2004) suggests that the initial impulse provided by short-term injections of medication and publicity may have few long-term benefits. This chapter is not a guide to how to design a deworming program, and thus I do not take a stand on the relative merits of medications versus publicity versus sanitation. Rather, I take the reduction in hookworm as given and evaluate the socioeconomic consequences.

the majority of these cases and the quality of performance in the county schools was raised considerably.

Typical of school officials' attitude was that of W. H. Smith, state supervisor of rural schools in Mississippi, who was thoroughly convinced that the economic prosperity of the people and the progress of educational development of the state depended largely on the successful eradication of the hookworm. The mental and physical growth of hundreds of children was evident. Smith asked for expansion of the program so that the thousands of children who were still suffering from mental and physical retardation might be saved.

And a report (RSC 1915) describes a Tidewater, Virginia, community's experience of "how the treatment of these children had transformed the school":

> Children who were listless and dull are now active and alert; children who could not study a year ago are not only studying now, but are finding joy in learning. These children were born of anemic parents; were themselves infected in infancy; for the first time in their lives their cheeks show the glow of health. With this has come a new light to the eye, a new spring to the step, a new outlook on life. All this shows itself in a new spirit in the school.... Some of the 15 children who had never attended school, having been treated, have come in during the year. Others have declared their intention to enter in the fall.

Identification Strategy

The first factor for identifying the effect of the hookworm eradication campaign is that different areas of the South had distinct incidences of the disease. Hookworm larvae were better equipped to survive in areas with sandy soil and a warm climate. Broadly, this meant that the residents of the coastal plain of the South were much more vulnerable to infection than residents of the piedmont or mountain regions. Populations in areas with high (preexisting) infection rates were in a position to benefit from the newly available treatments, whereas areas with low prevalence were not. This heterogeneity allows for a treatment-control strategy.

Second, the initiation of the campaign by the RSC was largely a function of factors external to the southern states.[3] The eradication campaign was made possible by critical innovations to knowledge: understanding how the disease worked and, more important, recognizing its presence. This contrasts with explanations that might have troublesome endogeneity problems, such as changes in government spending or positive income shocks in the infected areas. But even with the knowledge of the hookworm problem, there would have been formidable obstacles to taking action. The public health infrastructure of this period was extremely limited. Rockefeller's donation was an important precondition for attacking the problem.

Third, the antihookworm campaign achieved considerable progress against the disease in less than a decade. This is a sudden change on historical time scales. Moreover, I examine outcomes over a 50-year time span, which is unquestionably long relative to the five-year RSC intervention.

---

3 The historical presentation in this section draws heavily on the work of Ettling (1981).

These factors combine to form the central variable in this study:

$$(\text{Pretreatment Infection Rate})_j \times (\text{Indicator for Posttreatment})_t.$$

More compactly, call this variable $H_j^{\text{pre}} \times \text{Post}_t$, where j indexes the geographic area and t indicates the year. The variable H_j^{pre} denotes the level of hookworm infection among school-age children in area j at the time of the RSC's initial survey, and Post_t is a dummy variable indicating whether year t is later than the active years of the RSC campaign (1910–15).

I compare the evolution of outcomes (such as investment in human capital) across counties with distinct hookworm infection rates, in order to assess the contribution of the eradication campaign to the observed changes. Estimating equation 5.1 measures the reduced-form differences by pre-eradication hookworm for some outcome Y_{ijt} for person i in area j at time t.[4]

$$Y_{ijt} = \beta(H_j^{\text{pre}} \times \text{Post}_t) + \delta_t + \delta_j + X_{ijt}\Gamma + \varepsilon_{ijt}, \qquad (5.1)$$

in which Y_{ijt} is the outcome of interest, δ_t are time dummies, δ_j are geographic fixed effects, and X_{ijt} is some vector of individual-level controls.[5]

How realistic is the assumption that areas with high infection rates benefited more from the eradication campaign? Follow-up surveys found a decrease in hookworm infection of 30 percentage points across the infected areas of the South. Such a dramatic drop in the region's average infection rate, barring a drastic reversal in the pattern of hookworm incidence across the region, would have had the supposed effect of reducing infection rates *more* in highly infected areas than in areas with moderate infection rates. Figure 5.1 presents data on this issue.[6] The basic assumption here—that areas where hookworm was highly endemic saw a greater drop in infection than areas with low infection rates—is borne out across states and across counties.

---

4   All of the estimates of this equation are calculated using ordinary least squares regressions.

5   The model is derived as follows. For individual i, in area j, in year t, we start with an individual-level model with individual infection data and linear effects of hookworm:

$$Y_{ijt} = \alpha H_{ijt} + \delta_j + \delta_t + X_{ijt}\Gamma + \overline{\varepsilon}_{ijt},$$

where H_{ijt} is a dummy for being infected. Individual infection data are not available, so the hookworm infection rate, H_{ijt}, is replaced with its ecological (that is, aggregate) counterpart:

$$Y_{ijt} = \widetilde{\alpha} H_{jt} + \delta_j + \delta_t + X_{ijt}\Gamma + \overline{\varepsilon}_{ijt}.$$

(This equation can equally be run in aggregate form entirely, and, when estimated, it gives very similar results to those found here.) For the instrument $H_j^{\text{pre}} \times \text{Post}_t$, the reduced form of this system is equation 5.1. Alternatively, one could have written the individual-level model with separate terms for individual and aggregate infection variables, the latter reflecting some spillover from peer infection to own human capital. But both of these effects would be subsumed into the $\widetilde{\alpha}$ coefficient on the ecological infection rate, and it is this composite coefficient that I seek to measure in the present study. I have also experimented with nonlinear specifications, but no robust pattern emerges for the curvature of the response to hookworm. I report linear specifications below.

6   This figure embodies the first-stage relationship. Consider the aggregate first-stage equation:

$$H_{jt} = \gamma(H_j^{\text{pre}} \times \text{Post}_t) + \delta_j + \delta_t + \eta_{jt}.$$

This equation can be written in first-differenced form and evaluated in the post-RSC period:

$$\Delta H_j^{\text{post}} = \gamma H_j^{\text{pre}} + \text{constant} + v_{jt},$$

an equation that relates the observable variables graphed in figure 5.1.

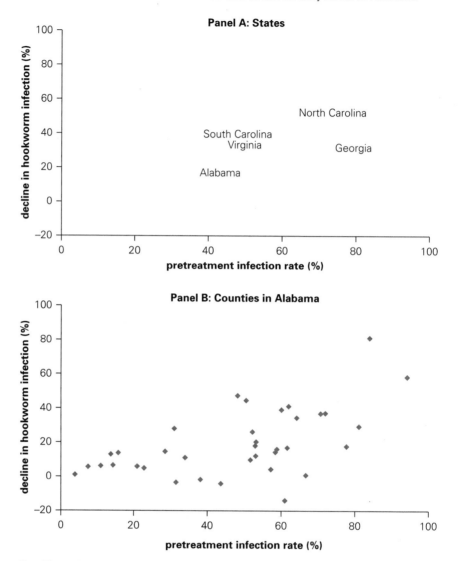

Figure 5.1 Hookworm Infection Rates Before and After Treatment at the State Level in Select Southern States and at the County Level in Alabama

Panel A: States

Panel B: Counties in Alabama

Note: The *y* axis displays the decrease in hookworm infection after intervention, as measured by follow-up surveys. The *x* axis is the pretreatment hookworm infection rate, as measured by the Rockefeller Sanitary Commission. Panel A displays data at the state level, as reported by Jacocks (1924). Panel B contains data from counties in Alabama, as reported by Havens and Castles (1930). Both follow-up surveys are from the early 1920s. The average number of children examined per country exceeds 450 in both studies.

Related Studies

Several pieces of contemporaneous evidence also complement the results from this study. Summarizing evidence from randomized trials in developing countries, Dickson and others (2000) find mixed evidence of the effect of hookworm infection on schooling, whereas Miguel and Kremer (2004) estimate the impact to be strong and positive using an experiment in Kenya. Miguel and Kremer argue that infection spillovers contaminated the earlier mixed results. Specifically, previous studies often randomized *within* schools, but failed to deal with the reinfection problem. As a result, they argue, follow-up surveys often found limited effects; no increase in school attendance was observed because there was little persistent difference in infection rates between control and treatment groups. (Philipson 2000 also discusses this evaluation issue in a general context.) Small-scale interventions that do not manage reinfection are therefore less likely to succeed. The RSC intervention was of such a scale that it brought about large reductions in hookworm disease in entire areas, and these gains were further consolidated through improvements in sanitation. In the context of economic development, it is precisely such a large and persistent reduction in disease burden that we would wish to consider.

Several other recent studies consider the early-twentieth-century reduction in tropical diseases in the American South. While childhood effects are the focus of this chapter, Brinkley (1994) examines the role that hookworm played in agricultural productivity. He finds a negative conditional correlation between hookworm infection and agricultural income per capita, although he does not specifically use the RSC intervention to identify this relationship. Bleakley (2002a) examines the interaction between malaria and hookworm. Bleakley and Lange (2004) consider the hookworm-related increase in returns to schooling in a quantity-quality model and examine the fertility behavior of households in response to hookworm eradication.

Data and Descriptive Statistics

This study links aggregate data on hookworm infection with individual socioeconomic data. Table 5.1 contains summary statistics of various outcomes. Because county boundaries change, I use aggregated county groupings, or "state economic areas" (SEAs), as the geographic unit.

The hookworm infection rates were computed by the Rockefeller Sanitary Commission for more than 550 counties across the South. The data collection took place between 1910 and 1914 (at a single point in time for each county), and the summary statistics were constructed from samples of school-age children in each county.[7] The RSC surveys measured an unweighted average infection rate across SEAs of 32 percent.

The number of individuals treated at least once by the RSC (scaled by 1910 SEA youth population) is reported in table 5.1. The second and third columns display the means by subsamples that are separated based on the intensity of their hookworm problem. Because of the policy of treating any infected person who presented himself or herself at a commission dispensary, the RSC directed more resources toward the areas with greater

---

7   The infection rates were based on microscopic examination of stool samples. (Several microscopists were generally part of the survey and dispensary teams.) The following quote is from the second annual report of the RSC (1911): "The survey is made by counties: it is based on a microscopic examination of foecal specimens from at least 200 children between the ages of 6 and 18 taken at random—that is, without reference to clinical symptoms—from rural districts distributed over the county."

Table 5.1 Summary Statistics

Indicator	Whole sample	By hookworm infection >40%	By hookworm infection <40%	Source
Hookworm infection rate	0.320 (0.230)	0.554 (0.137)	0.164 (0.117)	RSC annual reports
Individuals treated at least once by the RSC, per school-age child	0.206 (0.205)	0.342 (0.199)	0.109 (0.147)	RSC annual reports
School enrollment, 1910	0.721 (0.104)	0.711 (0.099)	0.729 (0.108)	IPUMS; author's calculations
Change in school enrollment, 1910–20	0.089 (0.080)	0.103 (0.090)	0.078 (0.072)	IPUMS; author's calculations
Full-time school attendance, 1910	0.517 (0.140)	0.469 (0.123)	0.551 (0.141)	IPUMS; author's calculations
Change in full-time school attendance, 1910–20	0.203 (0.097)	0.246 (0.093)	0.172 (0.089)	IPUMS; author's calculations
Literacy, 1910	0.853 (0.104)	0.824 (0.101)	0.875 (0.102)	IPUMS; author's calculations
Change in literacy, 1910–20	0.060 (0.067)	0.081 (0.075)	0.045 (0.057)	IPUMS; author's calculations
Share of the population that is black, 1910	0.357 (0.221)	0.41 (0.208)	0.318 (0.223)	IPUMS; author's calculations
Fraction of the population that is urban, 1910	0.174 (0.200)	0.167 (0.214)	0.180 (0.190)	ICPSR (1984)
School term, in months, c1910	5.251 (1.066)	5.055 (1.042)	5.391 (1.068)	State annual reports
Schools per square mile, c1910	0.195 (0.358)	0.142 (0.053)	0.233 (0.465)	State annual reports; ICPSR
Value of school property, per pupil, current dollars, c1910	5.518 (4.037)	4.699 (3.159)	6.104 (4.496)	State annual reports
Teacher-to-school ratio, c1910	1.336 (0.545)	1.397 (0.505)	1.293 (0.572)	State annual reports
Sample size	115	48	67	n.a.

Source: Author's calculations.

Note: Variable means are displayed in the first column. Standard deviations are displayed in parentheses below the mean. Sample selection for the Integrated Public Use Micro Sample (IPUMS) data consists of native-born whites and blacks, in the RSC-surveyed geographic units, for the indicated years. The school enrollment and attendance data are constructed for children ages 8–16; literacy data are for children ages 10–16, and the RSC reported infection rates are for children ages 8–16. See the appendix for further information on sources and construction of the variables. n.a. = not applicable.

hookworm infection. These numbers indicate that about 64 percent of the infected population received deworming treatments.[8]

The micro-level data come from the IPUMS, a project harmonizing the coding of historical census micro data (Ruggles and Sobek 1997). The RSC's

---

8 Similarly, a regression with these measures at the SEA level ($N = 113$; $R^2 = 0.495$) yields the following estimates:

$$Tr_j = 0.619 H_j^{\mathrm{pre}} + 0.003 + \varepsilon_j,$$
$$(0.064) \qquad (0.017)$$

where T_{rj} is the number of individuals treated at least once by the RSC, divided by the school-age population (ages 6 to 17, inclusive) in SEA_j. This indicates that, on the margin, about 62 percent of sufferers were treated.

activities took place from 1910 to 1915; therefore, the core component of the data come from the decennial censuses that bracket the intervention. The sensitivity analysis uses census micro data from 1900 to 1950, and the long-term follow-up comprises census samples from 1880 to 1990.

Three binary indicators of human capital are used here: school enrollment, regular or "full-time" school attendance, and literacy. The enrollment variable measures whether the child had gone to school for at least one day in the months preceding the census.[9] I proxy for regular or "full-time" school attendance by combining the enrollment variable with occupational information. Children are coded as attending school regularly if they were enrolled in school and they did not report an occupation. The literacy variable indicates whether the child could read and write.

The data show faster increases from 1910 to 1920 in the enrollment, attendance, and literacy rates in areas with high hookworm infection, coupled with lower average levels of these measures in 1910. The fact that this period coincides with the hookworm eradication campaign is prima facie evidence that the increase in school attendance was related to the reduction in hookworm disease.

Areas with greater hookworm burdens were different along other margins as well. For one, they were more rural and had higher proportions of black residents. Additionally, the hookworm-infested areas also had shorter school terms and a lower capital stock invested in primary education. There were also more teachers per school, in part because of the prevalence of one-room common schools. These variables and others constitute important controls in the sensitivity analysis below.[10]

Contemporaneous Effects on Children

Here I conduct regression analyses of changes in literacy, school enrollment, and school attendance between the 1910 and 1920 censuses by estimating equation 5.1. Using the two-period comparison, I find a substantial increase in school enrollment among children living in areas that had high levels of hookworm infection in 1910. This is true in absolute terms and also relative to areas with lower levels of infection. Specifically, the coefficient on $H_i^{pre} \times Post_t$ implies that a county with a 1910 infection rate of 50 percent would experience an increase in school enrollment of 3–5 percentage points, relative to a county with no infection problem. In 1910, the mean of school enrollment in the sample was 0.78, and the standard deviation across SEAs was 0.11. Moreover, the standard deviation of hookworm infection rates

---

9   The underlying census question used the word "attendance" rather than "enrollment," but I call the variable "enrollment" nonetheless. The rather low standard of attending at least one day maps more closely onto enrollment, as the word is used in the contemporary literature.

10 In previous versions of this study, I also compare hookworm infection with the prevalence of other disease conditions. I find a relationship between hookworm and malaria across the counties of the South. However, I find no robust relationship between hookworm and child mortality, pellagra morbidity, or typhoid deaths. These latter two variables were only available for the counties of one state each, and thus I cannot use them in the subsequent regression analysis. Malaria mortality rates are used below in the sensitivity analysis.

across SEAs in 1910 was 0.23; so a one-standard-deviation increase in lagged hookworm infection is associated with a post-RSC increase in school enrollment of one-quarter of a standard deviation.

These results are presented in table 5.2. Estimates of the variable of interest—$H_f^{pre} \times Post_t$—are displayed for various outcomes and specifications. Panel A presents the main results. The first row contains the estimates using the 1910 and 1920 censuses, which bracket the RSC intervention, while the second row contains similar estimates using the census micro data from 1900 to 1950. In addition to the results on school enrollment mentioned in the previous paragraph, I estimate positive effects of hookworm eradication on full-time school attendance and literacy as well. (The literacy variable is not available in later censuses, so column 3 is blank in the first and second rows of panel A; literacy results in panel B use the 1910–20 censuses.)

Table 5.2 Hookworm and Human Capital: Basic Results

Dependent variables	Estimating equation	School enrollment (1)	Full-time school attendance (2)	Literacy (3)
Panel A: Basic results				
Census years				
1910–20	5.1	0.0883*** (0.0225)	0.1591*** (0.0252)	0.0587*** (0.0186)
1900–50	5.1	0.0608*** (0.0261)	0.1247*** (0.0286)	
1900–50	5.2	0.0954*** (0.0233)	0.1471*** (0.0287)	
Panel B: Effects within and between states				
Change to specification				
Include state × Post dummies		0.1313*** (0.0245)	0.2144*** (0.0290)	0.0417** (0.0207)
Allow for state-specific mean reversion		0.1148*** (0.0265)	0.1813*** (0.0312)	0.0408** (0.0206)
Use infection from state of birth instead of SEA		0.0489 (0.0504)	0.2057*** (0.0765)	0.0907** (0.0451)
Census years		1900–50	1900–50	1910–20
Estimating equation		5.2	5.2	5.1

Source: Author's calculations.

Note: This table reports estimates of the interaction of pretreatment hookworm and a post-RSC dummy in the indicated equations. The dependent variables are the binary variables denoted in the column headings. Robust standard errors are in parentheses (clustering on area x $Post_t$). All regressions include fixed effects for area and time: controls for age, female, female × age, black, and black × age, and the interactions of the demographic controls with $Post_t$. The average school enrollment in 1910 (× $Post_t$) is used to control for mean reversion in the second and third rows of panel B. The base sample consists of all native-born white and black children in the IPUMS between the ages of 8 and 16 for 1900, 1910, 1920, 1940, and 1950. For panel A and the first two rows of panel B, the sample is drawn from the RSC-surveyed county groups (SEAs), all of which were in the South. For the third row of panel B, the sample consists of individuals in the 50 states and territories for which Kofoid and Tucker (1921) report hookworm infection rates, and all the area-level variables (hookworm, fixed effects, trend, mean-reversion control) are specified at the state-of-birth level. Because literacy is not available in the later censuses, no estimates are available for literacy in the first and second rows of panel A.

***Significant at the 1 percent level.
**Significant at the 5 percent level.

Figure 5.2 Hookworm Eradication and School Attendance, 1870–1950

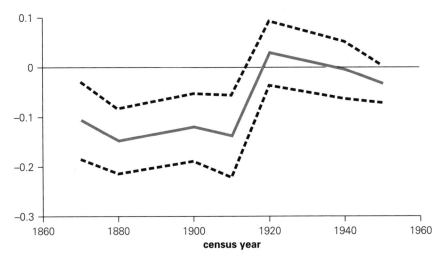

Source: Author's calculations.

Note: The y-axis plots the year-specific coefficients on the circa 1913 hookworm infection rate (solid line) plus the RSC-confidence intervals (dashed lines). The x-axis is the census year. The sample consists of all native-born white and black children in the IPUMS between the ages of 8 and 16 in the RSC-surveyed geographic units for 1870, 1880, 1900, 1910, 1920, 1940, and 1950. For each year, the coefficients are estimated in a regression of a school-attendance dummy on preintervention hookworm infection and demographic controls. Confidence intervals are constructed using standard errors that are clustered on SEA.

The surge in school attendance in high-hookworm counties coincided with the campaign for hookworm eradication. This can be seen in figure 5.2.[11] As shown in the graph, areas with more hookworm infection had lower levels of school attendance prior to the RSC, but these groups converge markedly thereafter. I further test this hypothesis adding SEA-specific trends to equation 5.1, resulting in the following equation:

$$Y_{ijt} = \beta(H_j^{\text{pre}} \times \text{Post}_t) + \tilde{\delta}_j \times t + \delta_t + \delta_j + X_{ijt}\Gamma + \varepsilon_{ijt}. \quad (5.2)$$

Trend differences across areas load onto the $\tilde{\delta}_j$, while differences that coincide with the antihookworm campaign load onto β. Estimates of equation 5.2 in row C of table 5.2 show little change in the estimated β.

The specification in the first row of panel B contains controls for state-level shocks and policy changes, most notably the compulsory schooling and child labor laws that were imposed in the first half of the twentieth century. Since these shifts were at the level of state × year, this specification implements a simple fix to purge the estimates of this effect, including (state × year) fixed effects. Throwing out all of the cross-state variation yields estimated effects that are essentially unchanged.

Another concern is mean reversion across areas: if some counties had high hookworm infection and low schooling because of a temporary shock, we might expect school attendance to rise in the following period even if hookworm had not affected the schooling decision. In the third row of

---

11 To construct this figure, I run a regression of school attendance on SEA-level hookworm, separately by census year from 1870 to 1950. Micro-level controls for age, female, female × age, black, and black × age are also included. The year-specific estimates on H_j^{pre} are plotted against year.

panel B of table 5.2, I add the interaction of $Post_t$ with 1910 average school attendance by SEA. Differential incidence of state policies (by average school attendance rates) are also absorbed by interacting state $\times$ year dummies with average attendance rates. There is evidence of mean reversion in schooling, but estimates of $H_j^{pre} \times Post_t$ are similar to above.

In the third row of panel B, I reestimate equation 5.2 using only state-of-birth-level variation in the antihookworm campaign. Because the RSC did not attempt a systematic survey of hookworm across the whole country, I use hookworm infection rates from Kofoid and Tucker (1921), who surveyed hookworm among army recruits. Because the full set of states is a much more heterogeneous sample, I also control for mean reversion as above. Restricting the analysis to the state level excludes much of the useful variation: the standard errors on the estimate of $H_j^{pre} \times Post_t$ are approximately twice those found above. There are two reasons for this: (a) there are fewer geographic units, and (b) the dispersion of infection rates across states is smaller than that across county groups.

However, point estimates of the effect of hookworm eradication are approximately the same magnitude as those in the county-level results. The result for enrollment is smaller than the estimates above, and we can reject neither zero nor the estimates from the SEA-level variation. In contrast, attendance and literacy do show statistically significant responses to hookworm, with magnitudes that are larger than previous estimates. The results indicate that, at the state-of-birth level, the effect of hookworm eradication worked principally through the intensive margin of human capital formation (literacy and full-time school attendance).[12]

Additional Specifications

The finding that highly infected counties experienced surges in school attendance is not sensitive to controlling for a variety of alternative hypotheses. I contrast these hypotheses with the effect of hookworm and the RSC by starting with equations 5.1 and 5.2 and adding plausible proxies for the supposed confounds. The control variables enter into the specification interacted with $Post_t$. These results are found in panel B of table 5.3. In every case, the added control variables are jointly significant at conventional confidence levels. The new controls include variables for health and health policy, educational resources, race and race relations, urbanization and land use, and parental background. (See the appendix for a complete list of controls and their sources.)

The estimated relationship between hookworm and human capital was not simply concentrated on one particular demographic group, although there are noteworthy differences. These results are seen in panel C of table 5.3. For preteens and adolescents, the estimates for enrollment and

---

12 This suggests that, if we examine these cohorts as adults, we will see increases in human capital, but the estimates (of years of schooling especially) may well be statistically insignificant. These results provide a natural benchmark for the cohort-based analysis below, since the retrospective-cohort analysis employs precisely the state-of-birth variation in hookworm.

Table 5.3 Hookworm and Human Capital: Sensitivity Tests and Results for Subgroups

| Specification or subsample | School enrollment | | Full-time school attendance | | Literate, 1910–20 |
	1900–50 (1)	1910–20 (2)	1900–50 (3)	1910–20 (4)	(4)
Panel A: Baseline results					
Baseline	0.0954***	0.0883***	0.1471***	0.1591***	0.0587***
	(0.0233)	(0.0225)	(0.0287)	(0.0252)	(0.0186)
Panel B: Specifications with additional controls					
Health and health policy	0.1200***	0.1187***	0.1628***	0.1646***	0.0724***
	(0.0291)	(0.0262)	(0.0355)	(0.0294)	(0.0233)
Education and race	0.1235***	0.0793***	0.1851***	0.1581***	0.0556***
	(0.0208)	(0.0208)	(0.0247)	(0.0250)	(0.0171)
Full controls	0.1014***	0.0850***	0.1408***	0.1026***	0.0513**
	(0.0349)	(0.0224)	(0.0421)	(0.0325)	(0.0213)
Panel C: Demographic subgroups					
Preteens	0.0932***	0.0890***	0.1416***	0.1549***	0.0912***
	(0.0255)	(0.0242)	(0.0302)	(0.0266)	(0.0253)
Adolescents	0.0986***	0.0877***	0.1573***	0.1682***	0.0323*
	(0.0280)	(0.0282)	(0.0336)	(0.0295)	(0.0165)
Blacks	0.2299***	0.1838***	0.2601***	0.2205***	0.1078***
	(0.0399)	(0.0337)	(0.0399)	(0.0320)	(0.0374)
Whites	0.0378	0.0270	0.1103***	0.1169***	0.0264*
	(0.0237)	(0.0267)	(0.0294)	(0.0294)	(0.0139)

Source: Author's calculations.

Note: This table reports estimates of the interaction of pretreatment hookworm and a post-RSC dummy in equation 5.1 (for the 1910–20 data) and equation 5.2 (for the 1900–50 data), for the indicated subsamples. The dependent variables are the binary indicators denoted in the column headings. Robust standard errors are in parentheses (clustering on SEA x Post). The sample consists of native-born black and white children in the IPUMS between the ages of 8 and 16 in the RSC-surveyed geographic units for the indicated years. The aggregate control variables enter into the specification interacted with Post$_t$. Control variables are described in the appendix. The number of clusters is 230. All regressions include fixed effects for area and time; controls for age, female, female × age, black, and black × age; and the interactions of the demographic controls with Post$_t$. Reporting of additional coefficient estimates is suppressed.

***Significant at the 1 percent level.
**Significant at the 5 percent level.
*Significant at the 10 percent level.

attendance are close in magnitude, which suggests a balancing of two offsetting effects: younger children were more likely to be infected, but adolescents were closer to the margin of not going to school.

There were also important differences between how blacks and whites responded to the antihookworm campaign. Whites appeared to have positive responses to hookworm eradication by all three measures of human capital, but the estimated effects of eradication were uniformly larger for blacks. There are several possible explanations for this result. One is that the general health of blacks was more sensitive to a given level of (own) hookworm infection. However, this explanation is inconsistent with existing medical evidence. The other possibility is that whites, because of higher average incomes and therefore better sanitary conditions, had lower rates of infection. Unfortunately, there is no direct published evidence on this hypothesis.

A third explanation is that whites, who were more likely than blacks to go to school and be literate, simply had less scope for improvement along these measures of human capital investment.[13] The long-term consequence of these racial differences is less clear because the return to schooling was lower for blacks than for whites during this period. I revisit this issue in a later section.

Interpretation

The estimates presented above imply plausible numbers for the effect of hookworm infection on school attendance. We can compare the reduced-form effect of $H_j^{\text{pre}} \times \text{Post}_t$ (about 0.09) to the estimated decline in infection as a function of the same variable (0.44). The latter number comes from the follow-up surveys discussed above and is shown in figure 5.1. Some of this relationship may be due to "Galton's fallacy" because it is a comparison of ΔH_t and H_{t-1}. This resulting upward bias in the first-stage relationship will cause a downward bias in the indirect least squares (ILS) estimates below.[14] However, the intervention may have lowered the rate of severe infections more than the overall rate, which would likely cause an upward bias in this estimator. Furthermore, in spite of the extensive set of controls employed, it is impossible to rule out that, for example, the RSC intervention differentially improved other sanitation-related diseases for hookworm-infested areas. Again, this presumably results in an upward bias on the ILS estimator.

Dividing the first number by the second gives us the indirect least squares estimate of infection on enrollment: 0.20. This indicates that a child infected with hookworm is 20 percent (that is, percentage points) less likely to be enrolled. Similarly, ILS estimates imply a 0.13 lower probability of being literate and 0.33 reduction in the probability of attending school full time.[15]

These estimates suggest that hookworm played a major role in the South's lagging behind the rest of the country. In computing the depressing effect of hookworm on the region's accumulation of human capital, I multiply the ILS estimates from above with an estimate of the area's hookworm burden. I assume a 40 percent regional hookworm infection rate, as reported by the RSC. The resulting numbers account for around half of the human capital gap.

---

13 Using logit and probit estimators rather than a linear probability model, I find that the hookworm effect was sometimes larger for whites, sometimes not, depending on the specification. This bolsters the hypothesis that the two groups were experiencing similar increases in some latent measure (human capital investment), but the binary nature of the census variables obscures this to some degree.

14 The mean-reversion bias on the reduced-form coefficients was shown to be negligible above, so there should be no mean-reversion bias in the ILS numerator.

15 These numbers suggest a larger effect than those obtained by Miguel and Kremer (2004), who report an IV estimate of –0.203 for the effect of intestinal-parasite infection on school participation. Their variable is based on spot checks of school attendance following the intervention and therefore is most comparable to the full-time school attendance variable used in this chapter. However, the estimates are not directly comparable because Miguel and Kremer use a combined infection rate that includes hookworm, roundworm, schistosomiasis, and whipworm.

Contemporaneous Effects on Adults

Next I examine how adult outcomes in the same time periods respond to the antihookworm campaign. This serves as a falsification exercise because adults were less likely to be directly affected by eradication. As an empirical matter, adults had much lower infection rates.[16]

Results for adults are displayed in table 5.4, which contains estimates of equation 5.1. For several outcomes, I cannot reject the null hypothesis that there was no differential change across counties with different hookworm infection rates. Neither adult literacy nor labor force participation was significantly affected by the treatment campaign. I obtain null results for the effect of hookworm on the occupational income score, an IPUMS variable that proxies income by occupation. I also do not find evidence that adults were more likely to live in urban areas. Finally, in results not shown, $H_j^{\mathrm{pre}} \times \mathrm{Post}_t$ does not predict whether adults residing in the area were in white-collar jobs or born out of state; neither do I find significant effects when I perform the analysis separately by broad age groupings.

Long-Term Follow-Up of Cohorts Exposed as Children

In this section, I follow up on the subsequent outcomes of the cohorts that, as children, were exposed to the hookworm eradication campaign. This analysis therefore represents a different approach to the question: instead of looking at the behavior of fixed age groups at different points in time, I analyze various year- and state-of-birth cohorts retrospectively. The

Table 5.4 Contemporaneous Effect on Adult Outcomes

parameter estimates

Dependent variables	Whole (1)	Male (2)	Female (3)	White (4)	Black (5)
Literacy	0.0062	−0.0107	0.0203	0.0107	−0.0014
	(0.0095)	(0.0108)	(0.0127)	(0.0112)	(0.0229)
Labor-force participation	−0.0069	−0.0069	−0.0056	−0.0212	0.0036
	(0.0134)	(0.0065)	(0.0284)	(0.0124)	(0.0249)
Occupational income score	0.0526	−0.0186	0.0581	0.0855	0.0224
	(0.2836)	(0.4912)	(0.4163)	(0.3903)	(0.3861)
Lives in an urban area	0.0157	0.0030	0.0280	0.0199	0.0132
	(0.0172)	(0.0190)	(0.0177)	(0.0226)	(0.0245)

Source: Author's calculations.

Note: Each cell reports the coefficient estimate on Hookworm × Post for the indicated sample and dependent variable. Robust standard errors are in parentheses (clustering on SEA × Post; the number of clusters is 230). None of the reported coefficients is statistically significant at conventional confidence intervals. The sample consists of all native-born white and black adults in the 1910–20 IPUMS between the ages of 25 and 55 (inclusive) in the RSC-surveyed geographic units. Reporting of additional coefficient estimates is suppressed. Specifications also include dummy variables for SEA, age, black, female, and year as well as interactions of the demographic variables with Post_t.

16 Smillie and Augustine (1925) show that hookworm infection among adults was very low in the southern United States. They also note the contrast with the experience of other countries, where hookworm infects across a broader range of ages.

comparisons are both across areas, based on different preexisting infection rates, and across cohorts, with older cohorts serving as a comparison group because they were not exposed to the RSC during childhood.

The geographic units employed in this analysis are place of birth rather than current residence. Matching individuals with hookworm infection rates of the area where they end up as adults would be difficult to interpret because of migration. Instead, I use the information on hookworm prevalence in an individual's state of birth to conduct the analysis. A problem with using states instead of counties is that there are fewer of them. As seen above, this reduces precision.

The effects of hookworm infection among children appear to extend into adulthood for the affected cohorts. This section contains several results supporting this conclusion.

Results for Earnings, Schooling, and Literacy

I consider a simple parameterization of the cross-cohort comparison: the number of *childhood* years potentially exposed to the antihookworm campaign times the pre-eradication hookworm intensity in the state of birth. Exposure to the RSC, Exp_{ik}, is zero for older cohorts, rises linearly for those born in the 19 years prior to 1910, and stops at 19 for younger cohorts.[17] Nineteen is chosen because most individuals in this period would have completed their schooling by that age, and hookworm infection was negligible at older ages. Thus the regression model is as follows:

$$Y_{ijk} = \beta(H_j^{pre} \times Exp_{ik}) + \delta_j + \delta_k + X_{ijk}\Gamma + \nu_{ijk} \qquad (5.3)$$

for state of birth j and cohort k. The demographic controls consist of indicator variables for each age $\times$ black $\times$ female cell plus interactions of state-of-birth dummies with black, female, and black $\times$ female.

Children with more exposure to the campaign, by being born later and in a state with greater pre-eradication hookworm, were more likely to be literate and earn higher incomes as adults. Results are mixed for years of schooling, but this is within the range of normal statistical variation. Table 5.5 contains these results. Panel A presents the estimates of equation 5.3.

The estimates do not appear to be an artifact of mean reversion. If the oldest cohorts had high hookworm infection and low productivity because of some mean-reverting shock, we might expect income gains for the subsequent cohorts even in the absence of a direct effect of hookworm on productivity. I use data on labor earnings by state in 1899 from Lebergott (1964). I interact the natural logarithm of this measure with age and include the interaction in the even-numbered columns of table 5.5. This analysis yields mixed evidence of mean reversion in the data, but the inclusion of these controls does not substantially affect the coefficient on $H_j^{pre} \times Exp_{ik}$.[18]

I argue that the earnings results are not contaminated by hookworm-induced changes in the probability of self-employment. The major difficulty

---

17 Specifically, the formula is $Exp_{ik} = max[min(19, 49 - age_i), 0]$, where age is measured in 1940.
18 Similar results are obtained by interacting the 1899 wage measure with the exposure variable instead of age or including the square of the average wage ($\times$ age) as well.

Evidence from Hookworm Eradication in the American South

Table 5.5 Long-Term Follow-up Based on Intensity of Exposure to the Treatment Campaign

Variable	Log earnings, 1939		Years of schooling, 1940		Literacy status, 1920	
	(1)	(2)	(3)	(4)	(5)	(6)
Controls for mean-reversion	No	Yes	No	Yes	No	Yes
Panel A: Main results						
Hookworm infection rate × years of exposure	0.0286*** (0.0066)	0.0234** (0.0093)	−0.0243 (0.0328)	0.0037 (0.0357)	0.0158*** (0.0019)	0.0115*** (0.0020)
Panel B: Changing returns to schooling						
Hookworm infection rate × years of exposure	0.0254*** (0.0044)	0.0219*** (0.0063)				
Infection × years of exposure × years of schooling	0.0023*** (0.0009)	0.0022** (0.0009)				
Panel C: Estimates of hookworm × exposure for demographic subgroups						
Males	0.0265*** (0.0056)	0.0253*** (0.0080)	−0.0690** (0.0326)	−0.0376 (0.0347)	0.0108*** (0.0018)	0.0083*** (0.0019)
Females	0.0322*** (0.0115)	0.0157 (0.0165)	0.0200 (0.0338)	0.0444 (0.0385)	0.0209*** (0.0027)	0.0148*** (0.0030)
Whites	0.0293*** (0.0071)	0.0232** (0.0103)	−0.0110 (0.0345)	0.0164 (0.0378)	0.0131*** (0.0022)	0.0086*** (0.0020)
Blacks	0.0220*** (0.0072)	0.0253** (0.0103)	0.1013*** (0.0387)	0.0133 (0.0461)	0.0314*** (0.0065)	0.0262*** (0.0063)

Source: Author's calculations.

Note: Each panel-column reports a separate regression for the indicated samples and dependent variables. State-average data are matched to individuals based on their state of birth. The measure of hookworm is from Kofoid and Tucker (1921). Unskilled-wage data from 1899, reported by Lebergott (1964), are used to control for mean reversion. The full sample consists of native-born blacks and whites in the age range [25, 60] and in the 1940 IPUMS database (except the literacy regressions, which include ages [16, 60] from the 1920 IPUMS data). Robust standard errors are in parentheses (clustering on state of birth). The demographic controls consist of indicator variables for each age × black × female cell, plus interactions of state-of-birth dummies with black, female, and black × female. Reporting of additional coefficient estimates is suppressed.

***Significant at the 1 percent level.
**Significant at the 5 percent level.

in using the earnings data from the 1940 census is that they are incomplete: labor income from self-employment is excluded. To gauge the impact of this problem, I estimate regression equations identical to those used for panel A of table 5.5, but with three new dependent variables: binary indicators for (a) self-employment, (b) missing data for log earnings, and (c) nonwage or salary income greater than $50. In doing so, I find no robust and statistically significant relationship between the hookworm measure and any of these three measures.[19] Additionally, I find evidence of a hookworm-related

---

19 Using controls for mean reversion, the coefficient (standard error) on $H_j \times \text{Exp}_{ik}$ is estimated to be −0.003 (0.003) for self-employment, 0.003 (0.004) for missing log-earnings data, and −0.001 (0.004) for nonwage or salary income exceeding $50.

increase in the total time worked (either for a wage or a salary or not), although once mean reversion controls are included, the increased labor supply does not account for a large fraction of the earnings effect.

I also consider the role played by the quantity of and returns to schooling in the wage results. Controlling directly for education does not significantly change the estimated effect of hookworm treatment. Additionally, I can easily reject, for conventional returns to schooling, the hypothesis that the wage effect is due entirely to a rise in education.[20] However, the fact that I estimate increases in literacy without concomitant rises in the *quantity* of schooling suggests an alternative hypothesis: changes in quality. In particular, it may be that students spend the same number of years in school, but that the time is better spent. For example, there might be less absenteeism, or students might be better equipped to absorb the material while in school. As shown above, students were less likely to work while in school and more likely to be literate following hookworm eradication. This suggests that the return to schooling was raised by the hookworm intervention.

There is indeed evidence that the return to schooling rose with the intervention. This can be seen in panel B of table 5.5. The crucial interaction is the triple interaction: between years of schooling and the treatment-intensity variable ($H_j \times \text{Exp}_{ik}$).[21] This new term is estimated to be positive and statistically significant in the labor-earnings regression.

This hookworm-related change in the return to schooling can potentially explain a large fraction of the increase in earnings described above. This regression, by comparing individuals with different terminal levels of attainment, estimates the average marginal effect of schooling in the sample (and how it changes following hookworm eradication). If the intervention had similar effects on the return to inframarginal schooling, we can compute the overall contribution through this channel. Multiplying the triple interaction (0.0022) by the average years of schooling in the South (7.72) yields 0.0170, almost 80 percent of the coefficient on $H_j \times \text{Exp}_{ik}$ in the first row of panel B.[22] Moreover, I cannot reject the hypothesis that all of the earnings effects worked through the rising return to schooling.

Several differences emerge among demographic groups. Results estimated from subsamples of males, females, whites, and blacks are contained in table 5.5, panel C. For no subgroup is there a robustly significant relationship

---

20 Similarly, I do not find evidence that the mechanism is migration out of the South, migration into an urban area, shifting to a white-collar occupation, or movement out of agriculture. I consider these potential channels by conditioning on the variables in the regressions above and find that their inclusion makes little difference for the estimate of $H_j \times \text{Exp}_{ik}$. Such variables are themselves endogenous, and therefore these results should be considered a decomposition of the hookworm effect, taking the regression estimates of the added variables as correct.

21 The additional second-order interactions are absorbed with a series of dummies for birth state × education and birth year × education. The first-order effects of education, state of birth, and year of birth are also absorbed with indicator variables.

22 Because the education variable was demeaned before interaction, the second-order term is evaluated at the mean of education.

---

between years of schooling and $H_j \times \text{Exp}_{ik}$. Estimates for literacy, in contrast, are positive and significantly different from zero for all demographic groups. Literacy responses are larger for females than for males, as well as for blacks than for whites, possibly because females and blacks had lower preexisting literacy rates. The estimate of $H_j \times \text{Exp}_{ik}$ in the earnings equation yields a positive and significant number for males, while the result for females is not sensitive to the inclusion of the mean-reversion control. In contrast, whites and blacks show similar earnings responses. This may be because blacks, while gaining more on measured human capital, faced lower returns to skill in the labor market.

Cohort-Specific Relationship between Income and Hookworm

In this subsection, I show that the shift in the relationship between income and pre-eradication hookworm coincides with childhood exposure to the eradication efforts. This can be seen graphically, and I also provide statistical tests comparing exposure to eradication with trends or autoregressive processes.

I use two income proxies that are available for a large number of censuses. The occupational income score and the Duncan socioeconomic index are both average indicators by disaggregated occupational categories that were calibrated using data from the 1950 census. The former variable is the average by occupation of all reported labor earnings. The measure due to Duncan (1961) is instead a weighted average of earnings and education among males within each occupation. Both variables can therefore measure shifts in income that take place between occupations. The Duncan measure has the added benefit of picking up between-occupation shifts in skill requirements for jobs. Occupation has been measured by the census for more than a century, and so these income proxies are available for a substantial stretch of cohorts.

Using these proxies, I construct a panel of average income by cohort. The units of observation of the panel are year of birth × state of birth, and I use microsamples from 10 censuses (1880 and 1900–90). This results in an unbalanced panel spanning the year-of-birth cohorts from 1825 to 1965 for 46 states of birth. (See the appendix for details of the data construction.)

For each year of birth, ordinary least squares (OLS) regression coefficients are estimated on the resulting cross section of states of birth. Consider a simple regression model of an average outcome, Y_{jk}, for a cohort with state of birth j and year of birth k:

$$Y_{jk} = \beta_k H_j^{\text{pre}} \times \delta_k + X_j' \Gamma_k + v_{jk}, \tag{5.4}$$

in which β_k is year-of-birth-specific coefficient on hookworm, X_j is a vector of other state-of-birth controls, and δ_k and Γ_k are year-of-birth-specific intercept and slope coefficients. (Note that there is no subscript i because I am working with average outcomes by cohort.) I estimate this equation using OLS for each year of birth k. This specification allows me to examine how the relationship between income and pre-eradication hookworm ($\hat{\beta}_k$) differs across cohorts.

I start with a simple graphic analysis using this flexible specification for cross-cohort comparison. Figure 5.3 displays a plot of the estimated β_k.

Figure 5.3 Cohort-Specific Relationship between Income and Pre-eradication Hookworm

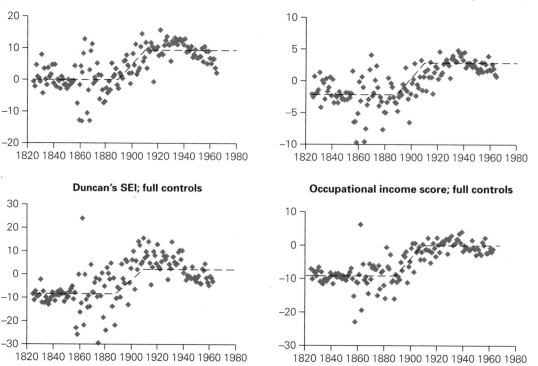

Source: Author's calculations.

Note: This figure summarizes regressions of income proxies on pre-eradication hookworm infection rates by state of birth. The y-axis for each graphic plots the estimated cohort-specific coefficients on the state-level hookworm measure. The x-axis is the cohort's year of birth. Each year-of-birth cohort's point estimate is marked with a dot. The dashed lines measure the number of years of potential childhood exposure to the Rockefeller Sanitary Commission's activities. For the underlying regressions, the dependent variables are constructed from the indicated income proxies (the Duncan socioeconomic indicator and the occupational income score). For each year-of-birth cohort, OLS regression coefficients are estimated on the cross-section of incomes by state of birth. In the basic specification, this state-of-birth average income is regressed onto hookworm infection, Lebergott's measure of 1809 wage levels, and regional dummies. The "full controls" specification contains, in addition, the various control variables described in the appendix. The regressions are estimated using weight equal to the square root of the cell size in the underlying micro data.

Each cohort's point estimate is marked with a dot. The top row of graphs contains estimates from the basic specification, in which the average income is regressed on hookworm infection, Lebergott's measure of 1899 wage levels, and dummies for census region. The bottom row displays estimates from the "full controls" specification, which, in addition to the basic variables, contains a number of control variables.[23]

---

23 These consist of the following state-of-birth-level variables: 1910 fraction black, fraction literate (among adults), fraction living in urban areas, 1890 child mortality rate, fraction of deaths in 1890 caused by scarlet fever, measles, whooping cough, diphtheria or croup, typhoid fever, malaria, diarrheal diseases, and pneumonia, 1910 fertility rates, 1930 unemployment rate, doctors per capita in 1898, state public health spending per capita in 1898, World War I recruits found "defective" at draft physical, and 1902–32 logarithmic changes in average monthly teacher salaries, length of school term, school expenditures per capita, and pupil-teacher ratios. See the appendix for details on these data.

Because hookworm was principally a childhood disease, cohorts that were already adults in 1910 were too old to have benefited from the reduction in hookworm. However, later cohorts experienced reduced hookworm infection during their childhood. This benefit increased with younger cohorts who were exposed to the RSC's efforts for a greater fraction of their childhood. The dashed lines therefore measure the number of years of potential childhood exposure (defined above) to the Rockefeller Sanitary Commission's activities.[24] Pre-eradication hookworm generally predicts lower income in earlier cohorts, while this is not the case for those born late enough to have potentially been exposed to the RSC during childhood.

Formal statistical tests indicate that the shift in the relationship between income and pre-eradication hookworm coincided with exposure to hookworm eradication, rather than with some trend or autoregressive process. I treat the $\hat{\beta}_k$ as a time series and estimate the following regression equation:

$$\hat{\beta}_k = \alpha \mathrm{Exp}_k + \sum_{i=1}^{n} \gamma_n k^n + \Phi(L)\hat{\beta}_k = \eta_{jk}, \tag{5.5}$$

in which Exp_k is exposure to hookworm eradication (defined similarly above), the k^n terms are nth-order trends, and $\Phi(L)$ is a distributed lag operator. To account for the changing precision with which the generated observations are estimated, observations are weighted by the inverse of the standard error for $\hat{\beta}_k$. Table 5.6 reports estimates of equation 5.5 under a variety of order assumptions about trends and autoregression. The dependent variables are $\hat{\beta}_k$, from the specification using the broad sets of controls. For the analysis using the occupational income score, the exposure term is similar across specifications, and there is no statistically significant evidence of trends or autoregression in these $\hat{\beta}_k$. The estimates using the Duncan socioeconomic indicator exhibit both trend and autoregression, but the exposure coefficient is stable once both are accounted for.[25]

Interpretation

In this section, I characterize the magnitude of the effect of the hookworm reduction in more easily interpretable units and contrast the estimates with cross-area differences in income per capita. I focus on the contrast between the cohort with no childhood exposure to the RSC and the cohort with full

---

24 The exposure variable is measured in different units than the cohort-specific regression coefficients, so to facilitate visual comparisons in figure 3.3, the line is rescaled in the y dimension so that the pre-1880 and post-1930 levels match those of the β_k. The calendar years for childhood exposure are fixed by the start of the RSC and the observed life cycle pattern of infection, and therefore the exposure line is not rescaled in the x dimension.

25 I obtain similar results from a variety of alternative specifications and methodologies for constructing the income data. These include constructing the cohort income data from narrower age ranges, excluding the 1990 census or including the 2000 census. The results are not sensitive to using an unweighted specification. Moreover, restricting the analysis to 100 and then 40 years of birth cohorts yields similar estimates on exposure, albeit with larger standard errors. I have experimented with higher-order polynomial trends and found no estimates of exposure that are statistically significant for $n \leq 5$.

Table 5.6 Exposure to RSC Versus Alternative Time-Series Relationships

time-series estimates of the exposure coefficient

Income proxy and specification	(1)	(2)	(3)	(4)	(5)
Occupational income score					
Basic	0.3113***	0.2915***	0.2612***	0.2497***	0.1912***
	(0.0214)	(0.0542)	(0.0384)	(0.0612)	(0.0622)
Full controls	0.2623***	0.3732***	0.2346***	0.3393***	0.2743***
	(0.0339)	(0.0858)	(0.0438)	(0.0960)	(0.1007)
Duncan's socioeconomic indicator					
Basic	0.5352***	0.7566***	0.3928***	0.5983***	0.4858***
	(0.0418)	(0.1069)	(0.0520)	(0.1124)	(0.1282)
Full controls	0.5007***	0.8820***	0.3544***	0.6616***	0.7081***
	(0.0661)	(0.1707)	(0.0735)	(0.1791)	(0.1969)
Additional controls					
Order of polynomial trend	0	1	0	1	2
Order of autoregressive process	0	0	1	1	2

Source: Author's calculations.

Note: This table reports the estimates of childhood exposure to the RSC in equation 5.5. The dependent variables are the cohort-specific regression estimates of income proxies on hookworm that are shown in figure 5.3. Robust standard errors are given in parentheses. Observations are weighted by the inverse of the standard error for β_k. In the basic specification, the income proxy was regressed onto hookworm infection, Lebergott's measure of 1899 wage levels, and dummies for the four census regions. The "full controls" specification contains, in addition, the various control variables listed in the appendix.

***Significant at the 1 percent level.

exposure. For example, comparing these cohorts in two areas that were one standard deviation (within the RSC-targeted area) apart in hookworm, we would expect wages to have increased 11 percent more in the area with the higher pre-period infection rate.

Using indirect least squares, I estimate the approximate effect of childhood hookworm infection on adult wages to be around 43 percent. Again, I compare the fully exposed and nonexposed cohorts to construct the estimate. The increase in wages as a function of the Kofoid measure of H_j^{pre} is 0.32, when comparing zero to full RSC exposure. Since hookworm was largely eradicated in the time span considered, I regress the pre-RSC hookworm (reported by Jacocks at the state level for certain states) on the Kofoid measure and estimate the decrease in infection rates as a function of H_j^{pre} to be 0.748.[26] This yields an ILS estimate of –0.43 in natural-log terms.

---

26 This is a departure from the methodology presented in the section on interpretation in that I scale the reduced-form coefficient by the preexisting hookworm infection rate rather than the change. For the ILS calculation, I used follow-up data on infection rates several years after the RSC to gauge the first-stage relationship between pre-RSC hookworm and the decline. In contrast, I consider in this section the effect of the intervention over a span of many more years, by which time hookworm had been mostly eradicated. Because eradication was slightly less than complete, this induces a slight downward bias of the ILS estimate. However, as in the previous ILS calculation, if the intervention decreased the severity of infections more than the overall rate, or the control strategy above did not correct for the correlation between hookworm eradication and other improvements in sanitation, there would be an upward bias in this estimator.

The ILS estimates using the occupational proxies for income are similar to the wage result. The shift in income related to RSC exposure is estimated in table 5.6. I compare these estimated changes with their respective averages for men born in the South between 1875 and 1895 and then construct the ILS coefficient as above. For the occupational income score, I estimate the proportional change in income related to childhood hookworm infection to be –0.23. The same estimate for the Duncan socioeconomic indicator is –0.42.

These results point to changes in the returns to schooling as well. I compute the drop in returns due to childhood hookworm exposure to be approximately 0.047, the ILS estimate for the changing returns to a year of education. This represents a substantial drop due to hookworm—around 50 percent of the estimated return to schooling in this period.

The estimated impact is large enough that it bears consideration in a macroeconomic context, although it is not so large that it unreasonably explains everything. The log income gap between the North and the South in 1900 was approximately 0.75. For a 40 percent infection rate in the South and an effect of hookworm on wages of 0.43, we would expect a reduction in southern incomes of approximately 17 log percentage points. In other words, some 22 percent of this income gap could be attributed to hookworm infection in the South. However, if we turn to contemporaneous evidence from developing countries, Miguel and Kremer estimate that the prevalence of intestinal-parasitic infection in the Busia region of Kenya is around 90 percent among school-age children. Applying our estimates to this area of Kenya suggests a log-income gain of approximately 0.38 from a complete eradication of intestinal worms from the country. This would be enough to raise income per capita to match the level of Zimbabwe, but obviously well short of the almost three natural log points needed to reach the levels of high-income countries. In any case, this calculation is probably optimistic in that the improvement in health in the U.S. South was translated into economic benefits in part because of functioning institutions like schools and labor markets that could effectively channel the new human capital. Whether this would happen in Kenya is less clear.

Conclusion

This study evaluates the economic consequences of the successful eradication of hookworm in the American South. The advantages of evaluating this intervention are that (a) its timing was relatively short and well defined, (b) geographic differences in infection permit a treatment-control design, and (c) sufficient time has passed that we can evaluate its long-term consequences.

I find that areas with higher levels of hookworm infection prior to the RSC experienced greater increases in school attendance and literacy after the intervention. This result is robust to controlling for a variety of alternative hypotheses, including differential trends across areas, changing crop prices, and shifts in certain education policies. No significant results are found for the sample of adults, who should have benefited less from the intervention owing to their substantially lower (prior) infection rates. Moreover, a long-term follow-up of affected cohorts indicates a substantial income gain as a result of the reduction in hookworm infection. This follow-up also shows a marked increase in the quality rather than the quantity of education.

This study contributes to two important questions in the literature. One is historical: Did the reduction in the relative disease burden play a role in the subsequent convergence between the American North and South? In this chapter, I show that the hookworm infection rate could account for around half of the literacy gap and about 20 percent of income differences, and so eradication would have closed it by a similar amount. Another question is contemporary: How much does disease contribute to underdevelopment in the tropics?[27] This chapter suggests potentially large benefits of public health interventions in developing countries, where hookworm is still endemic today. Nevertheless, using a simple calculation, I show that, although reducing hookworm infection could bring substantial income gains to some countries, the estimated effect is approximately an order of magnitude too small to be useful in explaining the global distribution of income.

While this broad decomposition of income per capita into institutions versus geography is interesting, one might argue that social scientists should instead focus on the efficacy of specific interventions. Changing the geography or the colonial history of a country is impossible, and unfortunately the literature on institutions has little to say about the complicated mess of intermediate variables that determine productivity. The present study quantifies the benefits of one such intervention and finds them to be substantial.

Nevertheless, it remains an open question whether the long-term gains from hookworm eradication estimated for the American South can be realized for developing countries in the present day. As noted, there have been other episodes in which externally supported eradication efforts failed because of a lack of local follow-up. Moreover, even if eradication could be achieved in less-developed areas, presumably a whole range of institutional infrastructure (functioning schools not least among them) needs to be in place to take advantage of the improvement in health. Investigating these interactions between health and institutions is therefore an important avenue of future study.

---

27 This possibility has been advanced recently by Jeffrey Sachs (2001) as part of an agenda highlighting the importance of geographic factors in development. This view has been challenged by Acemoglu, Johnson, and Robinson (2001), who argue in favor of the importance of institutions over geographic determinism.

Appendix: Data Sources and Construction

There are two major empirical components of this chapter, both of which involve combining micro and aggregate data. The first component is an analysis of sequential cross-sections (SCS) from different points in time. That is, I compare a particular age group in one year to that same age group later on and analyze changes over time differentially by area on the basis of each area's level of infection before the treatment campaign. The second component is a comparison of outcomes across cohorts. This retrospective cohort (RC) analysis is similarly combined with cross-area comparisons based on pretreatment disease burden. In this appendix, I discuss the micro data employed in first the SCS and then the RC analyses. I later describe the construction of the aggregate data on hookworm and the additional control variables that factor into the SCS and RC analysis.

Sources and Definitions for the Micro Data

The micro data for the SCS component are samples drawn from the censuses of 1900, 1910, 1920, 1940, and 1950, accessed through the IPUMS project (Ruggles and Sobek 1997). The sample consists of native-born whites and blacks in the age range [8, 16] in the case of children and in the age range [25, 55] in the case of adults. The age criteria for children serves to select children of school age who are likely not yet old enough to have migrated on their own. The lower age cutoff for adults removes those whose school-years were likely affected by the RSC in 1920. The outcome variables are defined as follows:

- *School enrollment.* This is an indicator variable for whether the child attended school at any time during a specified interval preceding the day of the census. The length of this interval varies across the censuses as follows: 1900, within the past year; 1910 and 1920, since September 1; 1940, since March 1; 1950, since February 1.
- *Full-time school attendance.* This is an indicator variable that is switched on if the child was attending school and not working. I consider a child to be working if the census recorded an occupation for him or her, which corresponds to a nonmissing "occ1950" code less than or equal to 970.
- *Literacy.* This variable is an indicator for the ability to read, write, or both.
- *Labor force participation.* A binary variable indicating whether the individual was working. Prior to 1940, this variable is based on whether the individual's reported occupation was classified as a "gainful" one. From 1940 on, the question corresponds more closely to the modern definition.
- *Occupational income score.* See below.

The micro data for the retrospective cohort analysis are drawn from the IPUMS data. The sample definitions and data construction for sections on the results for earnings, schooling, and literacy and on the cohort-specific relationship between income and hookworm are distinct and thus discussed separately.

The sample for table 5.5 was constructed as follows. The sample used in the section on earnings, schooling, and literacy consists of native-born whites and blacks in the age range [25, 60] in the 1940 census micro data, except for the literacy sample, which consists of native-born whites and blacks with ages [15, 45] from the 1920 census. (The data were accessed February 5, 2003.) The outcome variables are defined as follows:

- *Earnings.* The census earnings variable from 1940 measures the individual's wage and salary income from 1939. This measure excludes earnings from self-employment.
- *Years of schooling.* I recode the IPUMS "higrade" variable as follows: (a) kindergarten and below to zero and (b) the remaining values to be the number of years, starting with first grade.
- *Literacy.* Defined above.

The sample for figure 5.3 was constructed as follows. The underlying sample used consists of native-born whites in the age range [25, 60] in the 1900–90 IPUMS micro data and the 1880 micro data from the North Atlantic Population Project (NAPP 2004). (These data were last accessed November 14, 2005.) This results in a data set with year-of-birth cohorts from 1825 to 1965. The original micro-level variables are defined as follows:

- *Occupational income score.* The occupational income score is an indicator of income by disaggregated occupational categories. It was calibrated using data from the 1950 census and is the average by occupation of all reported labor earnings. See Ruggles and Sobek (1997) for further details.
- *Duncan socioeconomic index.* This measure is a weighted average of earnings and education among males within each occupation. The weights are based on analysis by Duncan (1961), who regressed a measure of perceived prestige of several occupations on the occupation's average income and education. This measure serves to proxy for both the income and the skill requirements in each occupation. It was similarly calibrated using data from the 1950 census.

These data are used to construct a panel of income by year of birth and state of birth. The cohort-level outcomes are constructed as follows:

1. The microdata from 1880–90 are first pooled together.
2. The individual income proxies are projected onto dummies for year of birth $\times$ census year, that is, I run the following regression: $y_{itk} = \delta_{tk} + \varepsilon_{itk}$ for individual i in cohort k when observed in census year t. This regression absorbs all cohort, age, and period effects that are common for the whole country.

3. I then define cells for each combination of year of birth and state of birth. Within each cell, I compute the average of the estimated income residuals (the t_{ijk}). Because these averages are constructed with differing degrees of precision, I also compute the square root of the cell sizes to use as weights when estimating equation 5.4.
4. I do this separately for both the occupational income score and the Duncan socioeconomic index.

These average income proxies by cohort form the dependent variables in the section on cohort-specific relationship between income and hookworm, specifically figure 5.3.

For the majority of the years of birth, I can compute average income proxies for all of the 51 states plus the District of Columbia. The availability of state-level hookworm data and the control variables restricts the sample further to 46 states of birth. Hawaii is excluded because of missing data on hookworm. Alaska, Colorado, the District of Colombia, and Oklahoma are excluded because of missing data for at least one of the other dependent variables. This leaves 46 states of birth in the base sample.

Several cohorts were born before 1885 for which as few as 37 states of birth are represented. For those born between 1855 and 1885, this appears to be due to small samples, because, while the NAPP data are a 100 percent sample for 1880, there are no micro data for 1890, and IPUMS data for 1900 are only a 1 percent sample. In contrast, for the 1843–55 birth cohorts, all but two of the years have all 46 states represented. Nevertheless, even with the 100 percent sample from 1880, there are as many as six states per year missing for those cohorts born before 1843. Several of the territories (all of which would later become states) were being first settled by people of European descent during the first half of the nineteenth century, and it is quite possible that, in certain years, no one eligible to be enumerated was born in some territories. (Untaxed Indians were not counted in the censuses.) Note that I use the term state to refer to states or territories. Territories were valid areas of birth in the earlier censuses and are coded in the same way as if they had been states.

While this procedure generates an unbalanced panel, results are similar when using a balanced panel with only those states of birth with the maximum of 141 valid observations. A comparison of the cohort-specific estimates from the balanced and unbalanced panels shows high correlation (over 0.96, for example, in the case of the full-controls specification for the occupational income score).

Sources and Definitions for the Aggregate Data

Because county boundaries change over time and because county of residence is not available in the later censuses, I use the state economic area (SEA) as the aggregate unit for the sequential-cross-section analysis. The SEAs are aggregations of counties, with an average number of 8.5 counties per SEA. SEA boundaries tend to be more stable, in part because they were often defined by a state boundary or significant natural feature (such as a river or mountain range). See Bogue (1951) for more detail.

The area-level data come from a variety of county-level sources, but principally from the RSC annual reports (RSC 1910–15) and ICPSR (1984), which is a collection of historical census tabulations. When relevant, the formulas for constructing the variable are presented below. (Variable names are those of the ICPSR study.) Data refer to 1910 unless otherwise noted. To construct SEA-level data, I sum the constituent counties or construct population-weighted averages, as appropriate. "Per capita" normalizations come from ICPSR (1984). The following is a list (in thematic groupings) of the aggregate variables with information on sources and definitions. The method of aggregation is noted if different from above. The source is indicated in parentheses at the end of each item.

The following data are used to describe hookworm and RSC treatments:

- *Hookworm infection rate.* The source data are at the county level and from the period 1911–15. The infection numbers in most cases are from surveys conducted by the Rockefeller Sanitary Commission as prelude to (or simultaneously with) dispensing treatments. In a few instances, the RSC dispensaries had already visited the county before conducting the survey. In this case, I use the examinations conducted by the dispensaries to construct the hookworm infection rate, rather than surveys collected after administration of the RSC treatments. (The hookworm infection rates constructed from survey and examination have a correlation coefficient greater than 0.95 for those cases in which the survey was done first. (RSC 1910–15.)

- *Individuals treated at least once by the RSC per capita.* The source data are at the county level and from the period 1911–15. The RSC dispensaries tracked how many individuals received deworming treatments. If an RSC dispensary visited a county twice, I sum the individuals treated from each visit. While it is possible that some children were double counted in this procedure, dispensaries generally made multiple visits to cover different areas. (RSC 1910–15.)

For health and health policy, the following data are used:

- *Number of individuals examined by RSC per capita.* The source data are at the county level and from the period 1911–15. The RSC tracked how many individuals were examined by the dispensaries' medical staff. (RSC 1910–15.)

- *Sanitary index.* The RSC conducted independent surveys of the condition of sanitation infrastructure, including whether buildings had proper latrines, clean water sources, and so forth. Several measures of sanitation were combined by the RSC to form an index. (RSC 1910–15.)

- *Full-time health officer.* These data are compiled at the county level and include information on the first year each county employed a full-time health officer. I code this variable as 1 if such an office was created between 1910 and 1920 inclusive. (Ferrell and others 1932.)

- *County spending.* Data are input at the county level on county-government spending on education and health or sanitation for the years 1902 and 1932. (The 1922 publication in the series does not include these categories of spending, and the 1913 publication does not include earmarked transfers from the state government.) The health spending is normalized by total population, while the education expenditure is normalized by school-age population. (U.S. Bureau of the Census 1915b, 1935.)

- *World War I cantonment size per capita.* I use data on the troop numbers that were mustered and trained at the major Army cantonments of mobilization or embarkation for World War I. Of the 32 cantonments, 19 camps were in the South. I input the highest value given for the number of soldiers within a camp during 1918–20. (Bowen 1928.)

- *Malaria mortality, 1919–21.* (Maxcy 1923.)

- *Change in fertility, 1900–10.* The fertility rate for 1910 is measured from census tabulations under the fraction of the population under six years of age, defined as $1 - (v41 + v53)/(v20 + v21)$. For 1900, the tabulations permit calculating the fraction of the population under five for 1900, or $1 - (v22 + v37 + v39 + v41 + v43)/(v8 + v10)$. When computing the approximate difference, I up-weight the 1900 number by five-fourths. (ICPSR 1984.)

For education, the following data are used:

- *Log change in school term length, c1905–25.* This measures the average length of school term, in weeks. Kentucky county data are imputed from cross-tabulated data on number of schools by month. The imputation is calibrated using Alabama data, which contain a continuous measure and a cross-tabulation. (Annual and biennial reports of the various state departments of education, 1905–30.)

- *Log change in average monthly salaries for teachers, c1905–25.* Generally these data were reported directly, but in a few cases, I had to construct the variable using annual salaries and term length. No adjustment for full-time equivalence was available from the source data. (Annual and biennial reports of the various state departments of education, 1905–30.)

- *Log change in school density, c1905–25.* Number of schoolhouses operating in the county, divided by land area in square miles. (Annual and biennial reports of the various state departments of education, 1905–30; ICPSR 1984.)

- *Log change in number of teachers per school, c1905–25.* (Annual and biennial reports of the various state departments of education, 1905–30.)

- *Log change in pupil-teacher ratio, c1905–25.* Average attendance divided by number of teachers. (Annual and biennial reports of the various state departments of education 1905–30.)

- *Log change in value of school plant and equipment, c1905–25.* (Annual and biennial reports of the various state departments of education 1905–30.)
- *Log change in county spending, c1905–25.* See the description above with the health controls.
- *Change in returns to literacy for adults, c1910–20.* This is measured from a regression of the occupational income score on literacy status, by SEA, for the 1910 and 1920 census samples of adults. (Author's calculations using the 1910 and 1920 IPUMS data.)
- *Literacy rates.* These data were compiled at the county level and come from the 1910 census. Child literacy refers to ages 10–20 and is constructed as follows: $1 - (v50/v49)$. Adult literacy refers to males of voting age, defined as $1 - (v37/v26)$. (ICPSR 1984.)

For race and race relations, the following data are used:

- *Fraction black.* These data come from the 1910 census and are defined as the fraction of the area's males who are black, out of the total population of blacks and whites. Specifically this is defined as $(v24 + v25)/(v24 + v25 + v22 + v23)$. (ICPSR 1984.)
- *Rosenwald schools per capita.* This measures the number of classrooms per capita built by the Julius Rosenwald Fund as of 1930. The denominator normalizes the number of classrooms by the population of blacks ages 5–19 in 1930. (Johnson 1941.)
- *Lynchings per capita, 1900–30.* The base data are the number of lynchings per 100,000 population by county in the years 1900–30. The denominator is the county population in 1930. (Johnson 1941.)

For agricultural-rural controls, the following data are used:

- *Population urban, 1900 and 1910.* From census tabulations measuring the population residing in metro areas. For 1910, the urban population is contained in variable $v9$ in the ICPSR data, which I scale by the total population as defined above. The 1900 fraction urban is also defined in the 1910 data as $v13/(v13 + v14)$. I construct the change in urbanization using the difference between the two variables. (ICPSR 1984.)
- *Crop acreage per capita.* The base data measure the total farmed acreage at the county level, regardless of tenancy. This is constructed with the formula $(v155 + v164 + v175)$ and scaled by total population. (ICPSR 1984.)
- *Sharecropped areas per capita.* The base data are a county-level measure of total acreage sharecropped ($v164$ using the ICPSR variable scheme). I scale this by total population. (ICPSR 1983.)
- *Farm value per capita.* The base data are a county-level measure of the value of farm land and buildings, regardless of tenancy. This is defined as $v177 + v166 + v157$. (ICPSR 1984.)
- *Cotton acreage per capita.* The base data are cotton acreage in 1910 by county. (U.S. Bureau of the Census 1915a.)

- *Tobacco acreage per capita.* The base data are tobacco acreage in 1910 by county. (U.S. Bureau of the Census 1915a.)
- *Parental-background controls.* The mother's and father's occupational income scores are used as indicators for socioeconomic status. These data are matched to children using the "momloc" and "poploc" variables in the IPUMS. I also construct dummies for parent missing and assign them incomes of zero. These variables are interacted with census year in the regressions.

For the retrospective-cohort analysis, I focus on state of birth, as birthplace is not available at further disaggregation. (The District of Columbia is included, where data are available.)

- *Hookworm infection.* Computed from examinations of army recruits. (Koford and Tucker 1921.)
- *Average wage, 1899.* I input the average monthly earnings (with board) for farm laborers by state in 1899. Various other wage measures are summarized by the same source, but they are generally not available for a complete set of states. (Lebergott 1964: table A-24.)
- *Region of birth.* These dummy variables correspond to the census definition of regions: Northeast, South, Midwest, and West.
- *Doctors per capita, 1898.* (Abbott 1900.)
- *State public health spending, 1898.* Per capita appropriations, by state, for state boards of health in 1898. (Abbott 1900.)
- *Child mortality, 1890.* The estimates of child mortality are constructed from published tabulations. Part 3 (table 3) contains enumerated deaths of children under one year. I scale this number by the estimated birth rate (part 1: 482) times the female population (part 1: table 2). (U.S. Bureau of the Census 1894.)
- *Recruits for World War I found rejected for military service because of health "defects," 1917–19.* Fraction of total recruits. (Love and Davenport 1920.)
- *Mortality from other diseases.* Separate variables are constructed for the following eight causes of death: scarlet fever, measles, whooping cough, diphtheria or croup, typhoid fever, malaria, diarrheal diseases, and pneumonia. Data are expressed as the fraction of total mortality in 1890. (U.S. Bureau of the Census 1894.)
- *Fertility rate, 1890.* The estimated birth rate (from part 1: 182). (U.S. Bureau of the Census 1894.)
- *Log change in school term length, c1902–32.* Average length of school term, in weeks. (U.S. Office of Education 1905–32.)
- *Log change in average monthly salaries for teachers, c1902–32.* (U.S. Office of Education 1905–32.)
- *Log change in pupil-teacher ratio, c1902–32.* Average attendance divided by number of teachers. (U.S. Office of Education 1905–32.)
- *Log change in school expenditure, c1902–32.* (U.S. Office of Education 1905–32.)

- *Adult literacy rate. Defined as above.*
- *Population urban. Defined as above.*
- *Fraction black.* Defined as above.
- *Male unemployment rate, 1930.* (ICPSR 1984.)

References

Abbott, Samuel W. 1900. "The Past and Present Condition of Public Hygiene and State Medicine in the United States." Monographs of American Social Economics 19. Boston: Wright and Potter.

Acemoglu, Daron, Simon Johnson, and James A. Robinson. 2001. "The Colonial Origins of Comparative Development: An Empirical Investigation." *American Economic Review* 91 (5): 1369–1401.

Alabama, Department of Education. Various years (1905–25). *Annual Report.* Montgomery, AL: State of Alabama.

Arkansas, Superintendent of Public Instruction. Various years (1905–25). *Biennial Report.* Little Rock, AR: State of Arkansas.

Bleakley, Hoyt. 2002a. "Malaria and Human Capital: Evidence from the American South." Unpublished manuscript, Massachusetts Institute of Technology, Cambridge, MA, May.

————. 2002b. *Three Empirical Essays on Investment in Physical and Human Capital.* Ph.D. dissertation, Massachusetts Institute of Technology, Cambridge, MA.

————. 2003. "Disease and Development: Evidence from the American South." *Journal of the European Economic Association* 1 (2-3): 376–86.

Bleakley, Hoyt, and Fabian Lange. 2004. "Chronic Disease Burden and the Interaction of Education, Fertility, and Growth." Unpublished manuscript, Yale University, New Haven, CT.

Bogue, Donald J. 1951. *State Economic Areas: A Description of the Procedure Used in Making a Functional Grouping of the Counties of the United States.* Washington, DC: U.S. Government Printing Office.

Bowen, Albert S. 1928. "Activities Concerning Mobilization Camps and Ports of Embarkation. Vol. IV." Prepared under the direction of the Surgeon General, M. W. Ireland. Washington, DC: U.S. Government Printing Office.

Brinkley, Garland L. 1994. *The Economic Impact of Disease in the American South, 1860–1940.* Ph.D. dissertation, University of California, Davis.

Dickson, Rumona, Shally Awasthi, Paula Williamson, Colin Demellweek, and Paul Garner. 2000. "Effects of Treatment for Intestinal Helminth Infection on Growth and Cognitive Performance in Children: Systematic Review of Randomised Trials." *British Medical Journal* 320 (June 24): 1697–701.

Duncan, Otis D. 1961. "A Socioeconomic Index for All Occupations." In *Occupations and Social Status,* ed. A. J. Reiss, 109–38. New York: Free Press.

Ettling, John. 1981. *The Germ of Laziness: Rockefeller Philanthropy and Public Health in the New South.* Cambridge, MA: Harvard University Press.

Farmer, Henry F. Jr. 1970. *The Hookworm Eradication Program in the South, 1909–1925*. Ph.D. dissertation, University of Georgia.

Ferrell, John A., Wilson G. Smillie, Platt W. Covington, and Pauline A. Mead. 1932. *Health Departments of States and Provinces of the United States and Canada*. Public Health Bulletin 184. Washington, DC: Government Printing Office.

Georgia, Department of Education. Various years (1905–25). *Annual Report*. Atlanta, GA: State of Georgia.

Havens, Leon C., and Ruth Castles. 1930. "The Evaluation of the Hookworm Problem of Alabama by Counties." *Journal of Preventive Medicine* 4: 109–14.

ICPSR (Inter-university Consortium for Political and Social Research). 1984. *Historical, Demographic, Economic, and Social Data: the United States, 1790–1970*. Ann Arbor, MI: ICPSR. Computer file. http://www.icpsr.org/.

Jacocks, W. P. 1924. "Hookworm Infection Rates in Eleven Southern States as Revealed by Resurveys in 1920–1923." *Journal of the American Medical Association* 82 (20): 1601–02.

Johnson, Charles S. 1941. *Statistical Atlas of Southern Counties: Listing and Analysis of Socio-Economic Indices of 1101 Southern Counties*. Chapel Hill, NC: University of North Carolina Press.

Kentucky, Superintendent of Public Instruction. Various years (1905–25). *Biennial Report*. Frankfort, KY: Commonwealth of Kentucky.

Kofoid, Charles A., and John P. Tucker. 1921. "On the Relationship of Infection by Hookworm to the Incidence of Morbidity and Mortality in 22,842 Men of the United States Army." *American Journal of Hygiene* 1 (1): 79–117.

Kremer, Michael, and Edward Miguel. 2004. "The Illusion of Sustainability." Working Paper 10324, National Bureau of Economic Research, Cambridge, MA.

Lebergott, Stanley. 1964. *Manpower in Economic Growth: The American Record since 1800*. New York: McGraw-Hill.

Louisiana, Superintendent of Public Education. Various years (1905–25). *Biennial Report*. Baton Rouge, LA: State of Louisiana.

Love, Albert C., and Charles B. Davenport. 1920. *Defects Found in Drafted Men: Statistical Information Compiled from the Draft Records Showing the Physical Condition of the Men Registered and Examined in Pursuance of the Requirement of the Selective Service Act*. Prepared under the direction of the Surgeon General, M. W. Ireland. Washington, DC: U.S. Government Printing Office.

Maxcy, Kenneth F. 1923. "The Distribution of Malaria in the United States as Indicated by Mortality Reports." *Public Health Reports* 308: 1125–38.

Miguel, Edward, and Michael Kremer. 2004. "Worms: Identifying Impacts on Education and Health in the Presence of Treatment Externalities." *Econometrica* 72 (1): 159–217.

Mississippi, Superintendent of Public Education. Various years (1905–25). *Biennial Report*. Jackson, MS: State of Mississippi.

NAPP (North Atlantic Population Project). 2004. NAPP: Complete Count Microdata, Preliminary Version 0.2. Minneapolis, MN: Minnesota Population Center. Computer file. http://www.nappdata.org/.

North Carolina, Superintendent of Public Instruction. Various years (1905–25). *Biennial Report*. Raleigh, NC: State of North Carolina.

Philipson, Tomas J. 2000. "External Treatment Effects and Program Implementation Bias." Working Paper T0250, National Bureau of Economic Research, Cambridge, MA.

RSC (Rockefeller Sanitary Commission). Various years (1910–15). *Annual Report*. New York: Rockefeller Foundation.

Ruggles, Steven, and Matthew Sobek. 1997. Integrated Public Use Microdata Series: Version 2.0. Minneapolis, MN: University of Minnesota, Historical Census Projects. http://www.ipums.umn.edu/.

Sachs, Jeffrey D. 2001. "Tropical Underdevelopment." Working Paper 8119, National Bureau of Economic Research, Cambridge, MA.

Smillie, Wilson G., and Donald L. Augustine. 1925. "Intensity of Hookworm Infection in Alabama: Its Relationship to Residence, Occupation, Age, Sex, and Race." *Journal of the American Medical Association* 85: 1958–63.

South Carolina, Superintendent of Education. Various years (1905–25). *Annual Report*. Columbia, SC: State of South Carolina.

Tennessee, Superintendent of Public Instruction. Various years (1905–25). *Biennial Report*. Nashville, TN: State of Tennessee.

Texas, Superintendent of Public Instruction. Various years (1905–25). *Biennial Report*. Austin, TX: State of Texas.

U.S. Bureau of the Census. 1894. "Vital and Social Statistics." In *Compendium of the Eleventh Census, 1890*. Vol. II. Washington, DC: U.S. Government Printing Office.

———. 1915a. "Report on the Statistics of Agriculture in the United States." In *Thirteenth Decennial Census of the United States 1910*. Vols. 6–7. Washington, DC: U.S. Government Printing Office.

———. 1915b. *Wealth, Debt, and Taxation*. Vol. 2. Washington, DC: U.S. Government Printing Office.

———. 1935. *Financial Statistics of State and Local Governments: 1932*. Washington, DC: U.S. Government Printing Office.

U.S. Office [Bureau] of Education. Various years (1894–1913). *Annual Report of the Commissioner Education*. Washington, DC: U.S. Government Printing Office.

Virginia, Superintendent of Public Instruction. Various years (1905–25). *Annual Report*. Richmond, VA: Superintendent of Public Printing.

CHAPTER 6

Early Life Nutrition and Subsequent Education, Health, Wage, and Intergenerational Effects

Jere R. Behrman

Three articles in a prominent 2007 series in *Lancet* summarize much of what is known about early childhood development in developing countries, including nutritional aspects. Grantham-McGregor and others (2007) claim that more than 200 million children under five in developing countries fail to reach their developmental potential because of risk factors associated with poverty. Walker and others (2007) argue that these risk factors include stunting, inadequate cognitive stimulation, iodine deficiencies, and iron deficiency anemia; they also claim that evidence is sufficient "to warrant interventions for malaria, intrauterine growth restriction, maternal depression, exposure to violence, and exposure to heavy metals" (Walker and

The author thanks participants at the health and growth workshop sponsored by the Commission on Growth and Development on October 16, 2007, at the World Bank in Washington, DC, for useful comments. The author also thanks the coauthors of the various studies summarized here for their collaboration on the work that underlies this paper, particularly Harold Alderman, Maria Cecilia Calderon, Suzanne Duryea, John Hoddinott, John Maluccio, Reynaldo Martorell, Sam Preston, Agnes Quisumbing, and Aryeh Stein. The research summarized in the section on Guatemala was supported by National Institutes of Health grants TW-05598 on "Early Nutrition, Human Capital, and Economic Productivity," HD-046125 on "Education and Health across the Life Course in Guatemala," and HD045627-01 on "Resource Flows among Three Generations in Guatemala," as well as National Science Foundation/Economics grants SES 0136616 and SES 0211404 on "Collaborative Research: Nutritional Investments in Children, Adult Human Capital, and Adult Productivities." The paper was previously published as Commission on Growth and Development Working Paper 33.

others 2007: 145). Engle and others (2007: 229) conclude that "governments and civil society should consider expanding high-quality, cost-effective early child development programmes" because there are potentially considerable gains from doing so in developing countries. Engle and others (2007) also note that in recent years developing countries and international development organizations have shown increased interest in early childhood development programs.[1]

In an even more recent *Lancet* series on the implications of infant and maternal undernutrition for outcomes over the life cycle, Victora and others (2008) review the associations among undernutrition, human capital, and risk of adult diseases in developing countries. The authors consider 14 adult outcomes: height; school attendance and educational performance; income and assets; birth weight of offspring; body mass index, body composition, and obesity; blood lipids; insulin resistance and type 2 diabetes; blood pressure; cardiovascular disease; lung function; immune function; cancers; bone mass, fracture risk, and osteoporosis; and mental illness. They also consider exposure variables measured during pregnancy (maternal height and weight before pregnancy, weight gain, micronutrient status, and diet), at birth (weight, length, ponderal index, and intrauterine growth restriction), and at two years of age (stunting, wasting, and underweight).

Victora and others (2008) also contribute new analysis of data from five long-standing prospective cohort studies from Brazil, Guatemala, India, the Philippines, and South Africa. They report that indexes of maternal and child undernutrition (maternal height; infant birth weight and intrauterine growth restriction; and weight, height, and body mass index at two years, using new standards from the World Health Organization) are related to several adult outcomes (height, schooling, income and assets, offspring birth weight, body mass index, glucose concentrations, and blood pressure).

The authors also identify 28 relevant published articles.[2] Based on this review, they report that undernutrition is strongly associated with shorter adult height, less schooling, reduced economic productivity, and lower offspring birth weight (the last for women only). They also report that associations with adult disease indicators are ambiguous. Increased size at birth and

---

1 "Awareness of child development is increasing in developing countries. The health sector has advocated for early child development programmes for children with low birth weight, [with] developmental delays, and from low-income disadvantaged environments. Child development information is often incorporated into growth monitoring charts. Government-supported preschool programmes for children are increasing; in the past 15 years, at least 13 developing countries have instituted compulsory preschool or pre-primary programmes. By 2005, the World Bank had financed loans to 52 developing countries for child development programmes, for a total of US$1,680 million, at least 30 developing countries had policies on early child development, and UNICEF [United Nations Children's Fund] was assisting governments in supporting parenting programmes in 60 countries" (Engle and others 2007: 229–30).

2 They searched in the Medline, Embase, Cumulative Index to Nursing and Allied Health Literature (CINAHL), EconLit, Psychinfo, and PsychArticles databases, with all possible combinations of exposures and outcomes, and identified more than 15,000 original articles and 700 reviews. The search was then limited to articles on developing countries where outcomes had been measured in adulthood or late adolescence, excluding studies with low statistical power or poor methodological quality, and identified 28 relevant articles.

in childhood is positively associated with adult body mass index and, to a lesser extent, blood pressure values, but not with blood glucose concentrations. In their new analyses and in the published work they review, low birth weight and undernutrition in childhood are risk factors for high glucose concentrations, high blood pressure, and harmful lipid profiles once adult body mass index and height are controlled for, suggesting that rapid postnatal weight gains, especially after infancy, are linked to these conditions.

The authors' review of published studies indicates that there is insufficient information about long-term changes in immune function, blood lipids, or osteoporosis indicators. Birth weight is positively associated with lung function and the incidence of some cancers, and undernutrition may be associated with mental illness. The authors note that height at two years is the best predictor of human capital and that undernutrition is associated with lower human capital.

Table 6.1 summarizes numerical associations between maternal and infant-child anthropometric measures of nutritional status, on the one hand, and selected adult outcomes, on the other.[3] The outcomes in the table only include one indicator of adult health outcomes—adult height, commonly considered an indicator of long-run nutritional status—because Victora and others (2008) do not provide such estimates for other adult health outcomes. The estimates are generally "adjusted" estimates, meaning that they include controls for other variables (which tends to lower the estimates). But other than those adjustments, these are estimates of associations without efforts to control for maternal and infant-child anthropometrics that are determined by behavioral choices in the presence of intergenerationally correlated endowments.[4] The estimates suggest some strong associations over the life cycle and across generations between early life nutrition and a range of adult outcomes.

Table 6.1 Select Associations between Maternal and Infant Anthropometric Measures and Adult Outcomes

Outcome	Measure
Adult height	0.7–1.0 centimeter per centimeter at birth 3.2 centimeters per HAZ at age 2 0.5 centimeter per centimeter of maternal height
Education attainment	0.3 grade per kilogram at birth 0.5 grade per HAZ at age 2 0.5 grade per WAZ at age 2
Labor income	8 percent per HAZ at age 2 for males 8–25 percent per HAZ at age 2 for females
Birth weight of offspring	208 grams per kilogram for mother at birth 70–80 grams per HAZ or WAZ of mother

Source: Victora and others 2008.

Note: HAZ refers to height-for-age *z* scores (that is, the number of standard deviations in the international reference population). WAZ refers to weight-for-age *z* scores.

---

3 The income estimates are based only on data from Brazil and Guatemala.

4 Although there are exceptions, as in the Guatemalan case discussed below.

Based on their review of the literature and the estimates in table 6.1, Victora and others (2008) conclude the following:

- Damage suffered in early life leads to permanent impairment and might also affect future generations.
- Preventing such damage would probably generate major health, educational, and economic benefits.
- Chronic diseases are especially common in undernourished children who experience rapid weight gain after infancy.

Thus these *Lancet* studies provide a limited, qualified, but still strong suggestion that better early life nutrition and health have intrinsic benefits that increase later welfare. Moreover, for developing-country populations, better early nutrition and health are associated with and may have good outcomes over the life cycle and across generations.

The rest of this chapter summarizes further supporting evidence. The next section summarizes some of the strongest micro-level evidence available based on panel data over 35 years from Guatemala. The second section summarizes some benefit-cost analyses for early life nutritional interventions. The studies reviewed in this chapter indicate that improved early life nutrition in poorly nourished populations may have substantial causal effects on improving productivity and saving resources over the life cycle and into the next generation and may have benefits that substantially outweigh the costs. Thus, in addition to important direct intrinsic welfare benefits, better early life nutrition in such contexts should be a high priority in strategies for increasing growth and productivity.

Evidence from Guatemala on Impacts of Early Life Nutrition and Other Aspects of Early Childhood Development over the Life Cycle

Some of the richest available evidence on the long-term impacts of early life nutrition comes from a study covering 35 years on an experimental nutritional project initiated in four Guatemalan villages in 1969 and running through 1977. This section first describes the project and related data and then summarizes recent estimates of its long-term effects.

The Nutritional Intervention and Follow-Up Data

In the early and mid-1960s protein deficiency was considered the most important nutritional problem facing poor people in developing countries, and there was considerable concern that this deficiency affected children's ability to learn. The Institute of Nutrition for Central America and Panama (INCAP), based in Guatemala, became the locus of a series of preliminary studies on this subject in the second half of the 1960s (see Habicht and Martorell 1992; Martorell, Habicht, and Rivera 1995; Read and Habicht 1992). These studies informed the development of a large-scale nutritional supplementation project that began in 1969.

The data used in the studies summarized in the following section are based on that project and initially were collected for children age birth to seven years during 1969–77 in four villages in eastern Guatemala.[5] In addition, follow-up data have repeatedly been collected for the same individuals.[6] Three of the villages—Conacaste, Santo Domingo, and San Juan—are in mountainous areas with shallow soils, while Espíritu Santo, located in a river valley, has somewhat higher agricultural potential. All four villages are located relatively near the Atlantic Highway, which connects Guatemala City to the country's Caribbean coast, ranging from 36 to 102 kilometers from Guatemala City.

Between January 1969 and February 1977, INCAP implemented a nutritional supplementation trial in these four villages and collected data on recipient children's growth and development. Data collection focused on all village children under seven and all pregnant and lactating women. Data on cohorts of newborns were collected until September 1977. Data stopped being collected when children turned seven. Thus the birth years of the children included in the 1969–77 longitudinal data collection ranged from 1962 to 1977, so their ages ranged from 0 to 15 years when the project ended. Accordingly, the length and timing of children's exposure to the nutritional interventions depended on their birth dates.

For example, only children born after January 1969 and before October 1974 were exposed to the nutritional interventions for the full first three years of their lives—considered a critical period for child growth (see Maluccio and others 2009; Martorell, Habicht, and Rivera 1995; Martorell and others 2005 and the references therein). Recent estimates summarized in the next section suggest that this is also a critical period for early life nutrition's impact on education achievement, adult cognitive skills, and wage rates and intergenerational effects (Behrman and others 2009; Hoddinott and others 2008; Maluccio and others 2009).

Conacaste and San Juan were randomly assigned to receive a high-protein energy drink, *Atole*, as a dietary supplement. *Atole* contained incaparina (a vegetable-protein mixture developed by INCAP and still widely available in markets in Guatemala), dry skim milk, and sugar and had 163 calories and 11.5 grams of protein per 180 milliliter serving. This design reflected the prevailing view of the 1960s that protein was the critical missing nutrient in most developing countries. *Atole*, the Guatemalan name for hot maize gruel, was pale gray-green and slightly gritty, with a sweet taste.

---

5 Some 300 villages were screened to identify those of appropriate size, compactness (to facilitate access to feeding stations, health centers, and psychological testing sites), ethnicity, diet, schooling levels, demographic characteristics, nutritional status, and physical isolation. This screening identified two sets of village pairs similar in these characteristics: Conacaste and Santo Domingo (relatively populous villages) and Espíritu Santo and San Juan (less populous villages).

6 This population has been studied intensively, with particular emphasis on the impacts of the nutritional intervention (Martorell and others 2005 provide references to many of these studies).

In designing the data collection efforts, there was considerable concern that the social stimulation associated with attending feeding centers—such as the observation of children's nutritional status, monitoring of their intake of *Atole*, and so on—might also affect children's nutritional outcomes, confounding efforts to understand the impacts of the supplement alone. To address this concern, in Espíritu Santo and Santo Domingo a different drink, *Fresco*, was provided. *Fresco* was a cool, clear, fruit-flavored drink. It contained no protein and only sufficient sugar and flavoring for palatability. It also contained far fewer calories per serving (59 calories per 180 milliliters) than did *Atole*. Several micronutrients were added to *Atole* and *Fresco* in equal concentrations. These additions were made to sharpen the contrast between the drinks in protein. Although the energy content differed, this was not recognized as being of much importance at the time.

The two nutritional supplements were distributed in supplementation centers and were available daily, on a voluntary basis, to all community members at times convenient to mothers and children that did not interfere with usual meal times.[7] For the studies summarized in the next section, a critical question is the extent to which the project's design resulted in differences in access to calories, proteins, and other nutrients. Averaging over all children in the *Atole* villages (that is, both those who consumed the supplement and those who never consumed any), children under one consumed 40–60 calories a day, children age one consumed 60–100 calories a day, and children age two consumed 100–120 calories a day as supplement. By contrast, children in the *Fresco* villages consumed almost no *Fresco* for the first two years of their lives, averaging at most 20 calories a day, rising to about 30 calories a day by age three (Schroeder, Kaplowitz, and Martorell 1992: fig. 4). Micronutrient intakes from the supplements were also larger in *Atole* than in *Fresco* lages.[8]

Multidisciplinary research teams conducted several follow-up rounds of data collection on participants from the 1969–77 sample as well as their children. Data collection in 1987–88 targeted the same individuals born

---

7   A program of free primary medical care was provided throughout the period of data collection. Periodic preventive health services, such as immunization and deworming campaigns, were conducted in all villages.

8   To assess whether total caloric intake by these children increased, Islam and Hoddinott (2009) estimate an ordinary least squares relation in which the dependent variable is the sum of calories consumed at home plus calories from supplements. In addition to controlling for maternal and paternal characteristics (age and completed grades of schooling) and household characteristics (a wealth index and distance from the feeding center), they include a dummy variable of 1 if the child resided in one of the two villages where *Atole* was provided, yielding a crude measure of the intent-to-treat effect of the intervention on intakes. For children age one to three years, the coefficient on *Atole* is positive and statistically significant, indicating that total caloric consumption for children exposed to *Atole* increased by 18 percent and total protein intake by 45 percent. Thus the intervention increased energy and protein intakes for young children in *Atole* villages relative to *Fresco* villages. In addition, for children under three the volume of *Atole* consumed was higher than the volume of *Fresco* consumed, implying that intakes of micronutrients were also greater for children in *Atole* villages. Thus the intervention improved nutritional intakes in general, rather than only protein intakes, as originally envisioned in 1969.

between 1962 and 1977 who had participated in the INCAP longitudinal data collection and were 11–26 years old in 1988, including those who remained in the original villages and those who had migrated to Guatemala City and to the provincial capital of the study area. Between 1991 and 1996, investigators studied the offspring of the original sample members in the original villages (migrants were not studied). In 1996, data collection was expanded to include surveillance of pregnancies and collect longitudinal data on these offspring. Between 1996 and 1999, information was collected on all children born between 1996 and 1999 and children born before this study's launch who were under three in 1996.

Next, a multidisciplinary team of investigators, including the author of this chapter, collected follow-up data in 2002–04 on all participants in the 1969–77 project through the Human Capital Study, the main source for the data on long-term outcomes in individuals' lives summarized below. In the 2002–04 sample, members ranged from 25 to 42 years old. By 2004, 1,855 (78 percent of the original sample) were found to be alive and living in Guatemala (11 percent had died, mostly due to infectious diseases in early childhood, 7 percent had migrated abroad, and 4 percent were not traceable). Of these 1,855 individuals, 1,113 lived in the original villages, 155 in nearby villages, 419 in or near Guatemala City, and 168 elsewhere in Guatemala. Of this sample, 1,051 (57 percent) had finished the complete battery of applicable interviews and measurements, and 1,571 (85 percent) completed at least one interview during the 2002–04 follow-up survey. For two-thirds of the 284 (15 percent) who completed no interviews, current addresses could not be obtained, and so contact could not be established. But the refusal rate for at least partial participation among those contacted was just 5 percent (Grajeda and others 2005).

Finally, an almost identical multidisciplinary team of investigators (again including the author of this chapter) conducted an additional survey between January 2006 and August 2007 of the original sample members, their children, and their aging parents, with an emphasis on intergenerational interactions— which is why this survey was called the Intergenerational Transfers Study (Melgar and others 2008 provide details). The data from this study are the source of the measures of intergenerational effects on children's anthropometric outcomes summarized below.

The sample frame for the Intergenerational Transfers Study builds directly on the original INCAP longitudinal study (1969–77), taking into account current information on residence status and information available for original respondents from later surveys, particularly the Human Capital Study (2002–04). The starting point was the sample of living individuals from the INCAP longitudinal study (hereafter referred to as original sample members) who met all of the following criteria:

- Were interviewed in the Human Capital Study and successfully completed the educational, marriage, and income history interviews
- Were living in one of the original study villages, another community in the department of El Progreso (where all the villages are located), or

Guatemala City or its suburbs, all of which are referred to as the Inter-generational Transfers Study area[9]

- Had a biological parent living in the Intergenerational Transfers Study area.

These criteria reflect a combination of cost considerations (such as tracing migrants to other parts of Guatemala) and study objectives (such as focusing on intergenerational interactions, particularly with the aging parents of the original sample members). Among other things, information was also collected on spouses or partners and children under 12 living in the same household as original sample members.[10] There were 1,090 individuals (46 percent of the original sample and 54 percent of those alive in 2007) from the original sample who satisfied all three criteria (or had a spouse or partner who did)[11] and 1,463 children of original sample members.

Estimates of Direct and Indirect Impacts of Early Childhood Nutrition

INCAP's data sets permit more confident assessment of the magnitude of causal impacts of improved early life nutrition on long-term outcomes in a low-income country context than do almost any other existing data sets. First, this is because of the experimental design in which—beyond the control of the households involved—some children were exposed to better nutrition than others during critical windows of their development (such as the first three years of life). This makes it possible to move beyond the associations underlying much of what is summarized in the introduction to this chapter.

The problem with interpreting associations between, for example, early life indicators of nutritional status and later outcomes as causal effects is that parents who invest more in early life nutrition of their children may also invest more in other aspects of their children's development—such as education—because of their greater interest in or capacity for investing in their children. Thus associations between early life nutrition and later life outcomes may reflect not just the impact of early life nutritional status on subsequent outcomes, but also in part—perhaps substantial part—parents' interest in and capacity for investing in their children.

---

9 This is in contrast to the Human Capital Study, for which original sample members anywhere in Guatemala were interviewed. This was not financially feasible for the Intergenerational Transfers Study, so about 10 percent of potential subjects were excluded under this criterion.

10 Spouses and partners include both formally married persons and cohabiting persons describing themselves as being in a union. Children include biological or adopted children of the original sample member or his or her spouse or partner. To be considered adopted, the child had to consider the original sample member to be his or her parent, and vice versa, and not consider anyone else to be his or her parent. All such children under 12 years of age who lived in the same household as the original sample member or his or her spouse or partner were included. In addition, children of original sample members who lived with a former spouse or partner who was not an original sample member were included in the target sample.

11 Among those who did not, 383 (16 percent) had died by the time of the survey and 624 (26 percent) were living outside the study area or could not be traced. The remaining 352 (15 percent) individuals were ineligible because they had not completed the relevant forms for the Human Capital Study, they did not have an eligible parent living in the study region, or both.

Table 6.2 Effects of Exposure in the First Three Years of Childhood to *Atole* Relative to *Fresco* Nutritional Supplements on Guatemalan Adults Age 25–42 and on Their Offspring

Dependent variable	Impact of exposure
Later in individuals' lives	
Female schooling attainment (grades)	**1.17**
	(2.13)
Female and male reading comprehension	**0.28**
	(2.52)
Female and male nonverbal skills	**0.24**
	(2.01)
Male income (US$ per year)	**870**
	(1.59)
Male wage rate (US$ per hour)	**0.67**
	(2.61)
Male hours worked (hours per year)	**−222**
	(−1.25)
Across generations: women's children	
Birth weight (grams)	**275**
	(2.58)
Weight (kilograms, 0–12 years old)	**1.91**
	(2.58)
Triceps skinfold thickness (millimeters), 0–12 years old	**1.38**
	(2.81)

Sources: Behrman and others 2009; Hoddinott and others 2008; Maluccio and others 2009.

Note: Impacts are in bold; t values (standard deviations) are in parentheses (t values > 1.65 indicate significance at the 0.10 level; t values > 1.96 indicate significance at the 0.05 level).

Second, INCAP data are unusually rich in some ways, covering about 35 years from childhood to adulthood, with biomedical and socioeconomic information on the original participants, their children, and parents.

Table 6.2 summarizes estimates of the direct impacts of the childhood nutritional interventions described above on outcomes over individual life cycles and the next generation. These are estimates of the causal impact of being exposed to the better nutritional supplement (*Atole*) instead of the other (*Fresco*) during the critical first two or three years of life.

The exposure to the *Atole* intervention (relative to *Fresco*) for the first three years of life has significant and substantial effects on a series of education-related outcomes. Female schooling increased by more than a full grade, and scores on reading comprehension and nonverbal cognitive skills tests rose by about one-quarter of a standard deviation for both men and women. For men—who are more likely to enter the formal labor market, with more than 95 percent participating—exposure to the *Atole* intervention during the first two years of life led to insignificant but substantial increases in annual income (nearly $900, compared with average income of about $3,500) and significant increases in hourly wages of $0.67, about a third of the average wage.

For women (there are no significant effects for men), exposure to the *Atole* intervention during the first three years of life increased their children's birth weight by 275 grams as well as indicators of fatness for children 0–12 years old. Thus early nutritional interventions can have substantial, long-lasting effects that are likely to enhance welfare, productivity, and growth, both over the life cycles of otherwise malnourished beneficiaries and across generations to their children.

Benefit-Cost Estimates of Improving Early Life Nutrition in Poorly Nourished Populations

The estimated outcomes suggest that, at least in contexts such as that in Guatemala, improving early life nutrition delivers considerable long-term gains. But these estimates by themselves do not indicate whether such gains are likely to be high relative to the costs or what priority such interventions might have among a larger set of possible interventions.

To provide some perspective on such matters, this section summarizes efforts by Behrman, Alderman, and Hoddinott (2004) to include such estimates as part of the "Copenhagen Consensus" (Lomborg 2004). The Copenhagen Consensus sought to set priorities among proposals for confronting 10 major global challenges (selected from a wider set of issues identified by the United Nations): civil conflicts, climate change, communicable diseases, inadequate education, financial instability, weak governance, hunger and malnutrition, migration, trade reform, and poor water and sanitation.

The procedure followed was that a panel of what the Copenhagen Consensus characterized as "eight of the world's most distinguished economists" (including four Nobel laureates) met in Copenhagen in May 2004. The panel was asked to address the 10 challenges noted above and to answer the following question: What would be the best ways of advancing global welfare, and particularly the welfare of developing countries, supposing that an additional $50 billion of resources were at governments' disposal? Before the meeting, 10 papers were commissioned from acknowledged experts to determine benefit-cost ratios for up to five proposals for each of the 10 challenge areas. The panel examined these proposals in detail. Each paper was discussed at length with the authors and with two other specialists who had been commissioned to write critical appraisals. The panel then met in private session and ranked the proposals.

Behrman, Alderman, and Hoddinott (2004) address the seventh challenge, hunger and malnutrition. The share of people in the developing world considered hungry fell from 20 percent in 1990–92 to 17 percent in 1999–2001, yet about 800 million people still do not consume enough food and nutrients to live healthy, productive lives. Most of these people live in Asia (505 million) or Sub-Saharan Africa (198 million). But while the prevalence of hunger has been falling in Asia, it has been rising in Africa. About half of the hungry live in farm households (often in high-risk production environments), with about a fifth each in rural landless and poor urban households. Malnutrition is a challenge related to, but in some ways distinct from, hunger.[12] Important manifestations of malnutrition include the following:

- Low birth weight, with more than 12 million infants a year born with low birth weights
- Slowed skeletal (linear) growth, inadequate weight gain, or both—resulting in stunted or wasted children, with 162 million stunted children under five around the world
- Micronutrient deficiencies, particularly iodine (2 billion people), iron (3.5 billion, including 67 million pregnant women a year), and vitamin A (128 million preschool children).

Reducing hunger and malnutrition can readily be justified because of the potential direct gains in welfare. But reducing hunger and malnutrition also offers potential productivity gains and economic cost reductions. These benefits and how they compare with the costs of achieving them are the focus here. For example,

- reducing the incidence of low birth weights and vitamin A deficiencies lowers the costs of infant mortality.
- reducing the incidence of low birth weights, inadequate postnatal growth, and vitamin A deficiencies lowers the costs of neonatal care and infant and child illnesses.
- lowering the incidence of stunting increases physical productivity.
- reducing the incidence of low birth weights, stunting, and iodine and iron deficiencies increases cognitive abilities and raises schooling and adult productivity.
- reducing the incidence of low birth weights lowers the costs of chronic adult diseases.

Moreover, adults who are better nourished in their early lives and child-bearing years transmit these benefits to subsequent generations. The estimates in the preceding section show some of the available evidence, albeit from just Guatemala, of some of these benefits.

Behrman, Alderman, and Hoddinott (2004) systematically review estimates of the impact of reducing hunger and malnutrition from all over the world, focusing on studies from which inferences can be made more confidently based on the studies' data and estimation methods. Ascertaining these effects is challenging because the effects may be manifested over the life cycle and across generations, but few data sets provide information on people and their children over such long periods. Instead, Behrman, Alderman, and Hoddinott piece together as best as the literature permits information on various impacts and channels through which they occur.

---

12 For example, the rapid spread of obesity in many parts of the developing world is a growing malnutrition problem but is quite distinct from hunger. But information was not available at the time to assess obesity in the same way as some other malnutrition problems.

Table 6.3 Estimated Present Discounted Values of Seven Major Benefits of Moving One Infant from Low Birth Weight, at Different Discount Rates

US$

Benefit	Annual discount rate		
	3 percent	5 percent	10 percent
Reduced infant mortality	95	99	89
Reduced neonatal care	42	42	42
Reduced costs of infant and child illness	36	35	34
Productivity gain from reduced stunting	152	85	25
Productivity gain from increased cognitive ability	367	205	60
Reduced costs of chronic diseases	49	15	1
Intergenerational benefits	92	35	6
Total	832	510	257
Share of total at 5% discount rate (%)	163	100	50

Source: Alderman and Behrman 2006.

Note: The 5 percent discount rate is the base-case estimate.

Table 6.3 shows seven major benefits of moving a baby from below to above the standard cutoff of 2,500 grams for low birth weight. Because the benefits occur over time, discounting is necessary to reflect the advantages in receiving benefits sooner rather than later, because the proceeds can be reinvested. With a 5 percent discount rate, the present discounted value of these benefits is $510.[13] But as the table shows, the present discounted value of benefits would be more than 60 percent higher with a discount rate of 3 percent—or just half as large with a discount rate of 10 percent.

The distribution of the components of the benefits among the seven categories is instructive. Much of the literature on the costs of low birth weight focuses either on early life or on later life—reducing chronic diseases through the so-called Barker (1998) effect. But under the assumptions underlying these estimates,[14] with a 5 percent discount rate, more than half of the impact comes from increased adult productivity, primarily through increased cognitive development (40 percent) and secondarily through reduced stunting (16 percent). Thus, under these assumptions, the direct productivity gains over the life cycle are the most important part of the benefits.

So from the perspective of increasing growth and productivity, are investments in reducing low birth weight good investments? The evidence seems strong that they have a positive impact by raising productivity and lowering costs. But having a positive impact is only part of the information needed to answer this question. One also needs to know the present

---

13 This is less than the $580 given in Behrman, Alderman, and Hoddinott (2004) because the estimates of Alderman and Behrman (2006) incorporate survival probabilities.

14 The most critical assumption is probably how to put a monetary value on averted mortality. Behrman, Alderman, and Hoddinott (2004) use the resource cost of the cheapest available alternative to averting mortality (infant inoculations, as in Summers 1994), but they present simulations to show how sensitive such estimates are to a range of alternatives.

discounted value of the costs of reducing low birth weight. If they are a lot less than $510, then reducing the prevalence of low birth weight is likely to be a high-priority investment in terms of productivity and growth. But if the present discounted value of the costs of reducing the prevalence of low birth weight is greater than $510, then in terms of productivity and growth such investments are not desirable, although they may be very desirable for intrinsic reasons.

Thus, Behrman, Alderman, and Hoddinott (2004) and Alderman and Behrman (2006) also try to obtain as good cost estimates as possible for reducing the prevalence of low birth weight in low-income countries. Many interventions have been proposed to address low birth weight problems (Alderman and Behrman 2006; Merialdi and others 2003; Steketee 2003), including antimicrobial treatments, antiparasitic treatments, insecticide-treated bed nets, maternal health records to track gestational weight gain, iron and folate supplements, targeted food supplements, and social awareness programs on birth spacing and timing of marriage.

Although some recommended interventions focus solely on low birth weight, some also address other goals, such as campaigns against smoking or the use of other drugs during pregnancy. To assess such interventions, one ideally would sum the expected present discounted value of all anticipated outcomes. Yet most lists of possible interventions provide little guidance on priorities, whether for using scarce public resources to alleviate problems related to low birth weight or for deciding which interventions have relatively high returns in which situations. This lack of clearly defined priorities likely reduces the influence of advocates of using scarce public resources to alleviate problems related to low birth weight. It also likely impedes agreement among advocates on how to use public resources to treat problems related to low birth weight.

Rouse (2003) provides a brief review of the cost-effectiveness of interventions to prevent adverse pregnancy outcomes, including low birth weight. He indicates, for example, that it costs $46 per case of low birth weight averted with treatments for asymptomatic sexually transmitted bacterial infections where they are prevalent. Consider also an extensive field trial of iron and folate supplementation in a Nepalese community with high rates of both low birth weight and anemia. Christian and others (2003) find that 11 women would need to be reached with micronutrient supplements to prevent one case of low birth weight. Although no cost data are provided in that study, Parul Christian and Keith West said in personal communications with Harold Alderman that the cost of $64 per pregnant woman reached in the experimental program could be reduced to $13 in an ongoing program. With just one in 11 births benefiting directly in terms of a case of low birth weight averted, the initial cost does not represent an economically efficient intervention. But if just one-third of the estimated cost reduction for an ongoing program could be realized, the intervention would be economically efficient. Moreover, economies of scope would allow the provision of vitamin A supplementation at little marginal cost and thus might reduce both infant and maternal mortality.

Behrman, Alderman, and Hoddinott (2004) estimate benefit-cost ratios for interventions to reduce hunger and malnutrition that lower the prevalence of low birth weight, improve infant and child nutrition, reduce micronutrient deficiencies (primarily for children and pregnant women), and invest in technological developments in low-income agriculture (which can improve nutrition by lowering prices for nutrients through more nutrient-rich foods and increasing incomes for poor farmers and farm workers; see table 6.4). The authors discuss a number of qualifications and caveats for these and other such estimates and explore the sensitivity of their estimates to some of the

Table 6.4 Estimated Global Benefit-Cost Ratios for Opportunities Related to Hunger and Malnutrition

Opportunities and targeted populations	Ratio of benefits to costs	Size of targeted population
Reducing low birth weight for pregnancies with high probabilities of it (particularly in South Asia)		12 million low birth weight births a year
Treatment for women with asymptomatic bacterial infections	0.6–4.9	
Treatment for women with presumptive sexually transmitted disease	1.3–10.7	
Drugs for pregnant women with poor obstetric history	4.1–35.2	
Improving infant and child nutrition in populations with high prevalence of child malnutrition		162 million stunted children under 5 years of age
Promotion of breastfeeding in hospitals where use of infant formula is the norm	4.8–7.4	
Integrated child care programs	9.4–16.2	
Intensive preschool programs, including meals and nutrition for poor families	1.4–2.9	
Reducing micronutrient deficiencies in populations suffering from them		
Iodine (per woman of child-bearing age)	15–520	2 billion people
Vitamin A (children under six)	4–43	128 million children
Iron (per capita)	176–200	3.5 billion people, including 67 million pregnant women
Iron (pregnant women)	6–14	
Investing in technology to develop agriculture		
Dissemination of new cultivars with higher yield potential	8.8–14.7	800 million undernourished who would benefit from price reductions, about 0.7 million of whom would benefit from any income increases due to productivity gains
Dissemination of iron- and zinc-dense rice and wheat	11.6–19.0	
Dissemination of vitamin A–dense "golden rice"	8.5–14.0	

Source: Behrman, Alderman, and Hoddinott 2004.

Table 6.5 Project Rankings in 2004 Copenhagen Consensus

Project rating	Ranking	Challenge	Opportunity
Very good	1	Diseases	Control HIV/AIDS
	2	Malnutrition	Provide micronutrients
	3	Subsidies and trade	Liberalize trade
	4	Diseases	Control malaria
Good	5	Malnutrition	Develop new agricultural technologies
	6	Water and sanitation	Develop small-scale water technology for livelihoods
	7	Water and sanitation	Provide community-managed water supply and sanitation
	8	Water and sanitation	Conduct research on water productivity in food production
	9	Government	Lower the costs of starting new businesses
Fair	10	Migration	Lower the barriers to migration for skilled workers
	11	Malnutrition	Improve infant and child nutrition
	12	Malnutrition	Reduce the prevalence of low birth weight
	13	Diseases	Scale up basic health services
Bad	14	Migration	Implement guest worker programs for the unskilled
	15	Climate	Impose optimal carbon taxes
	16	Climate	Adopt the Kyoto Protocol
	17	Climate	Impose a value-at-risk carbon tax

Source: Lomborg 2004.

most important assumptions.[15] They conclude that these estimates suggest that there is considerable potential for enhancing growth and productivity by investing more in early life nutrition—both before and after birth.

Various options exist for which the expected present discounted value of benefits exceeds the expected present discounted value of costs, suggesting the potential for major gains in productivity. Moreover, the benefit-cost ratios are high relative to those for many other interventions. In fact, based in part on the patterns of benefit-cost ratios across more than 30 proposed projects in the 10 challenge areas defined above, the Copenhagen Consensus panel gave high rankings to projects for reducing hunger and malnutrition (see table 6.5).[16]

---

15 Some of the assumptions might bias some estimates up and others down. For example, if higher discount rates are used, estimated benefit-cost ratios fall because many benefits are due to productivity improvements when infants and children become adults. The opposite holds if lower discount rates are used or if most other methods common in the literature for valuing averted mortality are used.

16 The Copenhagen Consensus 2008 rankings that were released on May 30, 2008, also include nutritional interventions, primarily directed toward early life, very high in their rankings. In fact, nutritional interventions occupy four of their six top-ranked interventions, the other two in the top six being "the Doha development agenda" (number two) and "expanded immunization coverage for children" (number four). See Copenhagen Consensus Center (2008).

References

Alderman, Harold, and Jere R. Behrman. 2006. "Reducing the Incidence of Low Birth Weight in Low-Income Countries Has Substantial Economic Benefits." *World Bank Research Observer* 21 (1): 25–48.

Barker, D. J. P. 1998. *Mothers, Babies, and Health in Later Life*. 2d ed. London: Churchill Livingstone.

Behrman, Jere R., Harold Alderman, and John Hoddinott. 2004. "Hunger and Malnutrition." In *Global Crises, Global Solutions,* ed. Bjørn Lomborg. Cambridge, U.K.: Cambridge University Press.

Behrman, Jere R., Maria Cecilia Calderon, John Hoddinott, Reynaldo Martorell, Samuel Preston, and Aryeh Stein. 2009. "Nutritional Supplementation of Girls Influences the Growth of Their Children: Prospective Study in Guatemala." University of Pennsylvania, Philadelphia.

Christian, Parul, Subarna Khatry, Joanne Katz, Elizabeth Pardhan, Steven LeClerq, Sharada Shrestha, Ramesh Adhikari, Alfred Sommer, and Keith West. 2003. "Effects of Alternative Maternal Micronutrient Supplements on Low Birth Weight in Rural Nepal: Double Blind Randomised Community Trial." *British Medical Journal* 326 (7389): 571–74.

Copenhagen Consensus Center. 2008. "Results (30th May 2008)." Copenhagen Consensus Center, Copenhagen Business School. http://www .copenhagenconsensus.com/Default.aspx?ID=788.

Engle, Patrice L., Maureen M. Black, Jere R. Behrman, Meena Cabral de Mello, Paul J. Gertler, Lydia Kapiriri, Reynaldo Martorell, and Mary Eming Young. 2007. "Strategies to Avoid the Loss of Potential among 240 Million Children in the Developing World." *Lancet* 369 (January): 229–42.

Grajeda, Ruben, Jere R. Behrman, Rafael Flores, John A. Maluccio, Reynaldo Martorell, and Aryeh D. Stein. 2005. "The Human Capital Study 2002–04: Research Design and Implementation of the Early Nutrition, Human Capital, and Economic Productivity Study." *Food and Nutrition Bulletin* 26(2, supplement 1): S15–S24.

Grantham-McGregor, Sally M., Yin Bun Cheung, Santiago Cueto, Paul Glewwe, Linda M. Richter, and Barbara J. Strupp. 2007. "Over Two Hundred Million Children Fail to Reach Their Developmental Potential in the First Five Years in Developing Countries." *Lancet* 369 (9555): 60–70.

Habicht, Jean-Pierre, and Reynaldo Martorell. 1992. "Objectives, Research Design, and Implementation of the INCAP Longitudinal Study." *Food and Nutrition Bulletin* 14 (3): 176–90.

Hoddinott, John, John A. Maluccio, Jere R. Behrman, Rafael Flores, and Reynaldo Martorell. 2008. "The Impact of Nutrition during Early Childhood on Income, Hours Worked, and Wages of Guatemalan Adults." *Lancet* 371 (February): 411–16.

Islam, Mahnaz, and John Hoddinott. 2009. "Evidence of Intra-household Flypaper Effects from a Nutrition Intervention in Rural Guatemala." *Economic Development and Cultural Change* 57 (2): 215–238.

Lomborg, Bjørn, ed. 2004. *Global Crises, Global Solutions*, Cambridge, U.K.: Cambridge University Press.

Maluccio, John A., John Hoddinott, Jere R. Behrman, Agnes Quisumbing, Reynaldo Martorell, and Aryeh D. Stein. 2009. "The Impact of Nutrition during Early Childhood on Education among Guatemalan Adults." *Economic Journal* 119 (537, April): 734–63.

Martorell, Reynaldo, Jere R. Behrman, Rafael Flores, and Aryeh D. Stein. 2005. "Rationale for a Follow-up Focusing on Economic Productivity." *Food and Nutrition Bulletin* 26 (2, supplement 1): S5–S14.

Martorell, Reynaldo, Jean-Pierre Habicht, and Juan A. Rivera. 1995. "History and Design of the INCAP Longitudinal Study (1969–1977) and Its Follow-up (1988–89)." *Journal of Nutrition* 125 (4): S1027–S41.

Melgar, Paúl, Luis Fernando Ramírez, Scott McNiven, Rosa Mery Mejía, John Hoddinott, and John A. Maluccio. 2008. "Resource Flows among Three Generations in Guatemala Survey: Definitions, Tracking, Data Collection, Coverage, and Attrition." International Food Policy Research Institute, Washington, DC.

Merialdi, Mario, Guillermo Carroli, José Villar, Edgardo Abalosi, Metin Gulmezoglu, Regina Kulier, and Mercedes de Onis. 2003. "Nutritional Interventions during Pregnancy for the Prevention or Treatment of Impaired Fetal Growth: An Overview of Randomized Controlled Trials." *Journal of Nutrition* 133 (5): S1626–S31.

Read, Merrill S., and Jean-Pierre Habicht. 1992. "History of the INCAP Longitudinal Study on the Effects of Early Nutrition Supplementation on Child Growth and Development." *Food and Nutrition Bulletin* 14 (3): 169–75.

Rouse, Dwight. 2003. "Potential Cost-Effectiveness of Nutrition Interventions to Prevent Adverse Pregnancy Outcomes in the Developing World." *Journal of Nutrition* 133 (5): S1640–S44.

Schroeder, Dirk G., Haley J. Kaplowitz, and Reynaldo Martorell. 1992. "Patterns and Predictors of Participation and Consumption of Supplements in an Intervention Study in Rural Guatemala." *Food and Nutrition Bulletin* 14 (3): 191–200.

Steketee, Richard. 2003. "Pregnancy, Nutrition, and Parasitic Disease." *Journal of Nutrition* 133 (5): S1661–S67.

Summers, Lawrence H. 1994. "Investing in All the People: Educating Women in Developing Countries." EDI Seminar Paper 45, World Bank, Economic Development Institute, Washington, DC.

Victora, Cesar G., Linda Adair, Caroline Fall, Pedro C. Hallal, Reynaldo Martorell, Linda Richter, and Harshpal Singh Sachdev. 2008. "Maternal and Child Undernutrition: Consequences for Adult Health and Human Capital." *Lancet* 371 (9609): 340–57.

Walker, Susan P., Theodore D. Wachs, Julie Meeks Gardner, Betsy Lozoff, Gail A. Wasserman, Ernesto Pollitt, and Julie A. Carter. 2007. "Child Development: Risk Factors for Adverse Outcomes in Developing Countries." *Lancet* 369 (9556): 145–57.

Index

Boxes, figures, notes, and tables are indicated by *b*, *f*, *n*, and *t*, respectively.

E

early child development, 17–20, 167–68,
168*n*, 170–76. *See also* nutrition
interventions
disease and undernutrition effects on
adulthood, 170
education returns from family
background, 20*f*
interventions, 17–20
hunger and malnutrition, 180*t*
investments, 17–19, 20
nutrition supplementation trial in
Guatemala, 170–75
orphanhood, 23
parental involvement, 174
economic growth, 53. *See also* health and
economic growth
and population growth, 61
assessing health impact, 15–16,
56–57, 63
causal effect of health and disease on, 78
health as indicator and interpretation of, 65
health input channels, 45
measuring contribution of disease-free
environment, 132
education, 4, 58. *See also* cognitive deficits
decline in due to stunting and poverty,
18, 19*f*
disease impacts on school participation,
146*n*
gender and biological and cultural
obstacles, 59
health effects through attendance and
cognition, 23, 57–58
hookworm eradication, 132–33, 135, 155
school attendance, 141–43,
142*t*, 143*f*
ill health effects, 53
increases wages, 59
lack of readiness and failure to learn, 58
malaria impacts on, 67
nutrition and levels of, 169*t*
nutritional supplements improve
outcomes, 175, 175*t*
returns from family background, 20*f*
epidemiological transition, 78, 78*n*, 79, 116

F

fertility, 161
foreign direct investment (FDI),
encouraging and discouraging, 60

G

girls, issues affecting health and
education, 59
government, health care spending, 2, 25,
50, 161
gross domestic product (GDP), 112, 112*f*
and GDP per capita for working-age
population, 93*t*
and life expectancy, 94, 112, 112*n*, 117*t*
per capita, 114*n*, 117*t*
by country wealth, 80*f*
growth. *See* economic growth; health and
economic growth

H

health, 7, 66
evidence-based policy making, 47–49
investments in early childhood, 19–20
monetary value of, 56
technology and disease prevention, 55
trends and income, 8–10
health and economic growth, 13*n*, 31
arguments against link, 66
disease eradication, 77–78
econometric approach, 11–12
estimation issues, 10–12, 118
four phases of perceptions of, 42
growth accounting assessment, 15–16
health and human capital, 7, 44–45, 56–58
health and income, 9, 9*f*, 21
causality, 12, 13, 13*n*, 53, 64–65, 78
data issues, 10–12
interpreting correlations between, 10–12
microeconomic approach, 16–17
Preston curve, 55
richer countries are healthier, 12
health and productivity link, 16–17
health and savings, 53, 59–60
health care financing, 25, 59
health care services, poor public quality,
28–29